THE MAMMOTH BOOK OF IQ PUZZLES

Nathan Haselbauer

RUNNING PRESS
PHILADELPHIA • LONDON

First published in the United States in 2005 by Carroll & Graf Publishers
This edition published in 2007 by Running Press Book Publishers

Printed and bound in the EU

9 8 7 6 5 4
Digit on the right indicates the number of this printing

Library of Congress Cataloging-in-Publication Data is available on file

ISBN: 978-0-7867-1481-0

Running Press Book Publishers
2300 Chestnut Street
Philadelphia, PA 19103-4371

Visit us on the web!
www.runningpress.com

THE INTERNATIONAL HIGH IQ SOCIETY

The International High IQ Society, the second largest high-IQ organization in the world, was founded in New York City by Nathan Haselbauer. He created the society in April 2000 to enable bright people from around the world to come together on the Internet. The society welcomes people from all walks of life who have an IQ in the top five per cent of the world's population and who want to be part of the society's global community. The society is unique in that its combined membership includes people of all ages, races and professions, and literally spans the globe.

The main goals of the society are to foster intellectual thinking and to provide opportunities for our members to socialize with each other. These goals are accomplished through the society's discussion forums, various tournaments, numerous online activities, a quarterly magazine, and functions held throughout the world.

Members have access to chat rooms, discussion forums, puzzles, numerous online activities, and are exclusive contributors to the society's publication, *Brainstorm Magazine*. Members also have the opportunity to become part of the Hamilton Institute, an online think tank which assists corporate, government and non-profit entities in the search for solutions to complex problems.

Membership in the International High IQ Society is open to persons who score within the top five per cent of the general population on one of the society's admissions tests. There is no other qualification for membership.

For more information visit www.highiqsociety.org or send an e-mail to membership@highiqsociety.org.

Also available

The Mammoth Book of Awesome Comic Fantasy
The Mammoth Book of Best New Erotica 3
The Mammoth Book of Best New Horror 14
The Mammoth Book of Climbing Adventures
The Mammoth Book of Comic Crime
The Mammoth Book of Egyptian Whodunnits
The Mammoth Book of Elite Forces
The Mammoth Book of Endurance and Adventure
The Mammoth Book of Explorers
The Mammoth Book of Eyewitness America
The Mammoth Book of Eyewitness Battles
The Mammoth Book of Eyewitness Everest
The Mammoth Book of Fantasy
The Mammoth Book of Fighter Pilots
The Mammoth Book of Future Cops
The Mammoth Book of Great Detective Stories
The Mammoth Book of Haunted House Stories
The Mammoth Book of Heroes
The Mammoth Book of Heroic and Outrageous Women
The Mammoth Book of Historical Whodunnits
The Mammoth Book of Humor
The Mammoth Book of Illustrated Crime
The Mammoth Book of Journalism
The Mammoth Book of Legal Thrillers
The Mammoth Book of Literary Anecdotes
The Mammoth Book of Locked-Room Mysteries and Impossible Crimes
The Mammoth Book of Maneaters
The Mammoth Book of Men O'War
The Mammoth Book of Mountain Disasters
The Mammoth Book of Murder and Science
The Mammoth Book of Native Americans
The Mammoth Book of Private Eye Stories
The Mammoth Book of Prophecies
The Mammoth Book of Pulp Action
The Mammoth Book of Roaring Twenties Whodunnits
The Mammoth Book of Roman Whodunnits
The Mammoth Book of Science Fiction
The Mammoth Book of Sea Battles
The Mammoth Book of Sex, Drugs and Rock 'n' Roll
The Mammoth Book of Short Erotic Novels
The Mammoth Book of Tales from the Road
The Mammoth Book of the Titanic
The Mammoth Book of UFOs
The Mammoth Book of Vampires
The Mammoth Book of Vampire Stories by Women
The Mammoth Book of War Correspondents
The Mammoth Book of Women Who Kill

CONTENTS

ACKNOWLEDGMENTS

This book wouldn't have been possible without support from the members of the International High IQ Society and proofreaders who were the testing ground for virtually all my puzzles. A special thank you also goes to Michael Dickheiser for the fine illustrations that he graciously contributed.

INTRODUCTION

The aim of *The Mammoth Book of IQ Puzzles* is to challenge and entertain your mind. As the president and founder of the International High IQ Society, I've been writing, gathering, and solving puzzles for years. I've tried my best to create puzzles for the beginner as well as the advanced puzzle solver, and this book represents a collection of my best puzzles.

Nothing beats the satisfaction of trying a new puzzle, giving it your best, and being able to come up with the solution. *The Mammoth Book of IQ Puzzles* offers that satisfaction to beginners and veterans. I hope you have as much fun solving these puzzles as I had creating them.

Each puzzle is rated according to its difficulty, and as the rating increases you'll need more insight and imagination to solve them. There's no time limit for any of these puzzles so take as long as you like.

The Mammoth Book of IQ Puzzles is really two books in one. The first section is a special challenge originally designed for the International High IQ Society. It features puzzles that are extremely difficult, even for the world's best puzzle solvers. The second section offers a variety of puzzles that will challenge both novice and expert puzzle solvers alike.

Many of the puzzle books in bookstores today are simply remakes of the old classics. Instead, I've made every effort to design each of my puzzles with a fresh, innovative approach. I hope you will let me know if I've accomplished my goal. I enjoy hearing from puzzle aficionados and welcome any correspondence.

Nathan Haselbauer
president@highiqsociety.org

PART I: THE GOAT CHALLENGE

THE SMARTEST PERSON IN THE WORLD COMPETITION

Every year the International High IQ Society holds the Smartest Person in the World Competition, nicknamed the GOAT (Greatest of All Time) Challenge. The GOAT Challenge features some of the hardest puzzles ever created. The first section of *The Mammoth Book of IQ Puzzles* contains thirty questions based on past GOAT Challenge competitions. Over half a million people from sixty different countries have taken the challenge and there has yet to be a perfect score. The questions vary in difficulty, but have been designed to stop everybody eventually.

Although a mastery of advanced mathematics is not required, proficiency in the general areas of mathematics is beneficial in solving many of the questions. Understanding the wording of the problem, which is occasionally rather intricate, and the ability to comprehend various complex concepts, are also essential. The use of reference materials, books, calculators and computers is permitted.

There are thirty questions in the GOAT Challenge, with difficulty ratings from one to five. Most of the questions with a rating of five were either not solved by anyone, or only by a small handful of puzzlers, so don't feel discouraged if you can't solve them right away. For additional help on some of the harder questions, see the puzzle section on the International High IQ Society's website (www.highiqsociety.org).

Good luck!

Goat Challenge Scoring

The combined difficulty levels of all thirty questions in the GOAT Challenge totals 122. Once you've completed the challenge, add up the difficulty levels of all the questions you answered correctly and match your total score against the scoring system below. The last column represents the rarity of your score.

SCORE	IQ	RARITY
1-10	100	1 out of 2
11-20	105	1 out of 3
21-30	110	1 out of 4
31-40	115	1 out of 6
41-50	120	1 out of 11
51-60	125	1 out of 21
61-70	130	1 out of 44
71-80	135	1 out of 102
81-90	140	1 out of 261
91-100	145	1 out of 741
101-110	150	1 out of 2,330
111-121	155	1 out of 8,137
122	160+	1 out of 31,560

CAMBRIDGE CRYPTOGRAM

Each letter has a numerical value attached to it, and the total of all the letters equals the professor's value. For example, if the letters N, E, W, T, O and N had values of 12, 7, 9, 14, 21 and 5, respectively, then Isaac Newton would have a numerical value of 68.

Your objective is to figure out Hawking's numerical value.

BARROW	71	TURTON	80
NEWTON	70	AIRY	46
WHISTON	104	BABBAGE	84
SAUNDERSON	129	KING	45
COLSON	51	LARMOR	58
WARING	92	DIRAC	52
MILNER	58	LIGHTHILL	130
WOODHOUSE	108	HAWKING	?

ANSWER:

Challenge 1	**Difficulty rating: 5**

CANNON-BALL STACKS

A park ranger has stacked cannon-balls in two tetrahedral pyramids for display at Gettysburg. He later decides to combine the cannon-balls in both of the pyramids in order to create one large pyramid. The smallest number of cannon-balls he can have if the two pyramids are the same size is twenty (assuming he uses every cannon-ball in both pyramids).

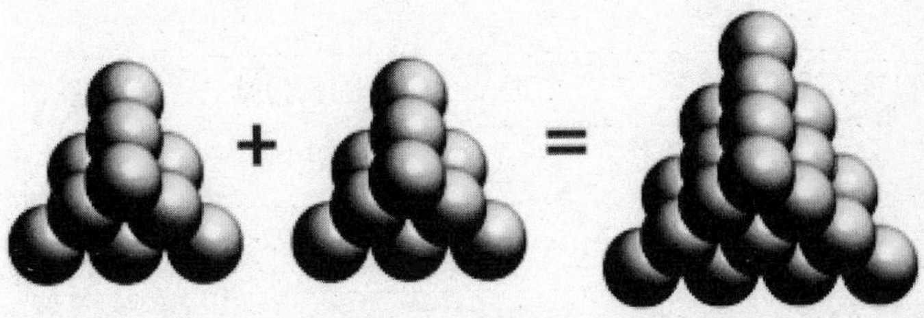

If the two smaller pyramids are different sizes, however, what would be the minimum number of cannon-balls he could use to make one large tetrahedral pyramid?

ANSWER:

Challenge 2	**Difficulty rating: 4**

TEN CHAIRS

A teacher has a square classroom with ten chairs in it that she wants to arrange for a class project. How can she arrange the ten chairs along the walls so that there is an equal number of chairs along each wall?

ANSWER:

Challenge 3	**Difficulty rating: 3**

CHECKER PROBLEM

How can you arrange nine checkers in nine rows of three checkers each?

ANSWER:

Challenge 4	**Difficulty rating: 4**

ARCHAEOLOGICAL DIG

Two teams of archaeologists have divided a site into eighty-one squares. The middle square has a sarcophagus in it and they are not allowed to enter that square. The teams must search the area to find artefacts, and examine every square except the one with the sarcophagus in it. Each team can visit each square only once. The first team moves from A to B and the second team moves from B to A. What path would both teams take so that each one searches the same number of squares?

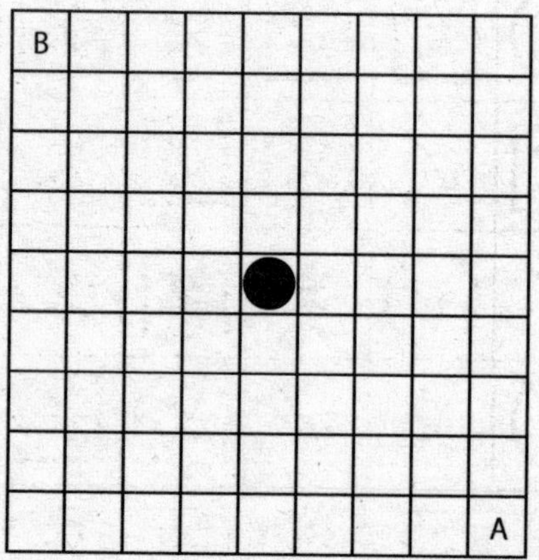

ANSWER:

Challenge 5	**Difficulty rating: 4**

MISSING ROW

Each of the six different symbols has a different value associated with it. When you add up the value of all the different symbols you get the total value for that row. The objective is to determine the value for each of the six symbols and fill in the missing value.

✓	✗	[✓]	(✗)	(✓)	74
(✗)	[✗]	[✓]	✗	[✗]	59
[✗]	✓	(✗)	[✓]	✗	?
✓	(✓)	✗	[✗]	✗	55
(✓)	✗	✓	(✗)	[✓]	74
72	55	60	69	62	

ANSWER:

Challenge 6	**Difficulty rating: 5**

HARDWARE STORE

A mathematician recently bought a hardware store and came up with an alternative method of pricing his goods. Can you figure out his method and determine the cost of the hammer?

SCREWDRIVER	**30**
BOLTS	**14**
NAILS	**13**
PLYWOOD	**19**
HAMMER	**?**

ANSWER:

Challenge 7	**Difficulty rating: 4**

WORD SCRAMBLE

There are six scrambled letters below that can be formed into seven English words. You must use all the letters in the word, and they can only be used once. Can you find all seven?

L A E S P T

ANSWER:

Challenge 8	**Difficulty rating: 3**

WORD JUMBLE

Take the first letter of each pair of words and replace it with another letter that will form two new words. Place the new letter in the box in the middle and you will form a new word vertically.

BIG	☐	TALE
NOSE	☐	TONE
MUCH	☐	HAT
VOTE	☐	HEAT
RAT	☐	JAR

ANSWER:

Challenge 9	Difficulty rating: 3

DOT COMPLEX

Complete the sequence.

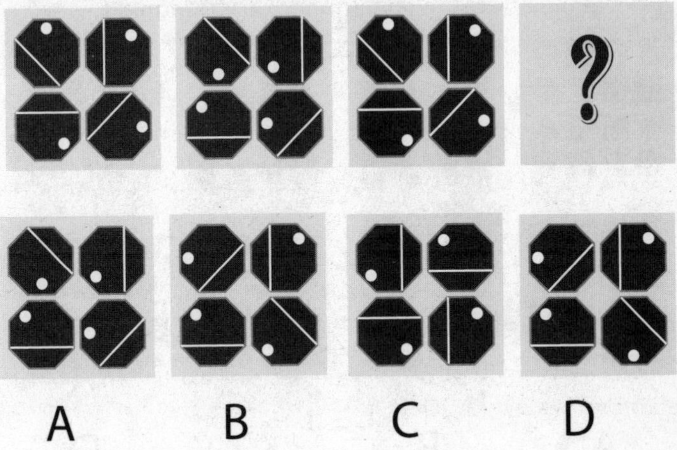

ANSWER:

Challenge 10	Difficulty rating: 4

PYRAMIDS AND SPHERES

Complete the sequence.

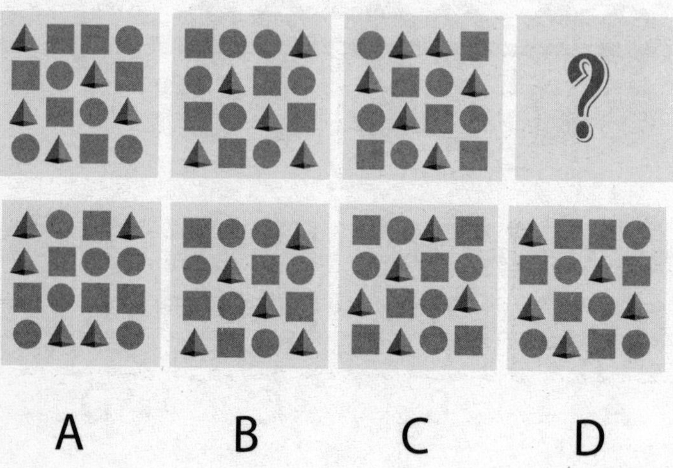

ANSWER:

Challenge 11	**Difficulty rating: 4**

GO ON, GO ON, GO ON

Complete the sequence.

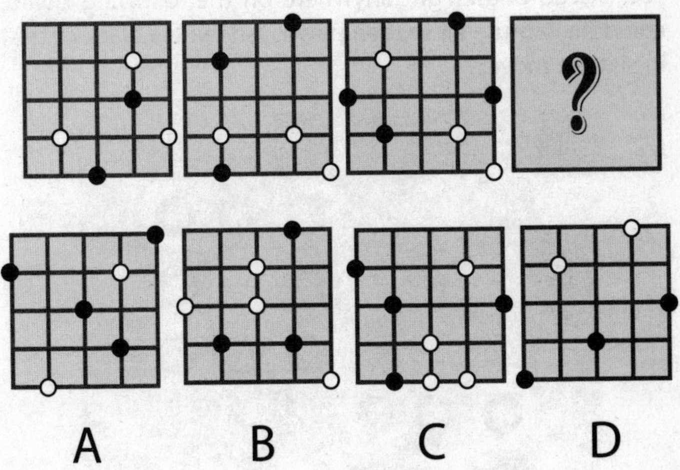

ANSWER:

Challenge 12 | **Difficulty rating: 4**

KNIGHT MOVES

On a chessboard, a knight moves two squares in one direction and one square at a right angle to the first direction. If you placed one knight anywhere on the following board, could he capture all sixteen pawns (shown as black circles) in sixteen moves?

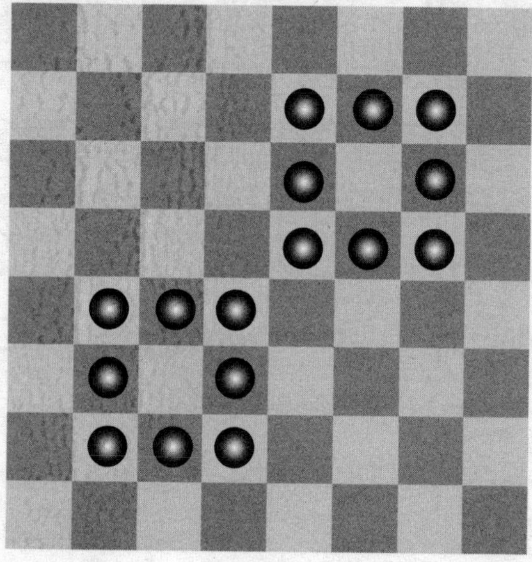

ANSWER:

Challenge 13	**Difficulty rating: 4**

DOT PLACEMENT

There is a single black dot on the board below. Place seven additional black dots in the white squares so that no two of the eight dots are in line horizontally, vertically, or diagonally.

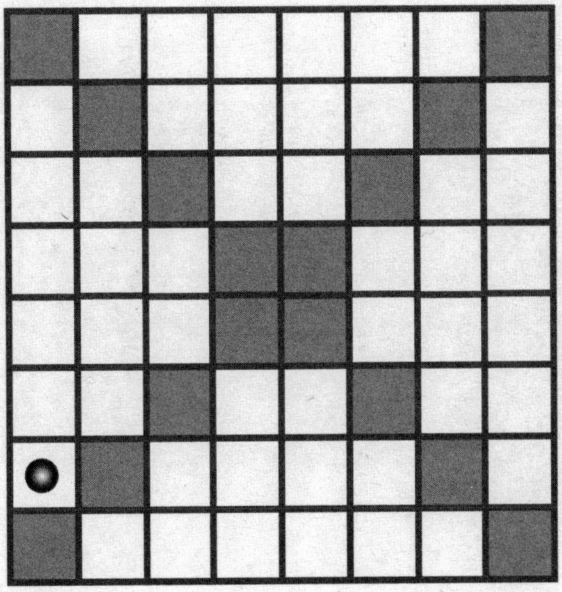

ANSWER:

Challenge 14	**Difficulty rating: 4**

MAKESHIFT CHESSBOARD

A young boy wanted to make a chessboard but only had this piece of wood. Without wasting any of the wood, can he make a chessboard with sixty-four equal squares? Each of the two protrusions can make two squares.

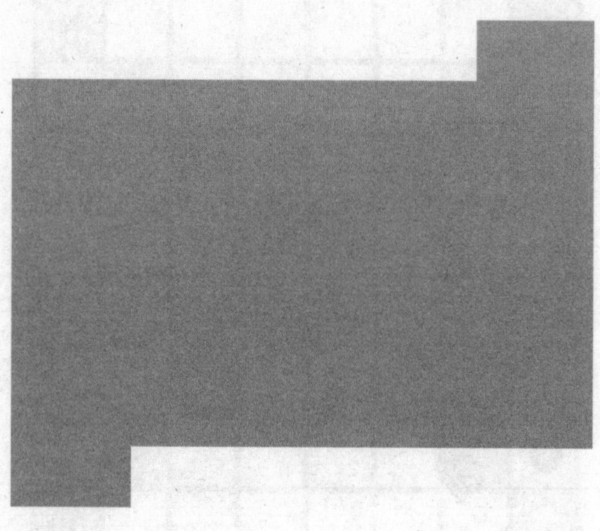

ANSWER:

Challenge 15	**Difficulty rating: 4**

FIND THE MISSING VALUE

= 13

= 30

= ?

ANSWER:

Challenge 16	**Difficulty rating: 4**

MISSING FIGURE

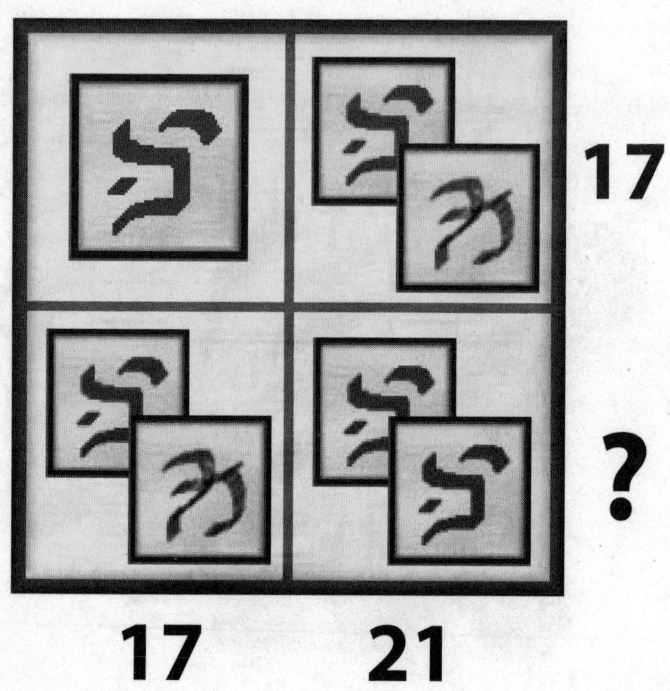

ANSWER:

Challenge 17	**Difficulty rating: 4**

MISSING VALUE

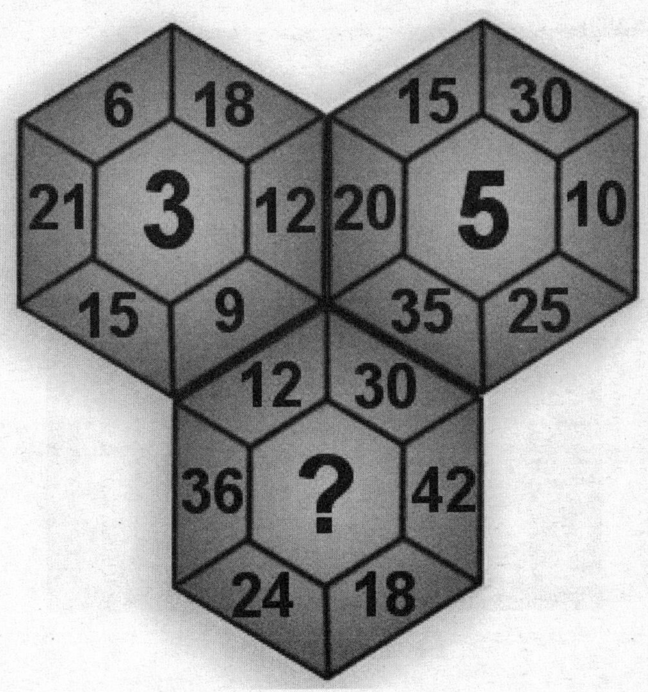

ANSWER:

Challenge 18	**Difficulty rating: 5**

MOLECULAR SEQUENCE

Use the diagram to determine the missing letter in the sequence.

A C ? G E

ANSWER:

Challenge 19	**Difficulty rating: 4**

ANALOGY PUZZLE

Determine the item that best completes the analogy.

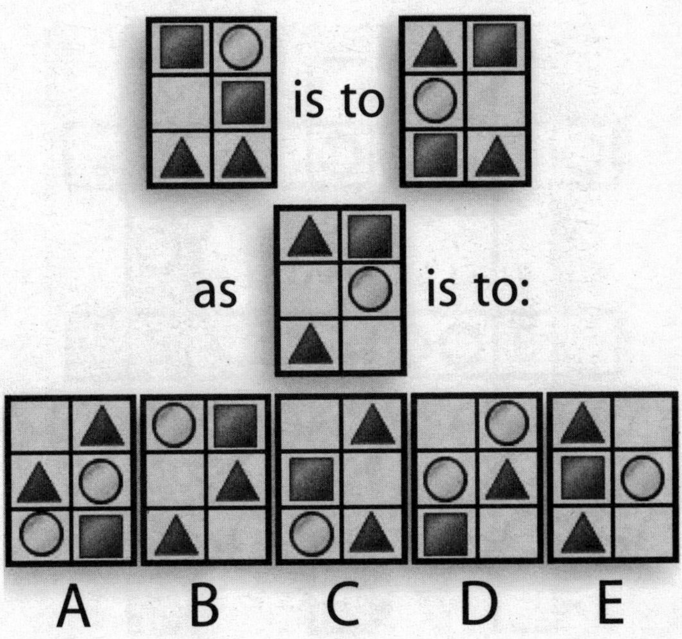

ANSWER:

Challenge 20	Difficulty rating: 3

TRELLIS PATTERN

Determine the system used to generate numbers in the grid below, and find the missing value.

ANSWER:

Challenge 21 | **Difficulty rating: 4**

WHEELS WITHIN WHEELS

Determine the system used to generate numbers in the diagram below, and find the missing value.

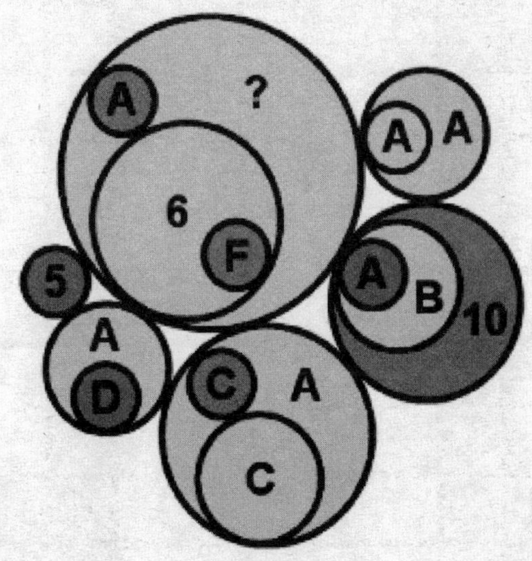

ANSWER:

Challenge 22	**Difficulty rating: 5**

HIDDEN NUMBERS

What is the missing number in the figure below?

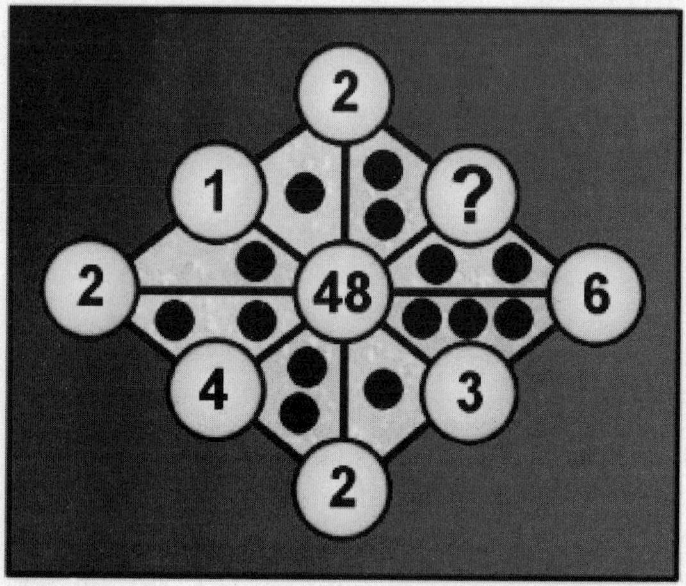

ANSWER:

Challenge 23	**Difficulty rating: 5**

STARBURST

Determine the relationship between the central star and the outer circles, and find the missing value.

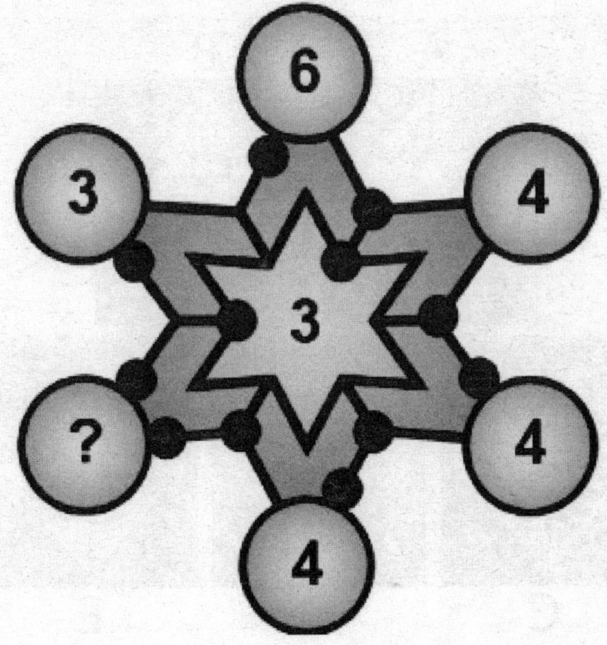

ANSWER:

Challenge 24	Difficulty rating: 4

ODD ONE OUT

Which of the following is least like the others?

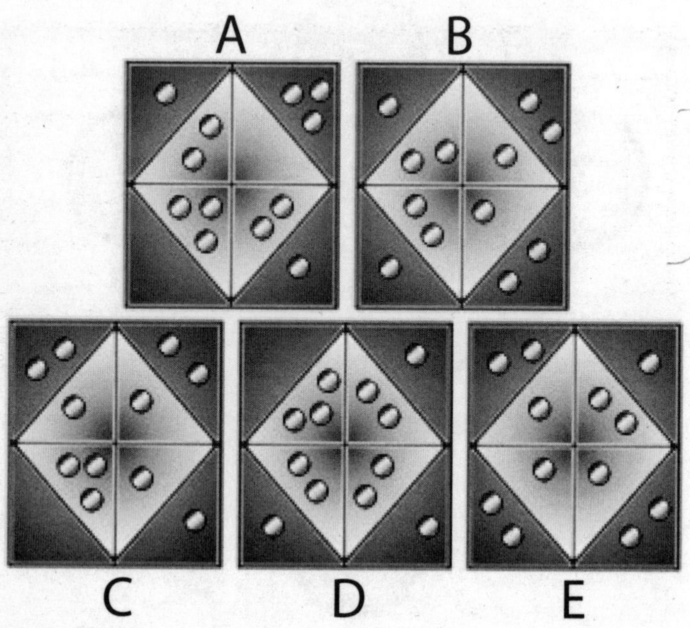

ANSWER:

Challenge 25	**Difficulty rating: 5**

FAST EXIT

Which of the circles in the maze is nearest to the exit?

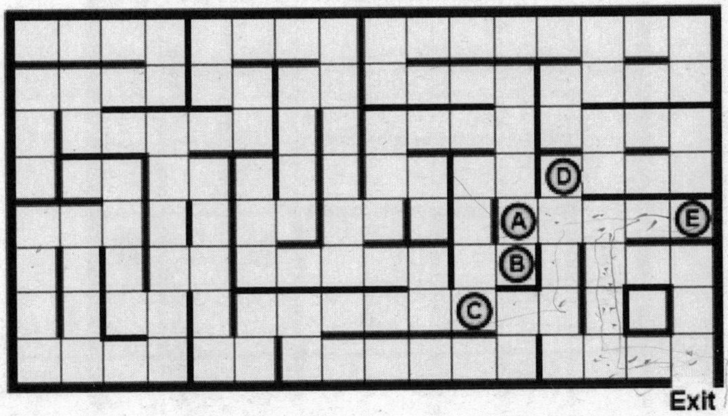

ANSWER:

Challenge 26	Difficulty rating: 3

MAZE

Discover the logic behind the placement of the circles within the maze and choose the best location for the last circle.

ANSWER:

Challenge 27	Difficulty rating: 4

BALANCING ACT

Shown below is an aerial view of a see-saw perfectly balanced by weights on both sides.

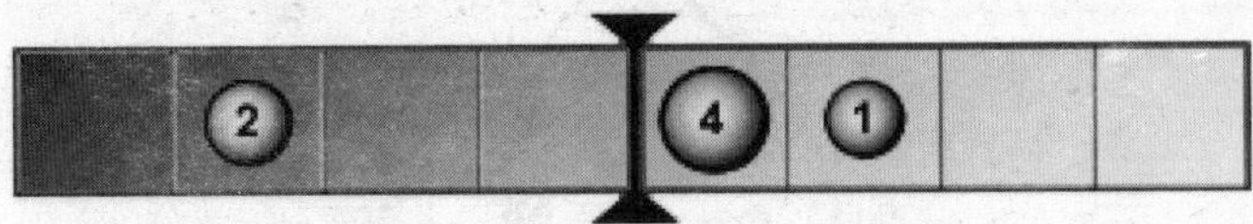

What weight must be placed at the indicated position to balance the following see-saw?

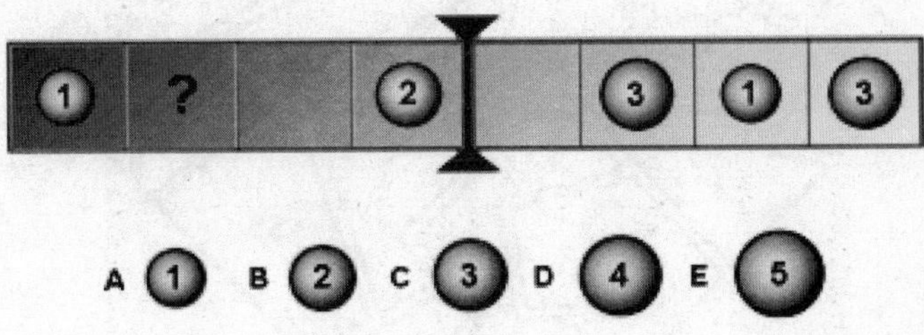

A (1) B (2) C (3) D (4) E (5)

ANSWER:

Challenge 28	**Difficulty rating: 3**

CORNER PLOT

Determine the missing value.

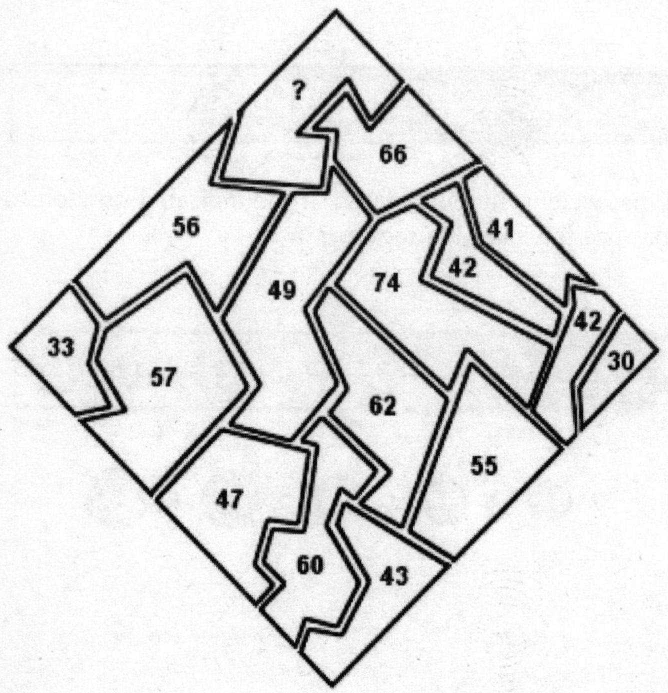

ANSWER:

Challenge 29 | **Difficulty rating: 5**

SEQUENTIAL HEADACHE

The following are the first twelve terms of a sequence generated from the diagram. Determine the 1000th term.

2 21 50 73 121 131 175 192 197 254 327 344

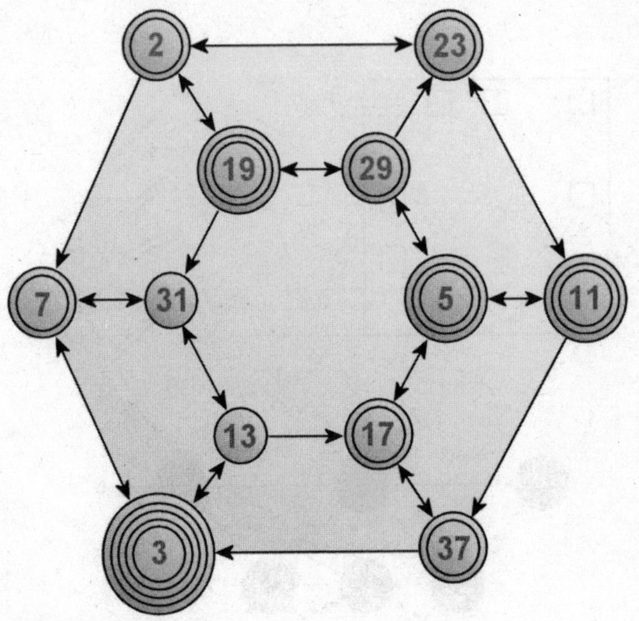

ANSWER:

Challenge 30	**Difficulty rating: 5**

CHALLENGE ANSWERS

1. 106. H=26, A=17, W=18, K=2, I=11, N=10, G=22

2. 680

3.

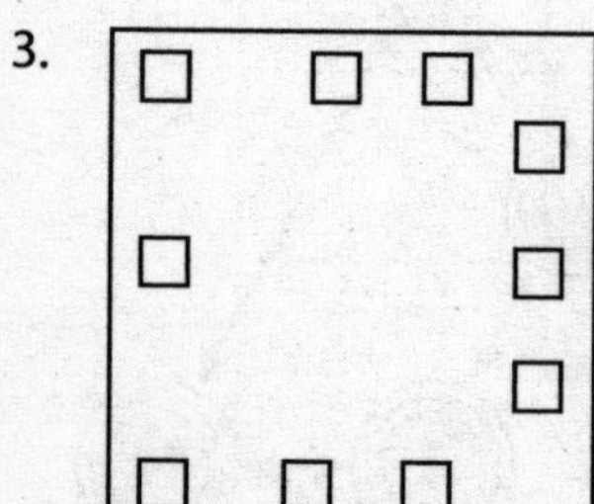

4.

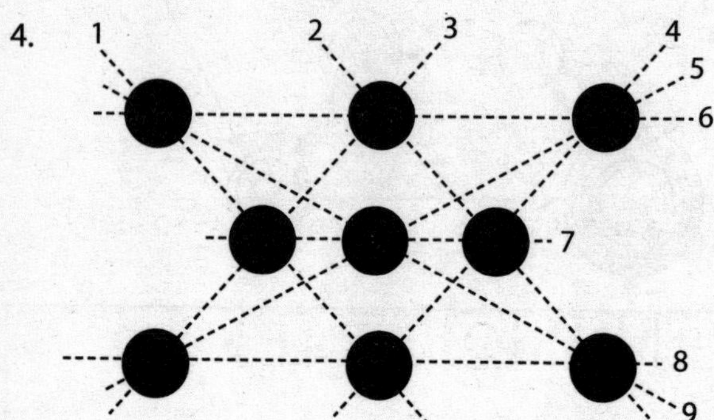

CHALLENGE ANSWERS

5. 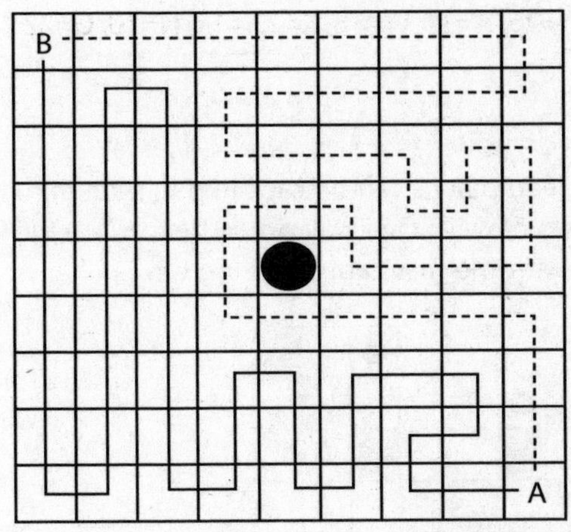

6. 56

7. 16 (vowels count as 2, consonants 3)

8. staple, petals, plates, pleats, pastel, palest, septal

9. P H O N E

10. A

CHALLENGE ANSWERS

11. D

12. C

13. All sixteen pawns can be captured in sixteen moves in a variety of ways. One way would be to place the knight at A3 with the first capture being C2.

14.

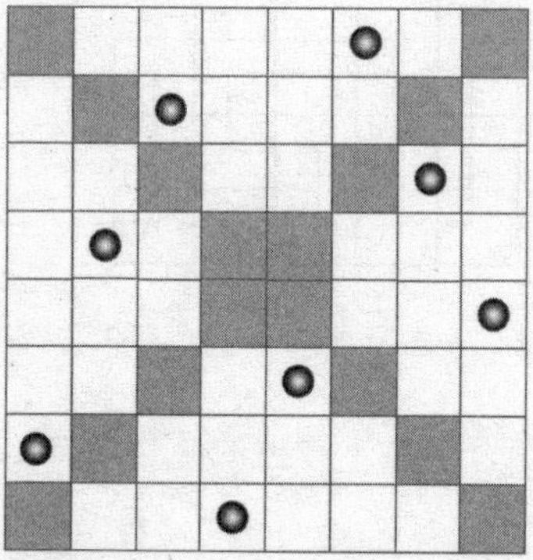

15.

CHALLENGE ANSWERS

16. 17
17. 21
18. 6
19. E
20. C
21. 1
22. 3
23. 4
24. 5
25. C
26. C
27. 1
28. E
29. 76
30. 29984

PART II: PUZZLES

DIFFICULTY RATING: 91

FIND THE HIDDEN VALUE

Each of the three different symbols has a different value associated with it. When you add up the value of all the different symbols you get the total value for that row. The objective is to determine the value for each of the three symbols and fill in the missing value.

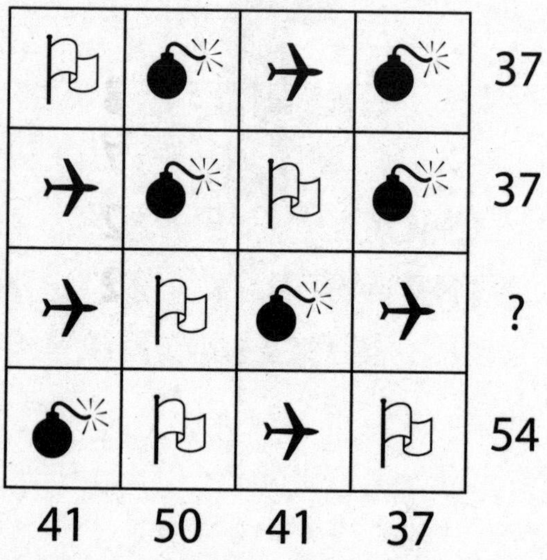

ANSWER:

Puzzle 1.1	**Difficulty rating: 3**

ICE CREAM STORE

There is a system of pricing at the ice cream store. How much should the mocha cost?

CHERRY	13
VANILLA	17
CHOCOLATE	22
STRAWBERRY	22
MOCHA	?

ANSWER:

Puzzle 1.2	**Difficulty rating: 4**

WORD SCRAMBLE

There are seven scrambled letters below that can be formed into four English words. You must use all the letters in the word, and they can only be used once. Can you find all four?

E D C R S E U

ANSWER:

Puzzle 1.3	**Difficulty rating: 3**

WORD MORPH

The word LIST can be turned into the word FISH in only three steps, changing only one letter at a time. Each time you change the word, it must form a valid word.

LIST

_ _ _ _

_ _ _ _

FISH

ANSWER:

Puzzle 1.4	Difficulty rating: 2

WORD ADDITION

What word inserted in the blank space will create two new words? Find at least one word for each set of words. *Example: QUICK sand PAPER*

NEWS ____ CLIP

BOOK ____ FRONT

ANSWER:

Puzzle 1.5	**Difficulty rating: 1**

BUBBLE TROUBLE

Complete the sequence.

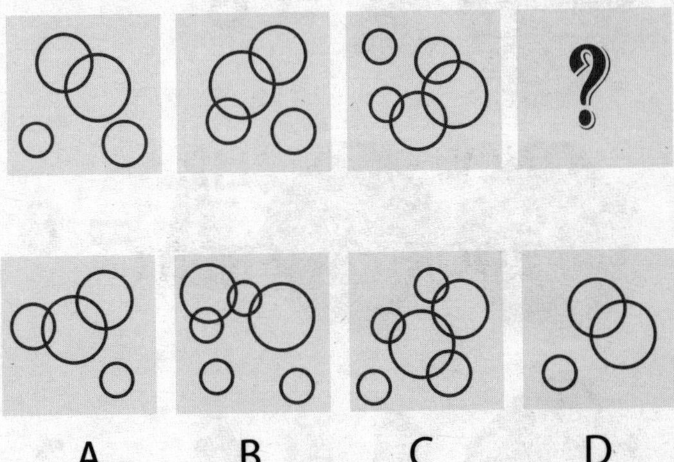

ANSWER:

Puzzle 1.6	**Difficulty rating: 2**

FIND THE MISSING VALUE

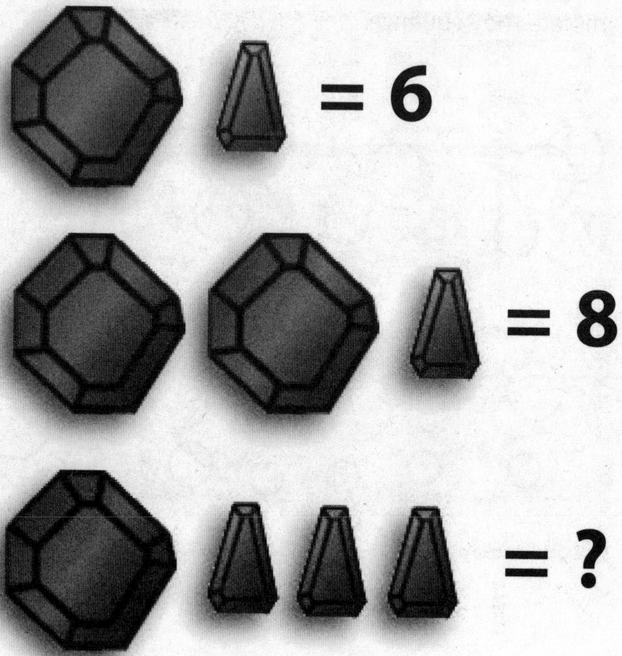

= 6

= 8

= ?

ANSWER:

Puzzle 1.7	**Difficulty rating: 2**

MISSING FIGURE

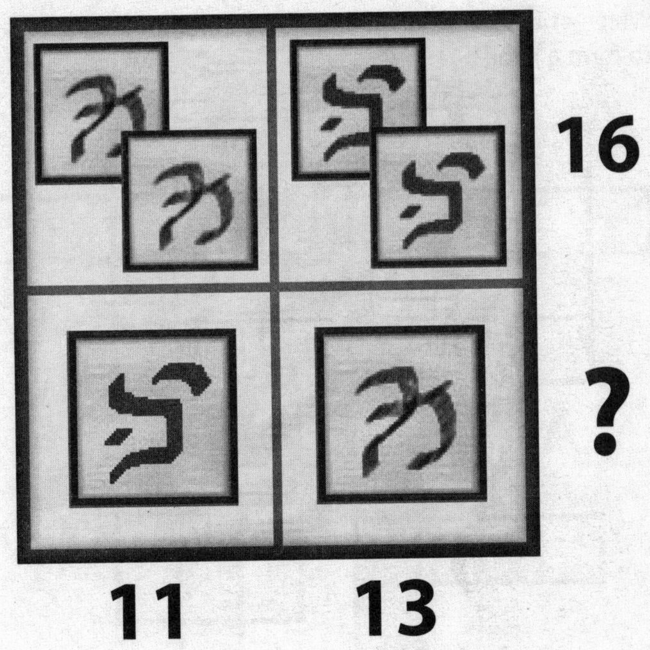

ANSWER:

Puzzle 1.8	Difficulty rating: 3

CUBE-ISM

Which of the following can be folded along the given lines to form a cube?

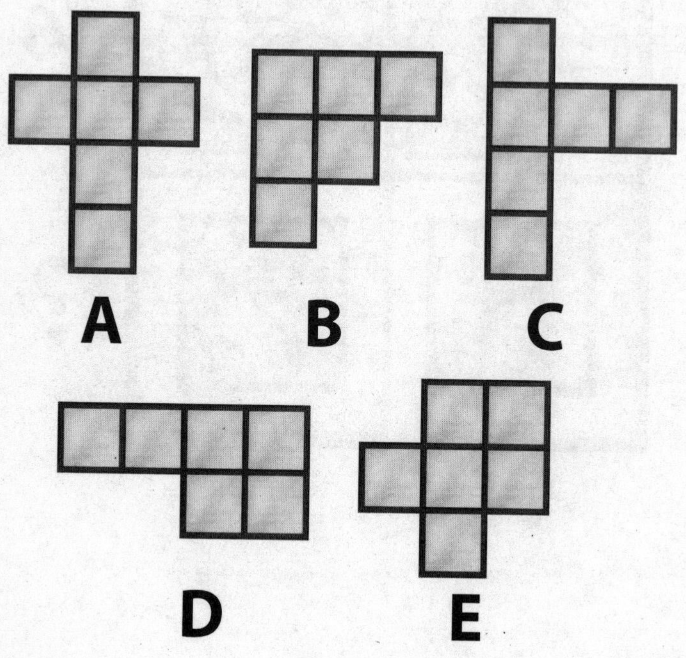

ANSWER:

Puzzle 1.9	**Difficulty rating: 1**

MISSING NUMBER

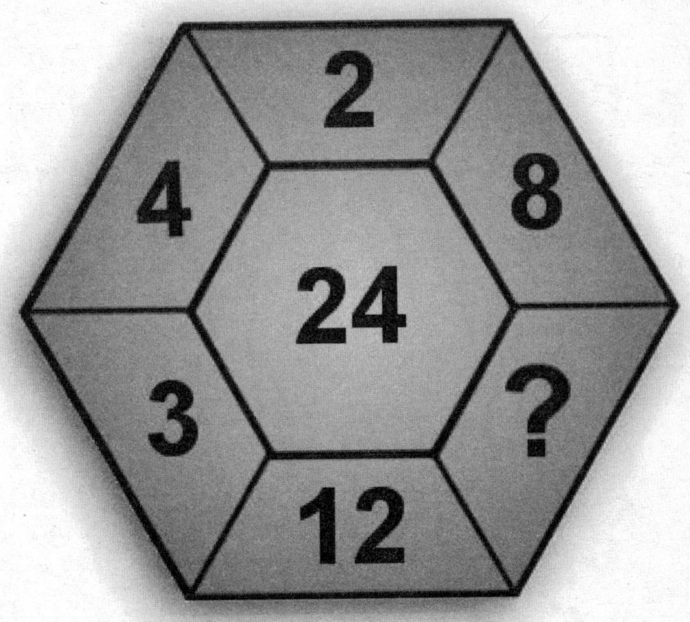

ANSWER:

Puzzle 1.10	Difficulty rating: 2

FACE FIT

Which of the following is least like the others?

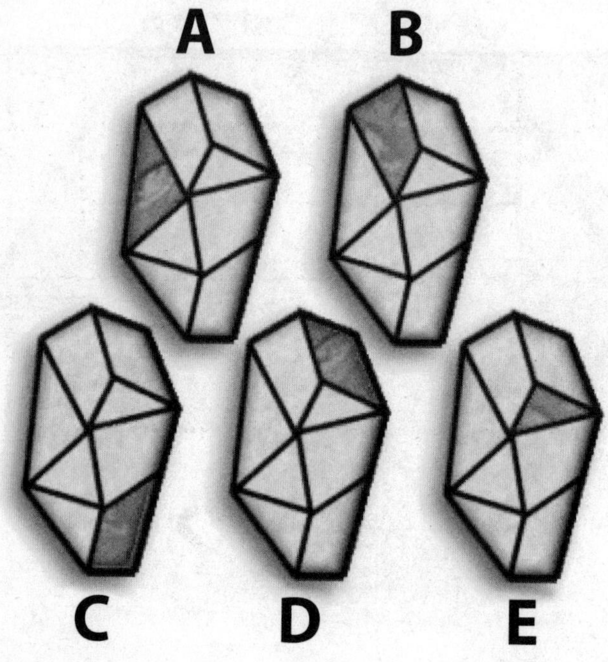

ANSWER:

Puzzle 1.11	Difficulty rating: 2

MISSING PIECES

Given the puzzle piece shown, determine the maximum number of times the piece can fit into the missing areas of the puzzle.

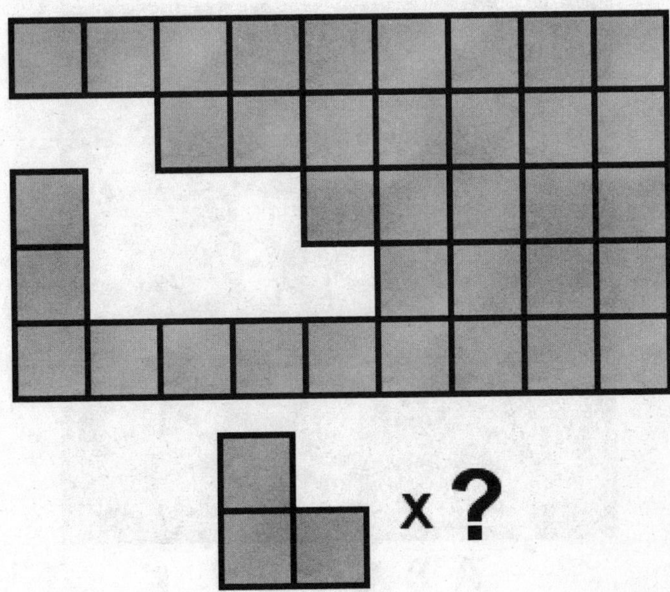

ANSWER:

Puzzle 1.12	**Difficulty rating: 1**

MOLECULAR SEQUENCE

Use the diagram to determine the missing letter in the sequence.

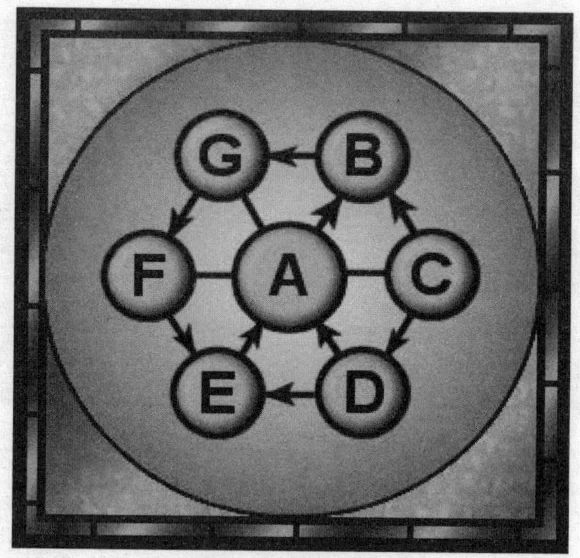

A B G F E ?

ANSWER:

Puzzle 1.13	**Difficulty rating: 4**

STARGAZING

Which item is the best continuation of the sequence?

ANSWER:

Puzzle 1.14	**Difficulty rating: 1**

TWO INTO EIGHT

Which item is the best continuation of the sequence?

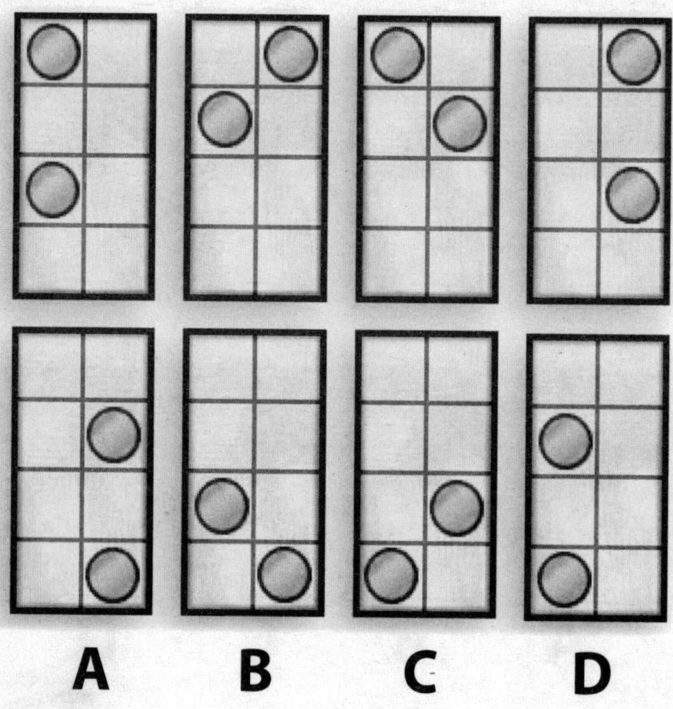

ANSWER:

Puzzle 1.15	**Difficulty rating: 1**

INTERLOCKING HEXAGONS

Which item is the best continuation of the sequence?

ANSWER:

Puzzle 1.16	**Difficulty rating: 1**

ANALOGY PUZZLE

Determine the item that best completes the analogy.

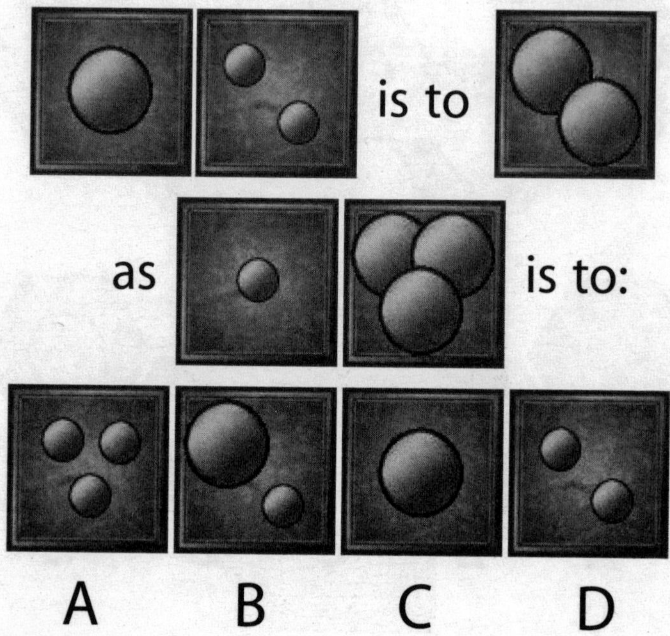

ANSWER:

Puzzle 1.17	**Difficulty rating: 2**

CUBE STACKING

The object below was created by gluing together several cubes. What is the total number of sides that are NOT glued to another cube?

You may assume that no cubes are hidden from view.

ANSWER:

Puzzle 1.18	**Difficulty rating: 1**

CHILD'S PLAY

Determine the missing item.

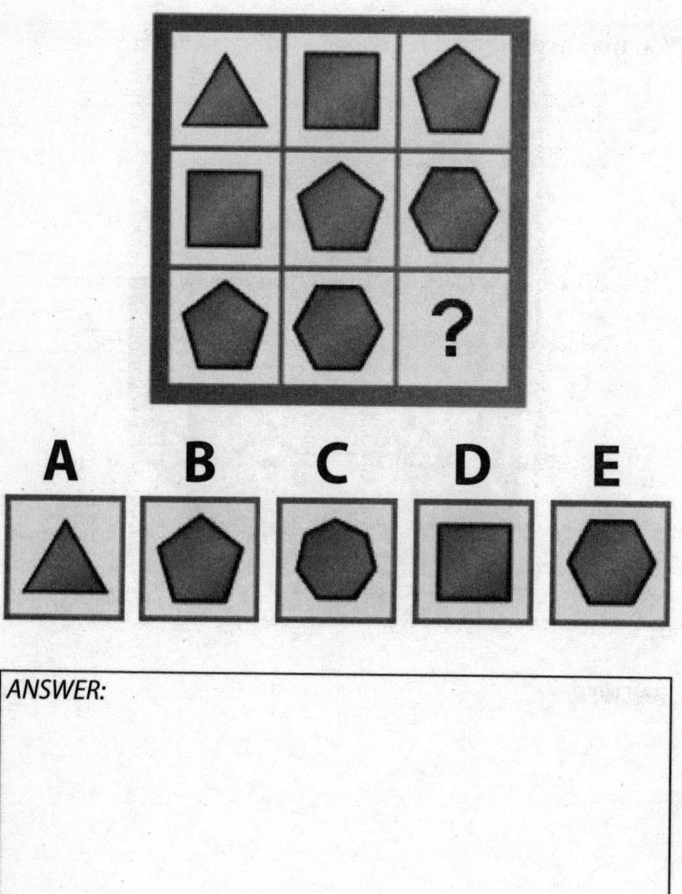

ANSWER:

Puzzle 1.19	**Difficulty rating: 2**

TRELLIS PATTERN

Determine the system used to generate numbers in the grid below, and find the missing value.

ANSWER:

Puzzle 1.20	Difficulty rating: 3

WHEELS WITHIN WHEELS

Determine the system used to generate numbers in the diagram below, and find the missing value.

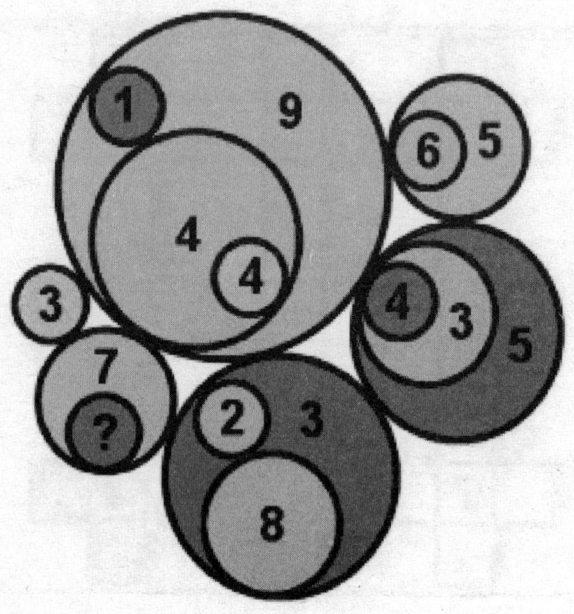

ANSWER:

Puzzle 1.21	Difficulty rating: 4

HIDDEN NUMBERS

What is the missing number in the figure below?

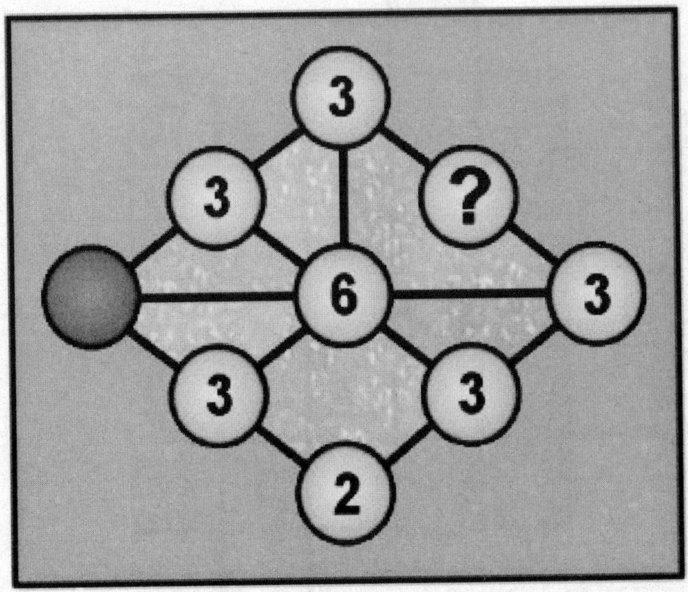

ANSWER:

Puzzle 1.22	**Difficulty rating: 2**

HIDDEN VALUES

Determine the system used to generate numbers in the grid below, and find the missing value.

ANSWER:

Puzzle 1.23	**Difficulty rating: 4**

CIRCUITOUS NUMBERS

Determine the system used to generate numbers in the grid below, and find the missing value.

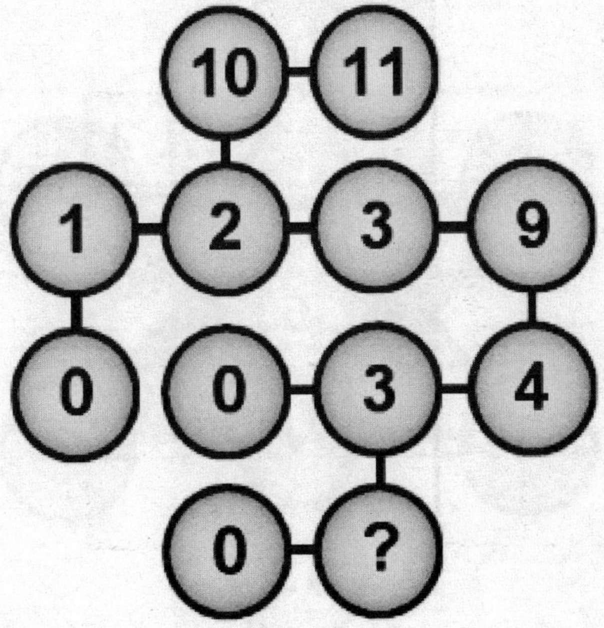

ANSWER:

Puzzle 1.24	**Difficulty rating: 3**

STARBURST

Determine the relationship between the central star and the outer circles, and find the missing value.

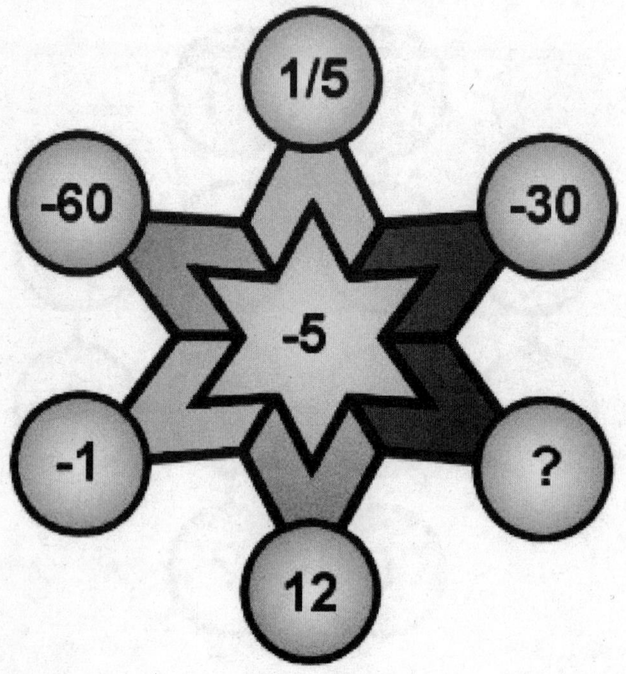

ANSWER:

Puzzle 1.25	**Difficulty rating: 3**

FACE FIT

Which one is most like the first four?

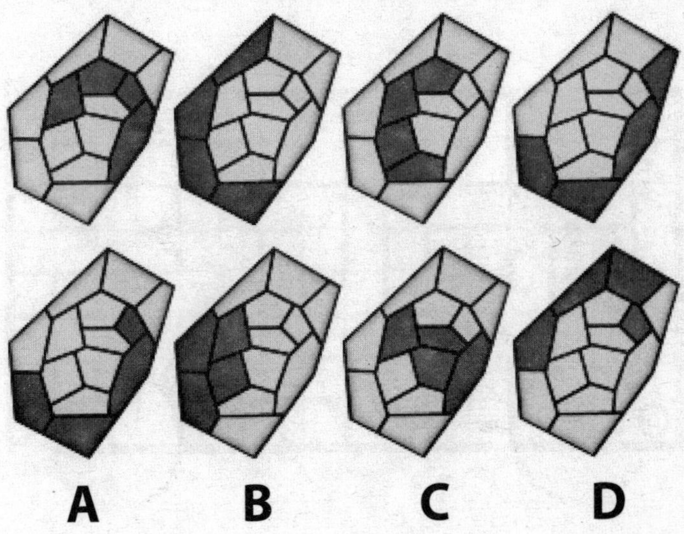

ANSWER:

Puzzle 1.26	**Difficulty rating: 2**

FAST EXIT

Which of the circles in the maze is nearest to the exit?

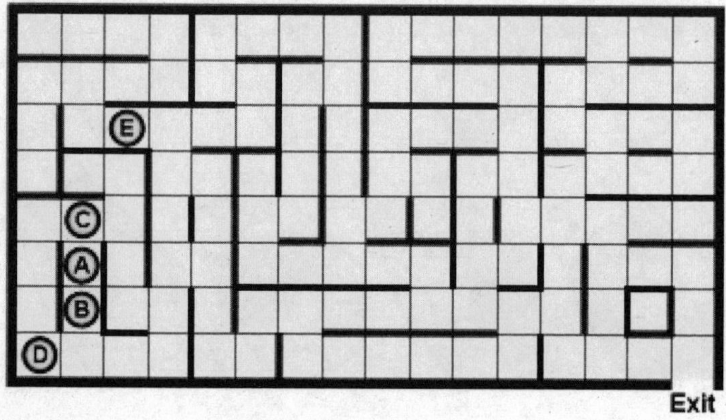

ANSWER:

Puzzle 1.27	Difficulty rating: 2

BALANCING ACT

Shown below is the aerial view of a see-saw perfectly balanced by weights on both sides.

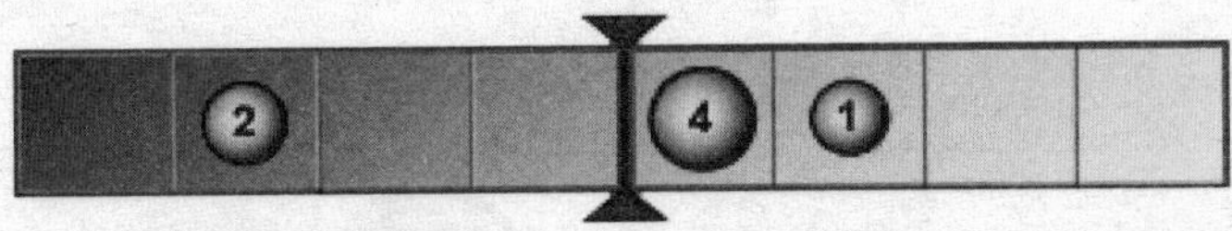

What weight must be placed at the position indicated, to balance the following see-saw?

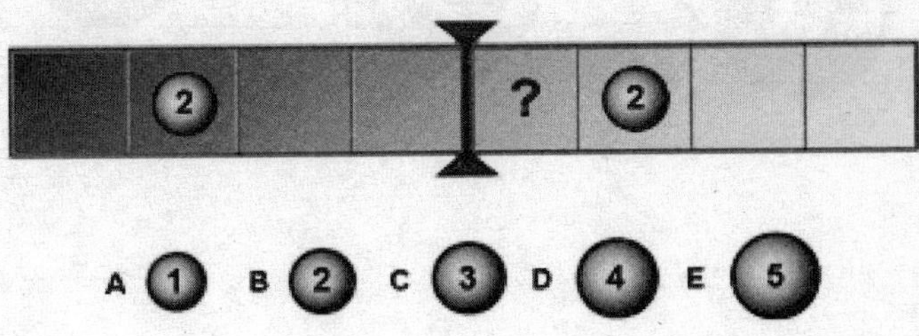

ANSWER:

Puzzle 1.28	Difficulty rating: 2

TURNING WHEELS

Shown below is a system of wheels connected by belts. The circumference of the outer rim of each wheel is exactly twice that of the inner rim. If wheel A turns at 100 revolutions per minute, how fast will wheel E turn?

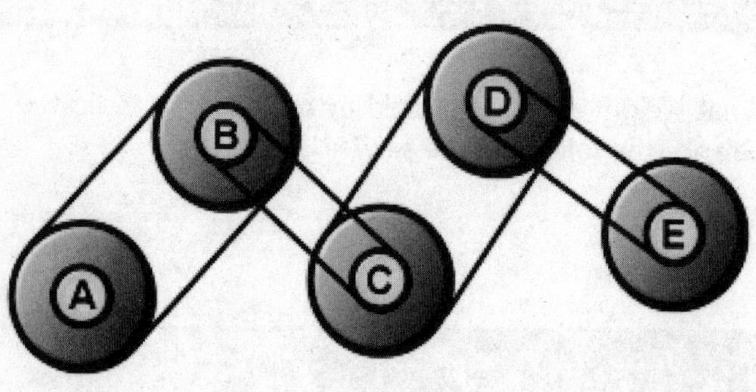

ANSWER:

Puzzle 1.29	Difficulty rating: 1

MORTS AND SKUDS

Some Morts are Skuds and all Skuds are Ralphs.
Therefore:

A. Some Morts are Ralphs
B. No Morts are Ralphs
C. All Morts are Ralphs
D. Few Morts are Ralphs

ANSWER:

Puzzle 1.30	**Difficulty rating: 2**

ABCs

I can buy two Bs for one A and one C for one A. I have four Bs. How many Cs can I buy?

ANSWER:

Puzzle 1.31	**Difficulty rating: 2**

FIND THE HIDDEN VALUE

Each of the three different symbols has a different value associated with it. When you add up the value of all the different symbols you get the total value for that row. The objective is to determine the value for each of the three symbols and fill in the missing value.

🌢	❄	☼	❄	102
☼	❄	❄	☼	98
🌢	🌢	❄	☼	91
❄	☼	🌢	🌢	91
91	?	102	87	

ANSWER:

Puzzle 1.32	**Difficulty rating: 3**

GROCERY STORE

The owner of a grocery store hired a young student who was studying cryptology at the university. The student decided to change the prices on some of the goods. Can you figure out his method and determine the cost of the pears?

PINEAPPLE 14

POTATOES 12

FLOUR 8

MILK 7

PEARS ?

ANSWER:

Puzzle 1.33	**Difficulty rating: 3**

WORD SCRAMBLE

There are seven scrambled letters below that can be formed into four English words. You must use all the letters in the word, and they can only be used once. Can you find all four?

E A T D S R H

ANSWER:

Puzzle 1.34	**Difficulty rating: 3**

WORD MORPH

The word BOOK can be turned into the word GOAT in only three steps, changing only one letter at a time. Each time you change the word, it must form a valid word.

BOOK

_ _ _ _

_ _ _ _

GOAT

ANSWER:

Puzzle 1.35	**Difficulty rating: 3**

WORD ADDITION

What word inserted in the blank space will create two new words? Find at least one word for each set of words. *Example: QUICK sand PAPER*

BREAK ____ HOUSE

AIR ____ MAN

ANSWER:

Puzzle 1.36	**Difficulty rating: 2**

FIND THE MISSING VALUE

ANSWER:

Puzzle 1.37	**Difficulty rating: 2**

DOT COMPLEX

Complete the sequence.

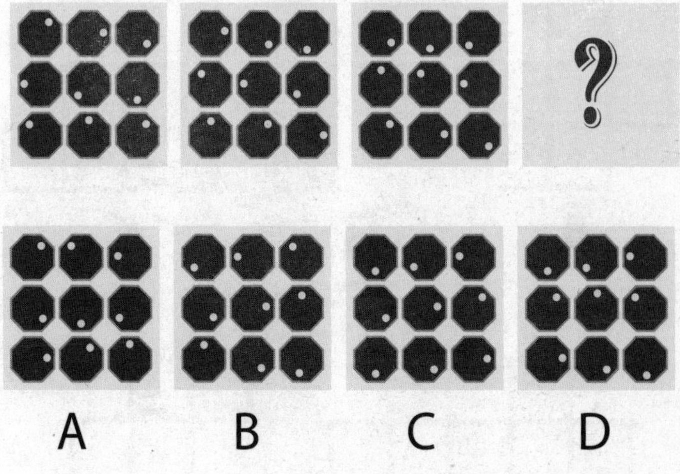

ANSWER:

Puzzle 1.38	Difficulty rating: 3

CUBE-ISM

Which of the following can be folded along the given lines to form a cube?

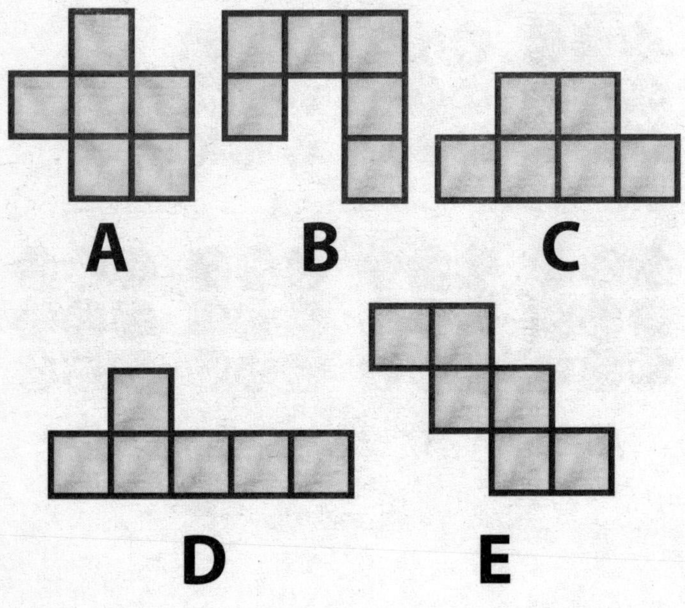

ANSWER:

Puzzle 1.39	Difficulty rating: 1

MISSING NUMBER

ANSWER:

Puzzle 1.40	**Difficulty rating: 3**

CHAPTER 1 ANSWERS

1.1. 41
1.2. 12 (vowels count as 3; consonants 2)
1.3. Rescued, Reduces, Secured, Seducer
1.4. LIST
MIST
FIST
FISH
1.5. News (paper) clip
Book (store) front
1.6. C
1.7. 14
1.8. 8
1.9. A
1.10. 6
1.11. E
1.12. 3
1.13. A
1.14. D
1.15. A
1.16. E
1.17. A
1.18. 18
1.19. C
1.20. 3
1.21. 2
1.22. 2
1.23. 4
1.24. 1
1.25. 6
1.26. A
1.27. E
1.28. B
1.29. 100 revolutions per minute.
1.30. A
1.31. 2
1.32. 102
1.33. 8 (Vowels count as 1; consonants 2)
1.34. Trashed, Hardest, Hatreds, Threads
1.35. BOOK
BOOT
BOAT
GOAT
1.36. Break (out) house
Air (mail) man
1.37. 9
1.38. D
1.39. E
1.40. 8

DIFFICULTY RATING: 95

FACE FIT

Which of the following is least like the others?

ANSWER:

Puzzle 2.1	**Difficulty rating: 2**

MISSING PIECES

Given the puzzle piece shown, determine the maximum number of times the piece can fit into the missing areas of the puzzle.

x ?

ANSWER:

Puzzle 2.2	**Difficulty rating: 1**

MOLECULAR SEQUENCE

Use the diagram to determine the missing letter in the sequence.

A C F A D G A E ?

ANSWER:

Puzzle 2.3	**Difficulty rating: 3**

STARGAZING

Which item is the best continuation of the sequence?

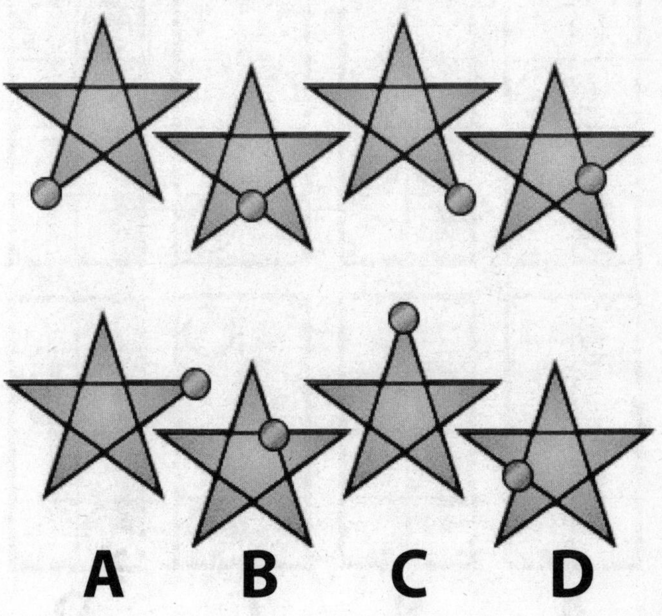

ANSWER:

Puzzle 2.4	**Difficulty rating: 1**

TWO INTO EIGHT

Which item is the best continuation of the sequence?

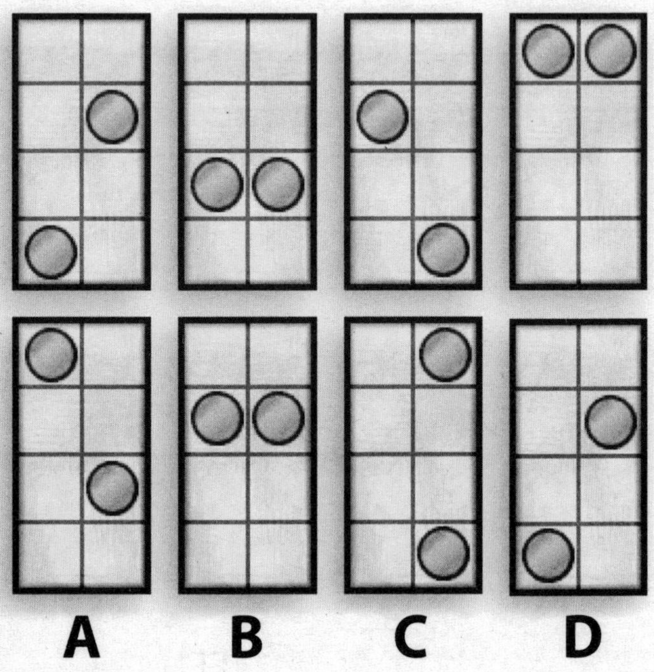

ANSWER:

Puzzle 2.5	Difficulty rating: 4

INTERLOCKING HEXAGONS

Which item is the best continuation of the sequence?

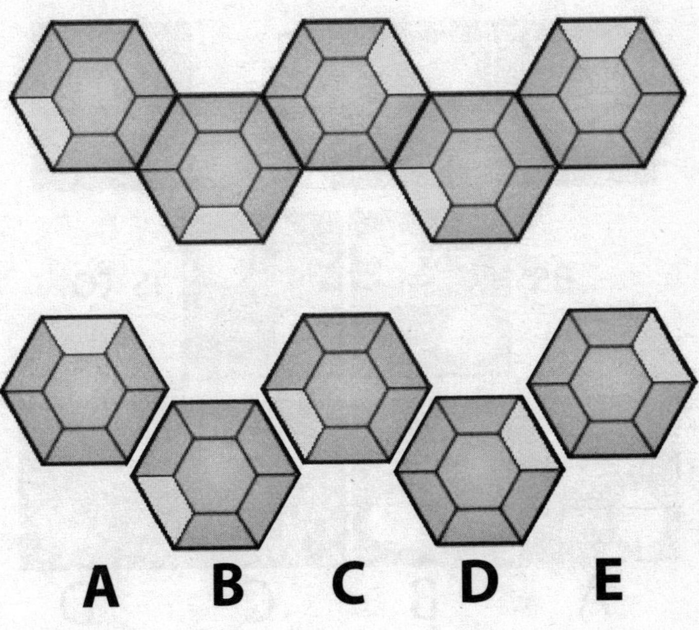

ANSWER:

Puzzle 2.6	Difficulty rating: 2

ANALOGY PUZZLE

Determine the item that best completes the analogy.

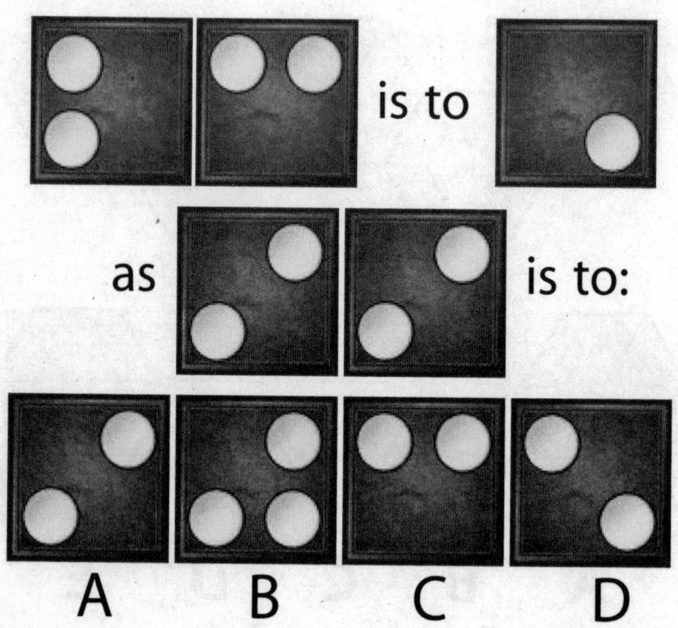

ANSWER:

Puzzle 2.7	**Difficulty rating: 3**

CUBE STACKING

The object below was created by gluing together several cubes. What is the total number of sides that are NOT glued to another cube?

You may assume that no cubes are hidden from view.

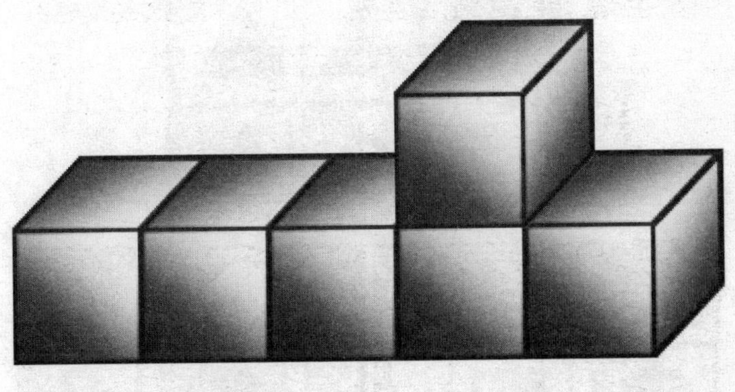

ANSWER:

Puzzle 2.8	**Difficulty rating: 1**

Determine the missing item.

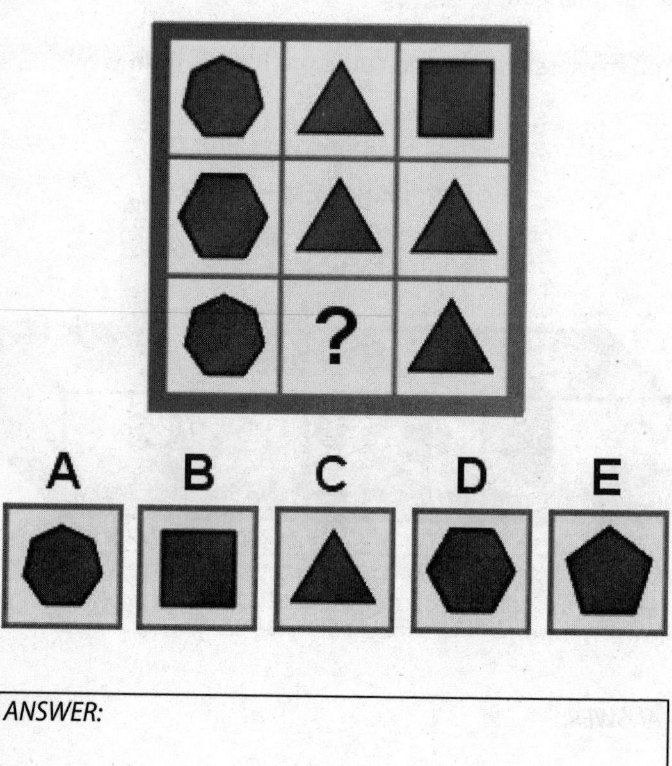

ANSWER:

Puzzle 2.9	**Difficulty rating: 2**

TRELLIS PATTERN

Determine the system used to generate numbers in the grid below, and find the missing value.

ANSWER:

Puzzle 2.10	**Difficulty rating: 4**

WHEELS WITHIN WHEELS

Determine the system used to generate numbers in the diagram below, and find the missing value.

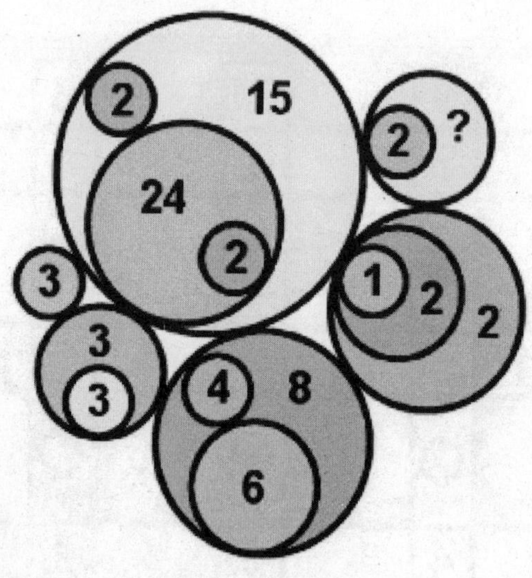

ANSWER:

Puzzle 2.11	**Difficulty rating: 3**

HIDDEN NUMBERS

What is the missing number in the figure below?

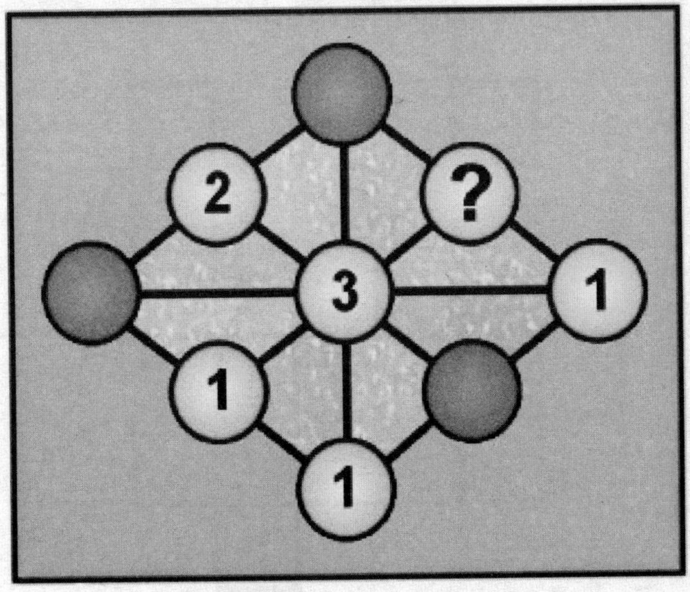

ANSWER:

Puzzle 2.12	**Difficulty rating: 3**

HIDDEN VALUES

Determine the system used to generate numbers in the grid below, and find the missing value.

ANSWER:

Puzzle 2.13	**Difficulty rating: 3**

CIRCUITOUS NUMBERS

Determine the system used to generate numbers in the grid below, and find the missing value.

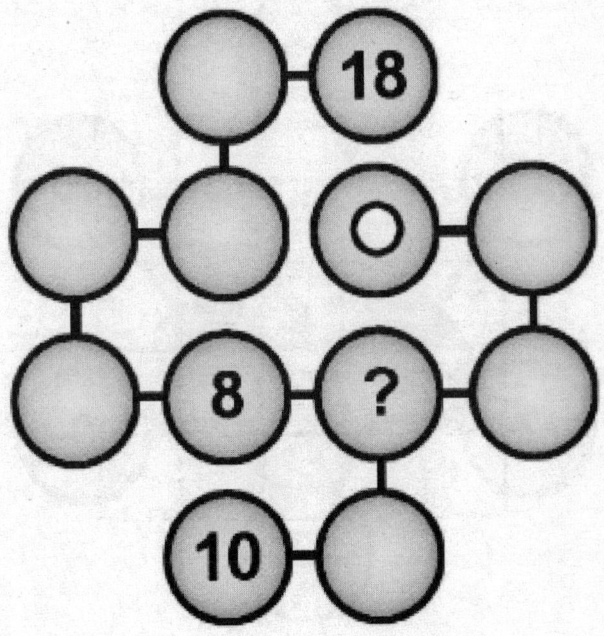

ANSWER:

Puzzle 2.14	**Difficulty rating: 3**

STARBURST

Determine the relationship between the central star and the outer circles, and find the missing value.

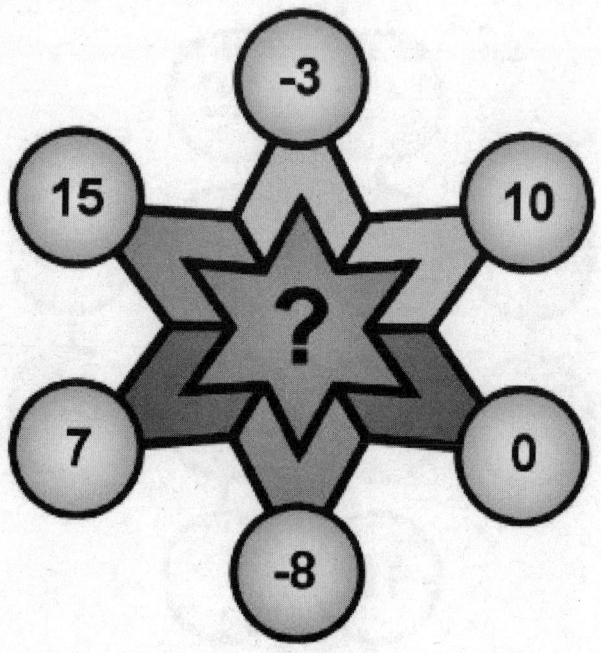

ANSWER:

Puzzle 2.15	**Difficulty rating: 3**

FACE FIT

Which one is most like the first four?

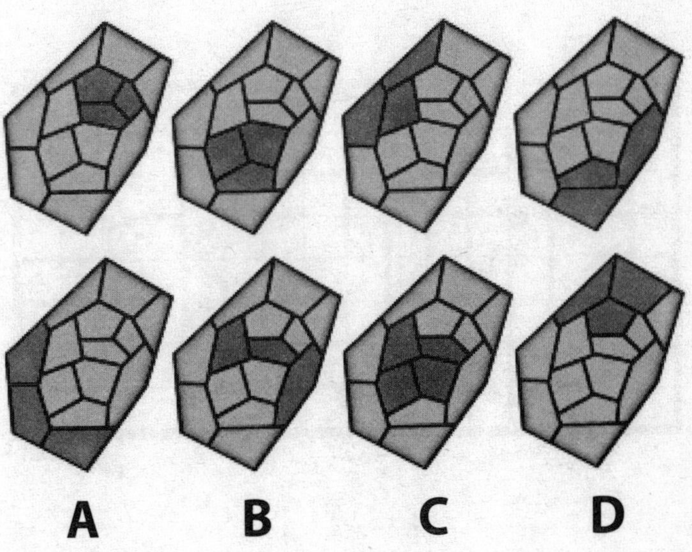

ANSWER:

Puzzle 2.16	**Difficulty rating: 2**

FAST EXIT

Which of the circles in the maze is nearest to the exit?

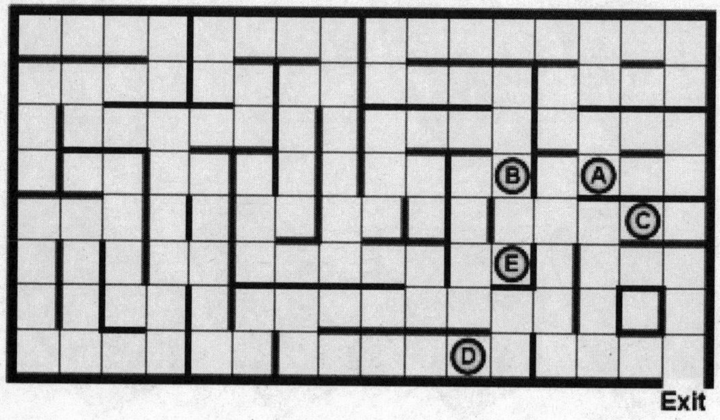

ANSWER:

Puzzle 2.17	Difficulty rating: 2

BALANCING ACT

Shown below is the aerial view of a see-saw perfectly balanced by weights on both sides.

What weight must be placed at the position indicated, to balance the following see-saw?

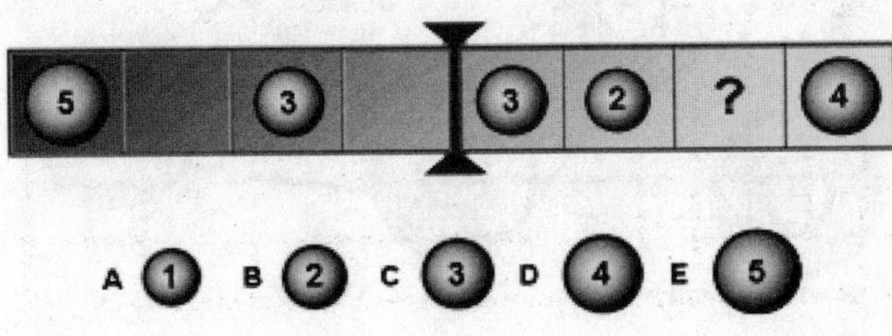

ANSWER:

Puzzle 2.18	**Difficulty rating: 2**

TURNING WHEELS

Shown below is a system of wheels connected by belts. The circumference of the outer rim of each wheel is exactly twice that of the inner rim. If wheel A turns at 100 revolutions per minute, how fast will wheel E turn?

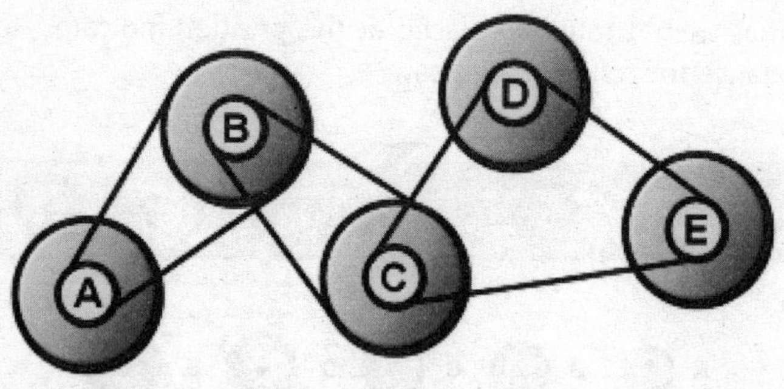

ANSWER:

Puzzle 2.19	**Difficulty rating: 3**

HAIL, CAESAR

A cat named after Caesar gets sleepy in the month of his name. What month is this?

ANSWER:

Puzzle 2.20	**Difficulty rating: 1**

THE EYES HAVE IT

Which word does not belong?

EYE
EAR
BOB
OBO

ANSWER:

Puzzle 2.21	**Difficulty rating: 2**

FIND THE HIDDEN VALUE

Each of the three different symbols has a different value associated with it. When you add up the value of all the different symbols you get the total value for that row. The objective is to determine the value for each of the three symbols and fill in the missing value.

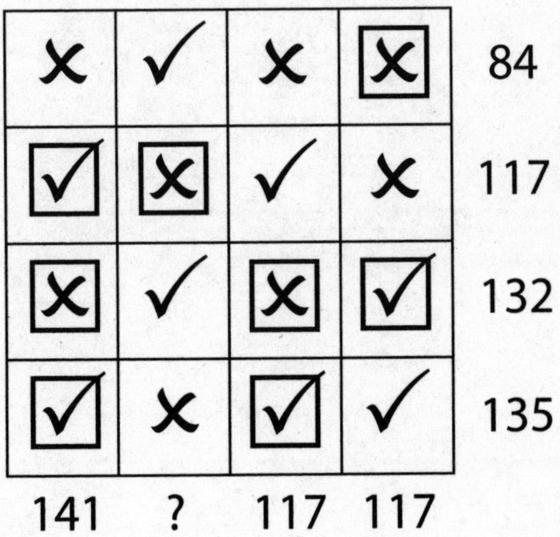

ANSWER:

Puzzle 2.22	**Difficulty rating: 3**

WORD SCRAMBLE

There are five scrambled letters below that can be formed into four English words. You must use all the letters in the word, and they can only be used once. Can you find all four?

R N I E S

ANSWER:

Puzzle 2.23	**Difficulty rating: 3**

WORD ADDITION

What word inserted in the blank space will create two new words? Find at least one word for each set of words. *Example: QUICK sand PAPER*

BATTLE _____ LINE

BREAD _____ CAR

ANSWER:

Puzzle 2.24	**Difficulty rating: 2**

DOT COMPLEX

Complete the sequence.

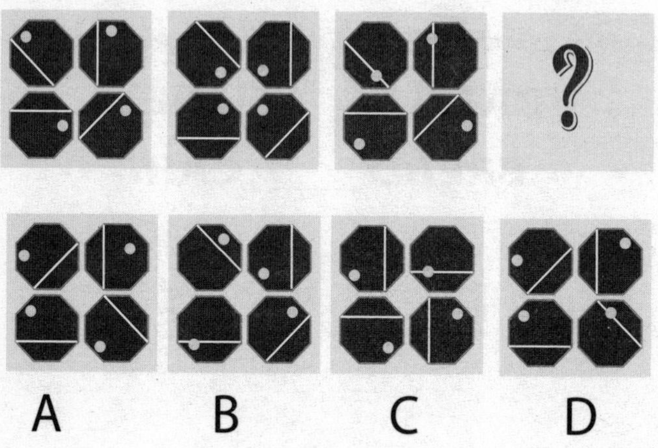

ANSWER:

Puzzle 2.25	**Difficulty rating: 3**

FIND THE MISSING VALUE

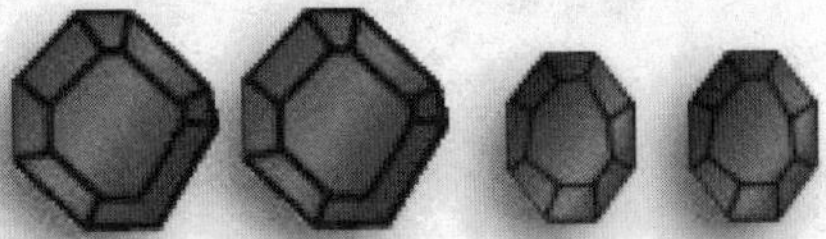

= 18

= 11

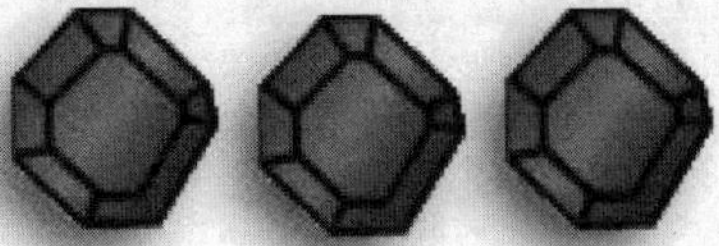

= ?

ANSWER:

Puzzle 2.26	Difficulty rating: 2

MISSING FIGURE

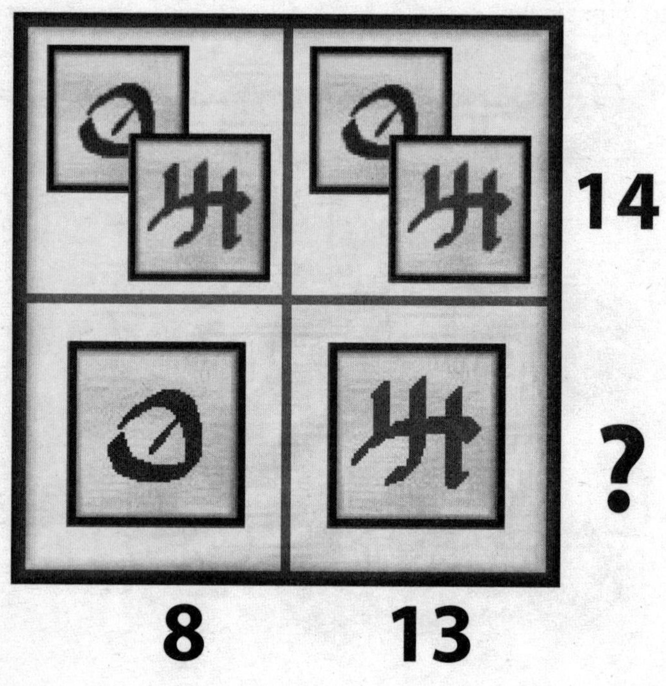

ANSWER:

Puzzle 2.27	**Difficulty rating: 3**

CUBE-ISM

Which of the following can be folded along the given lines to form a cube?

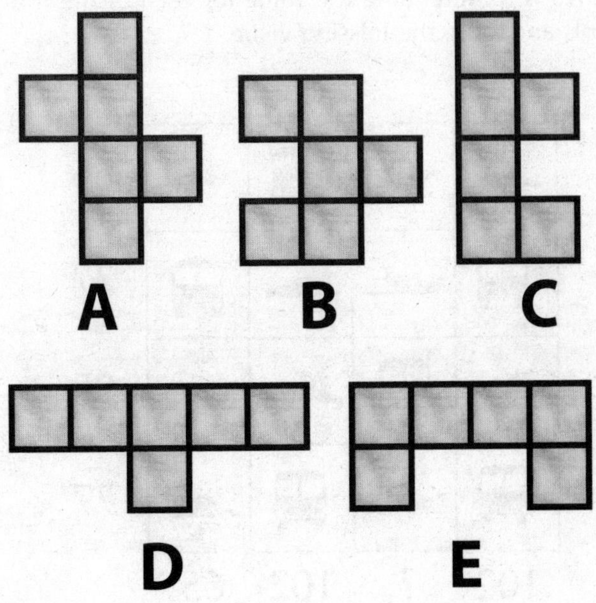

ANSWER:

Puzzle 2.28	**Difficulty rating: 1**

FIND THE HIDDEN VALUE

Each of the three different symbols has a different value associated with it. When you add up the value of all the different symbols you get the total value for that row. The objective is to determine the value for each of the three symbols and fill in the missing value.

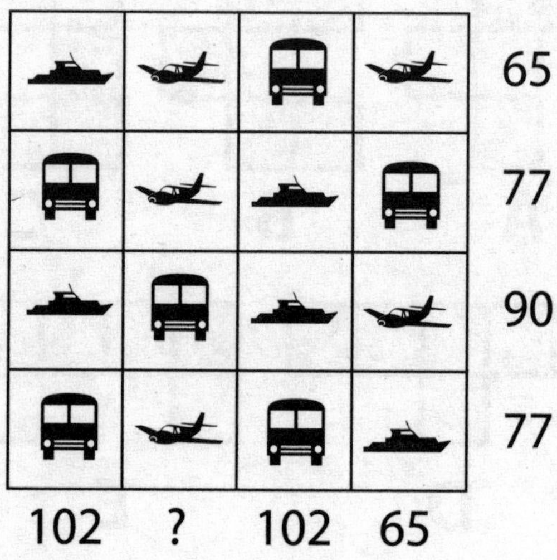

ANSWER:

Puzzle 2.29	**Difficulty rating: 3**

WORD ADDITION

What word inserted in the blank space will create two new words? Find at least one word for each set of words. *Example: QUICK sand PAPER*

BACK ____ MULE

BANK ____ WORM

ANSWER:

Puzzle 2.30	**Difficulty rating: 2**

WORD SCRAMBLE

There are five scrambled letters below that can be formed into three English words. You must use all the letters in the word, and they can only be used once. Can you find all three?

I N S L A

ANSWER:

Puzzle 2.31	**Difficulty rating: 3**

MOSAIC

Complete the sequence.

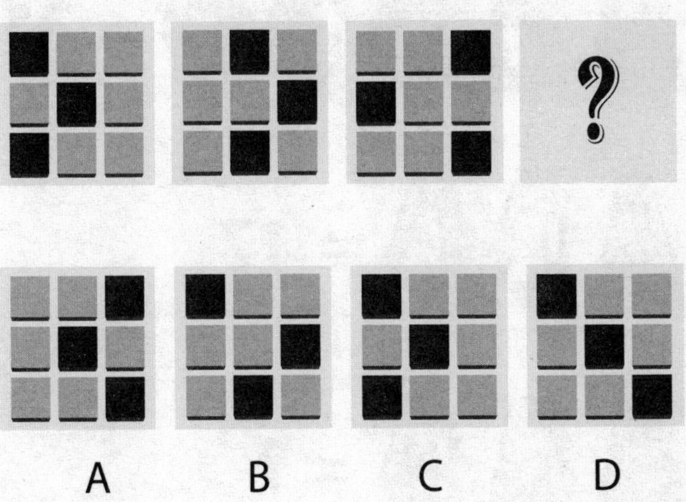

ANSWER:

Puzzle 2.32	**Difficulty rating: 2**

FIND THE MISSING VALUE

= 31

= 17

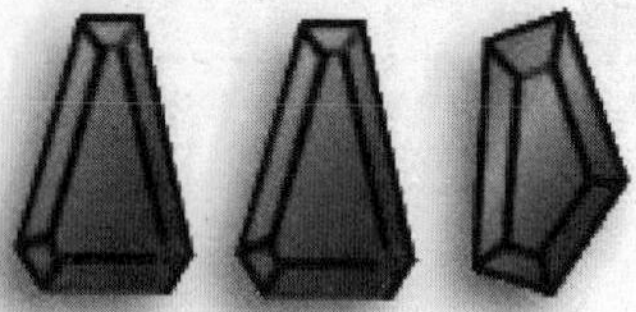

= ?

ANSWER:

Puzzle 2.33	**Difficulty rating: 2**

CUBE-ISM

Which of the following can be folded along the given lines to form a cube?

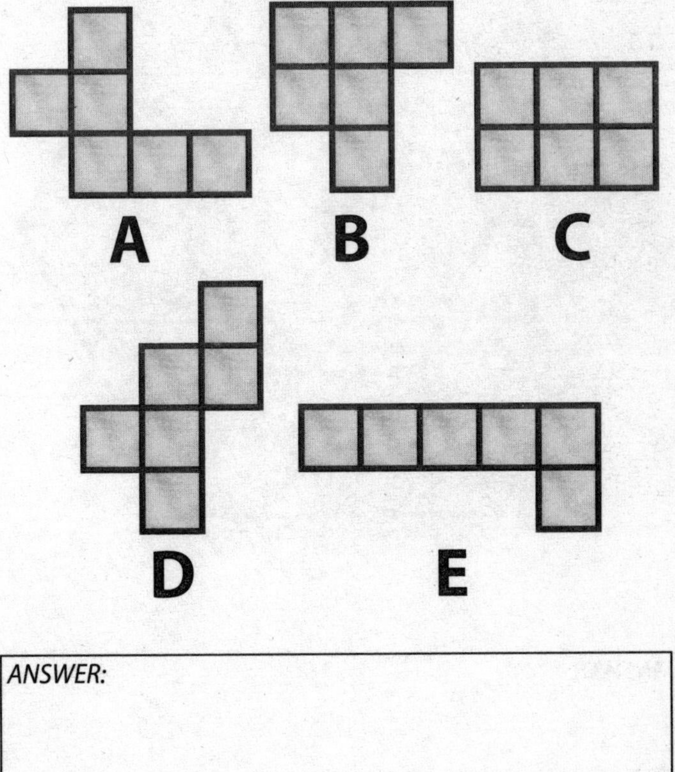

ANSWER:

Puzzle 2.34	**Difficulty rating: 1**

MISSING NUMBER

ANSWER:

Puzzle 2.35	Difficulty rating: 3

FACE FIT

Which of the following is least like the others?

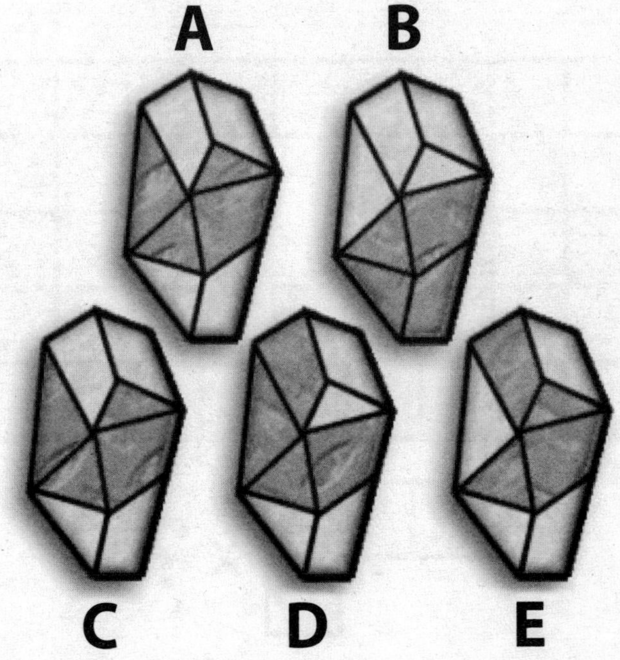

ANSWER:

Puzzle 2.36	**Difficulty rating: 2**

MISSING PIECES

Given the puzzle piece shown, determine the maximum number of times the piece can fit into the missing areas of the puzzle.

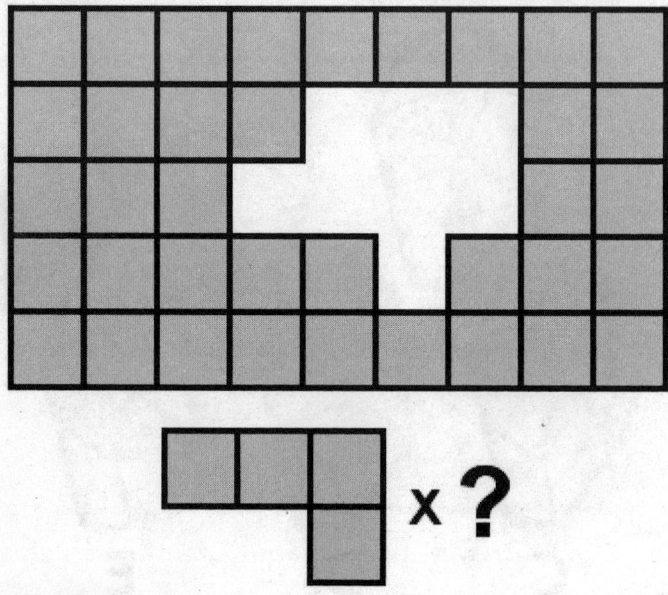

ANSWER:

Puzzle 2.37	Difficulty rating: 1

MOLECULAR SEQUENCE

Use the diagram to determine the missing letter in the sequence.

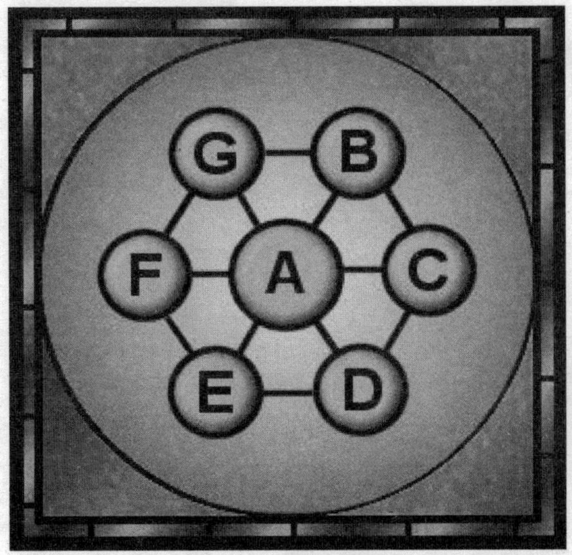

G A F C A B E A ?

ANSWER:

Puzzle 2.38	**Difficulty rating: 3**

STARGAZING

Which item is the best continuation of the sequence?

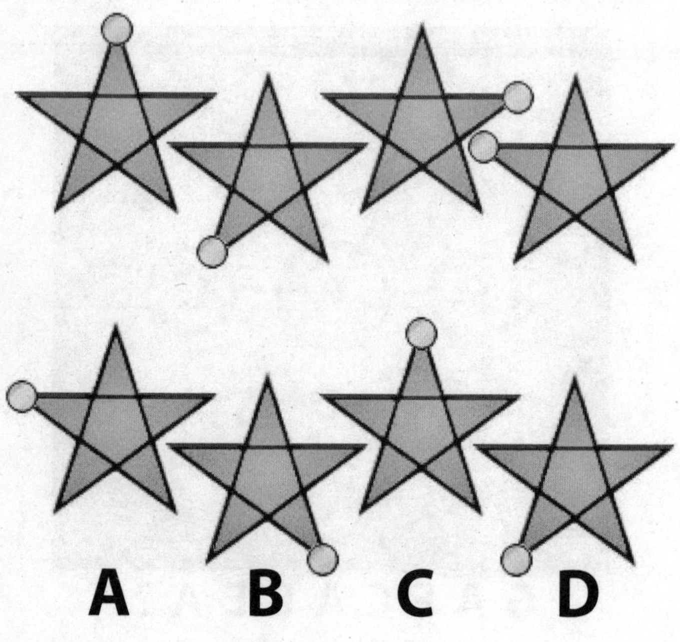

ANSWER:

Puzzle 2.39	**Difficulty rating: 2**

THREE INTO EIGHT

Which item is the best continuation of the sequence?

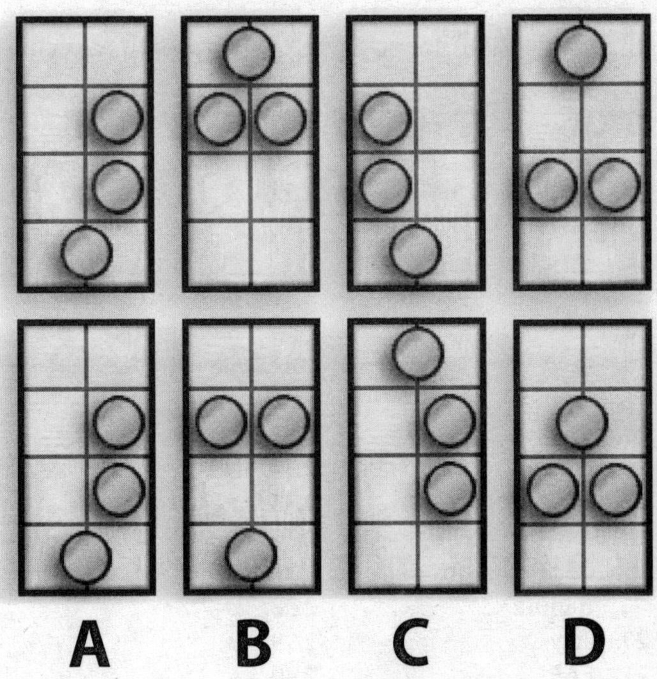

ANSWER:

Puzzle 2.40	**Difficulty rating: 4**

CHAPTER 2 ANSWERS

2.1. E
2.2. 4
2.3. B
2.4. A
2.5. D
2.6. D
2.7. D
2.8. 26
2.9. B
2.10. 4
2.11. 5
2.12. 1
2.13. 4
2.14. 6
2.15. 7
2.16. D
2.17. C
2.18. A
2.19. 25 revolutions per minute.
2.20. July
2.21. EAR
2.22. 93
2.23. Siren, Rinse, Risen, Reins
2.24. Battle (front) line
Bread (box) car
2.25. B
2.26. 24
2.27. 7
2.28. A
2.29. 40
2.30. Back (pack) mule
Bank (book) worm
2.31. Slain, Nails, Snail
2.32. C
2.33. 25
2.34. D
2.35. 12
2.36. D
2.37. 2
2.38. D
2.39. B
2.40. A

DIFFICULTY RATING: 97

LITTLE AND LARGE

Which item is the best continuation of the sequence?

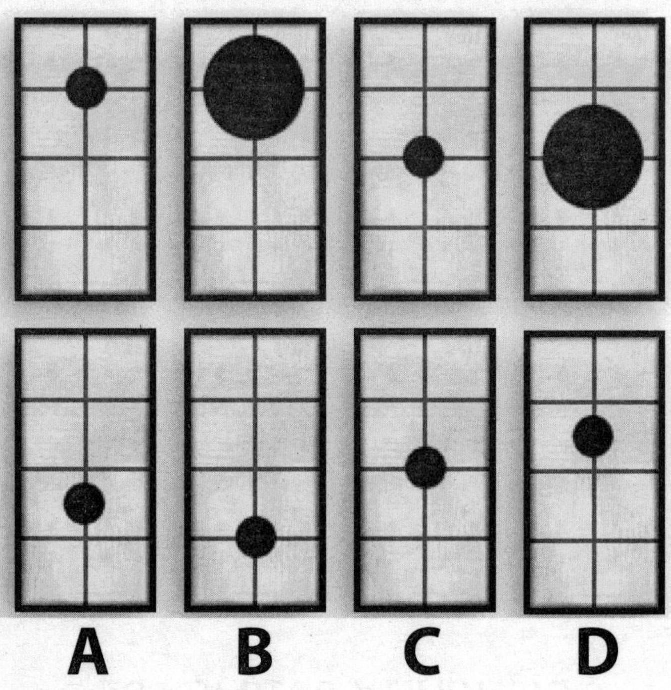

ANSWER:

Puzzle 3.1	Difficulty rating: 2

ANALOGY PUZZLE

Determine the item that best completes the analogy.

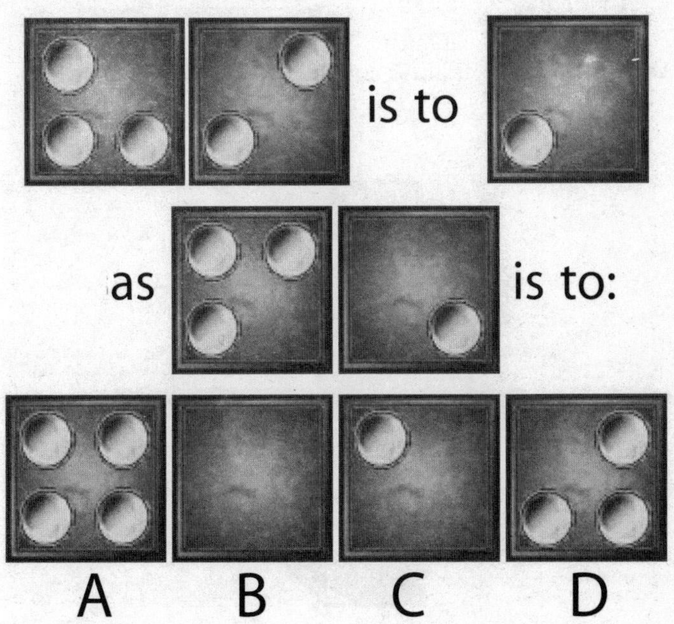

ANSWER:

Puzzle 3.2	**Difficulty rating: 3**

CUBE STACKING

The object below was created by gluing together several cubes. What is the total number of sides NOT glued to another cube?

You may assume that no cubes are hidden from view.

ANSWER:

Puzzle 3.3	**Difficulty rating: 2**

CHILD'S PLAY

Determine the missing item.

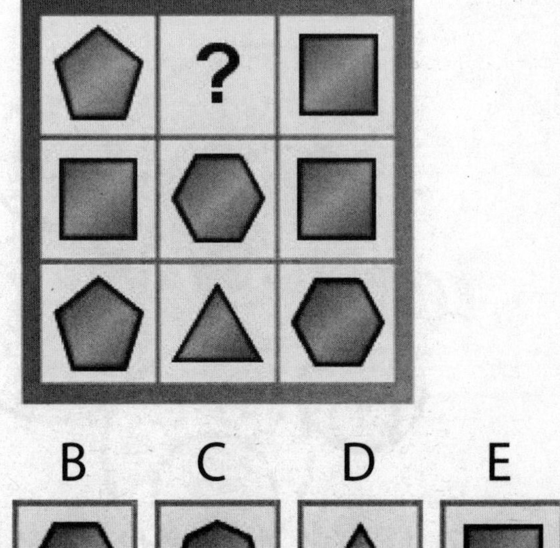

ANSWER:

Puzzle 3.4	**Difficulty rating: 1**

WHEELS WITHIN WHEELS

Determine the system used to generate numbers in the diagram below, and find the missing value.

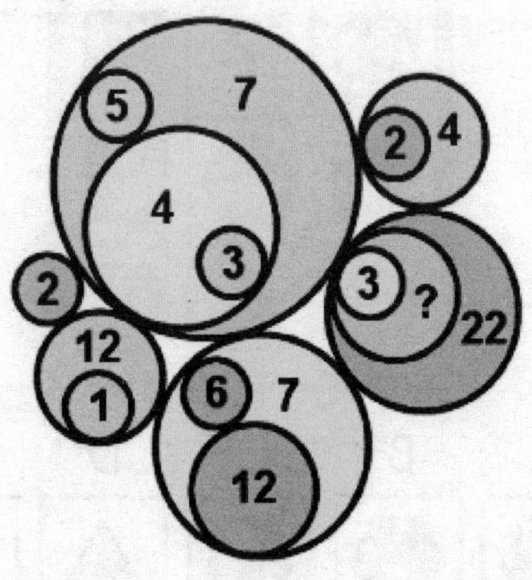

ANSWER:

Puzzle 3.5	**Difficulty rating: 3**

HIDDEN NUMBERS

What is the missing number in the figure below?

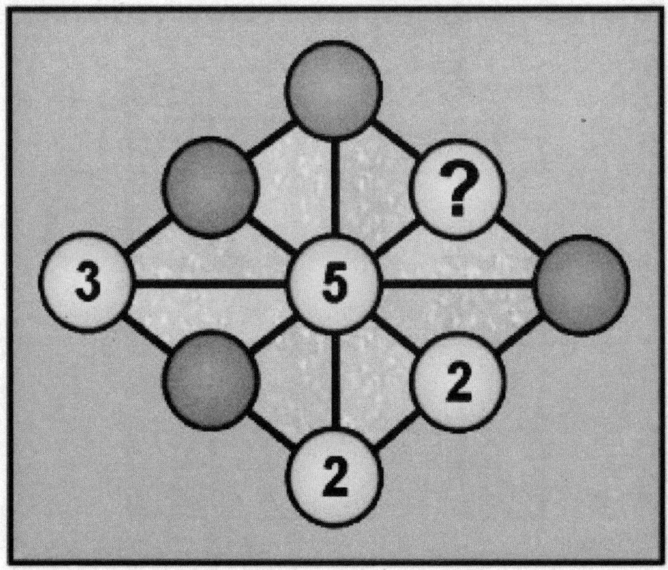

ANSWER:

Puzzle 3.6	**Difficulty rating: 3**

HIDDEN VALUES

Determine the system used to generate numbers in the grid below, and find the missing value.

ANSWER:

Puzzle 3.7	**Difficulty rating: 3**

CIRCUITOUS NUMBERS

Determine the system used to generate numbers in the diagram below, and find the missing value.

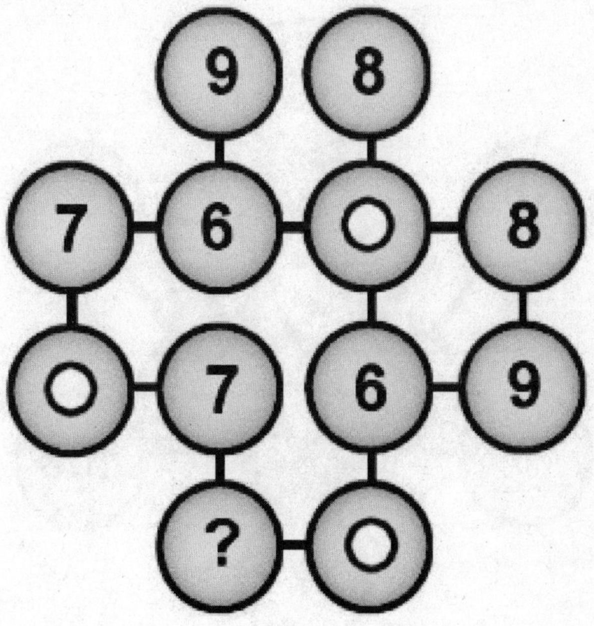

ANSWER:

Puzzle 3.8	**Difficulty rating: 3**

STARBURST

Determine the relationship between the central star and the outer circles, and find the missing value.

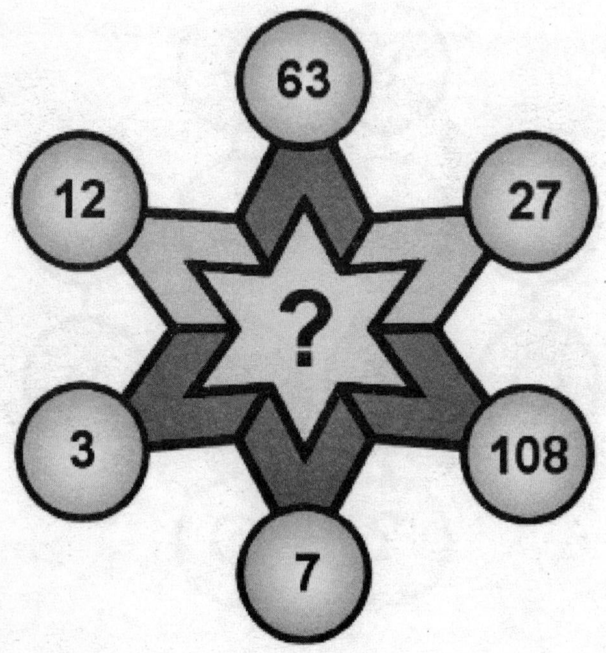

ANSWER:

Puzzle 3.9	**Difficulty rating: 3**

FACE FIT

Which one is most like the first four?

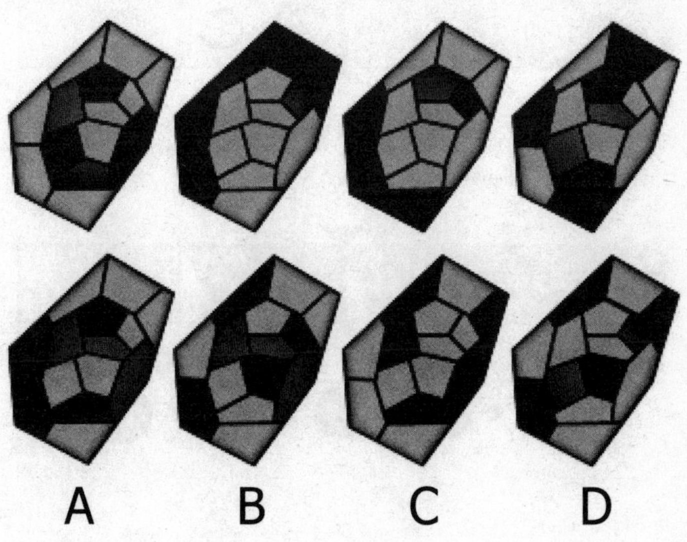

ANSWER:

Puzzle 3.10	Difficulty rating: 2

BALANCING ACT

Shown below is the aerial view of a see-saw perfectly balanced by weights on both sides.

What weight must be placed at the position indicated to balance the following see-saw?

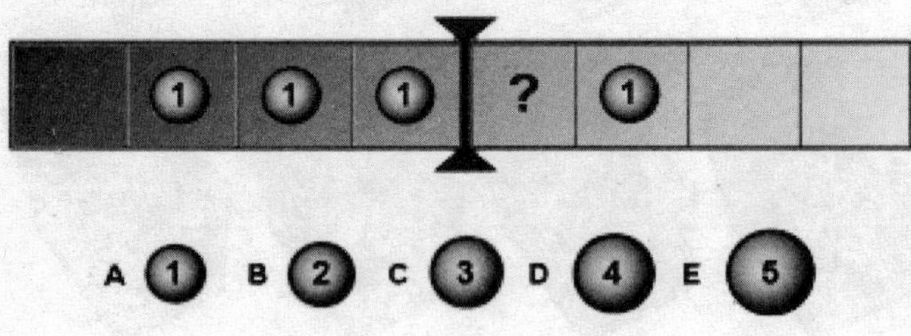

ANSWER:

Puzzle 3.11	Difficulty rating: 2

TURNING WHEELS

Shown below is a system of wheels connected by belts. The circumference of the outer rim of each wheel is exactly twice that of the inner rim. If wheel A turns at 100 revolutions per minute, how fast will wheel E turn?

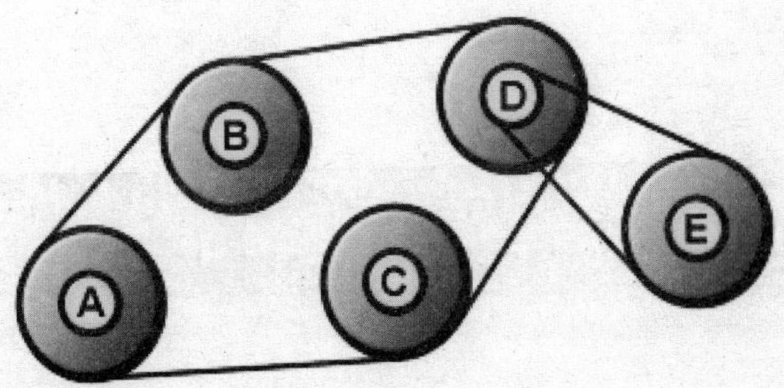

ANSWER:

Puzzle 3.12	**Difficulty rating: 2**

WHAT'S NEXT?

Complete the sequence.

2, 5, 26, 677, ?

ANSWER:

Puzzle 3.13	**Difficulty rating: 4**

MISPLACED LETTER

Which letter does not belong?

O T E M

ANSWER:

Puzzle 3.14	**Difficulty rating: 2**

FIND THE HIDDEN VALUE

Each of the three different symbols has a different value associated with it. When you add up the value of all the different symbols you get the total value for that row. The objective is to determine the value for each of the three symbols and fill in the missing value.

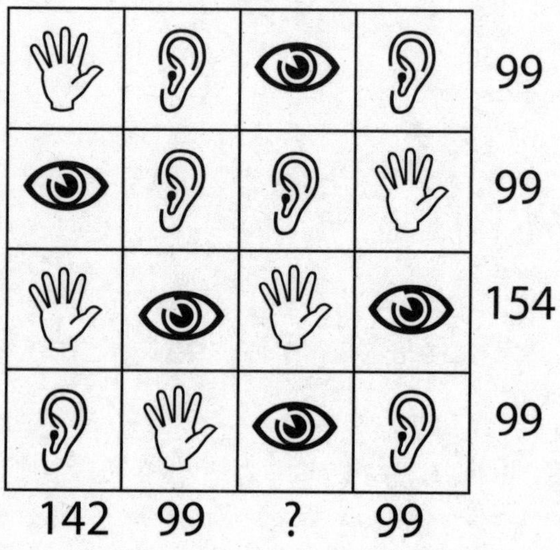

ANSWER:

Puzzle 3.15	**Difficulty rating: 3**

WORD SCRAMBLE

There are five scrambled letters below that can be formed into four English words. You must use all the letters in the word, and they can only be used once. Can you find all four?

S I E M L

ANSWER:

Puzzle 3.16	**Difficulty rating: 3**

WORD ADDITION

What word inserted in the blank space will create two new words? Find at least one word for each set of words. *Example: QUICK sand PAPER*

BARN _____ STICK

CAMP _____ PLACE

ANSWER:

Puzzle 3.17	Difficulty rating: 2

COMPLETE THE SEQUENCE

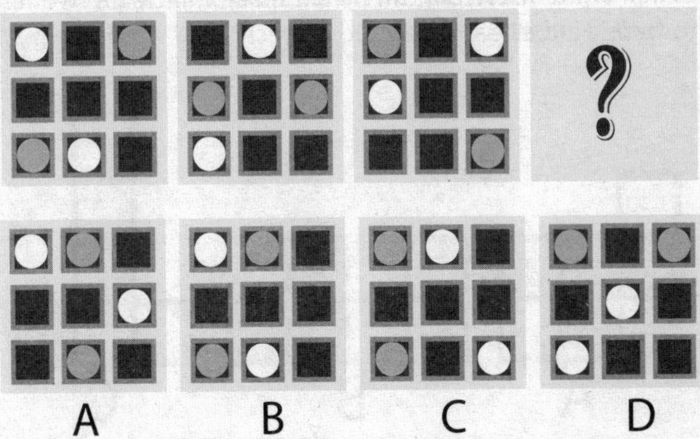

A B C D

ANSWER:

Puzzle 3.18 | **Difficulty rating: 3**

CUBE-ISM

Which of the following can be folded along the given lines to form a cube?

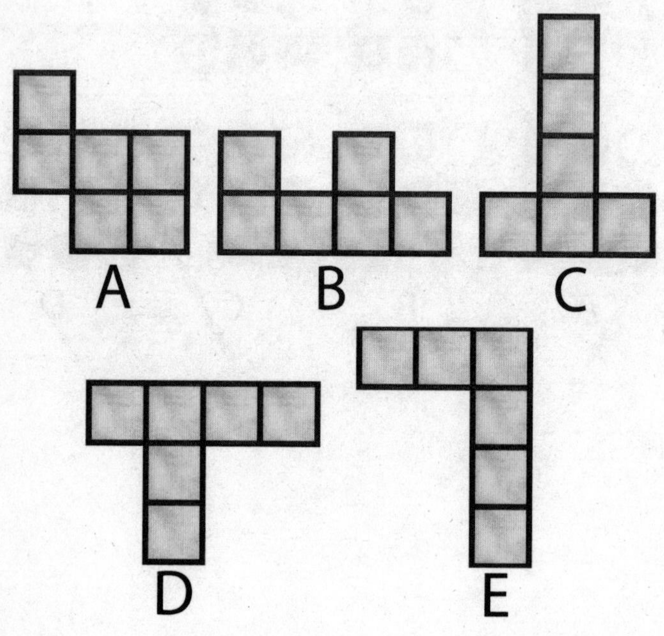

ANSWER:

Puzzle 3.19	Difficulty rating: 1

MISSING NUMBER

ANSWER:

Puzzle 3.20	Difficulty rating: 3

ODD BALL

Which of the following is least like the others?

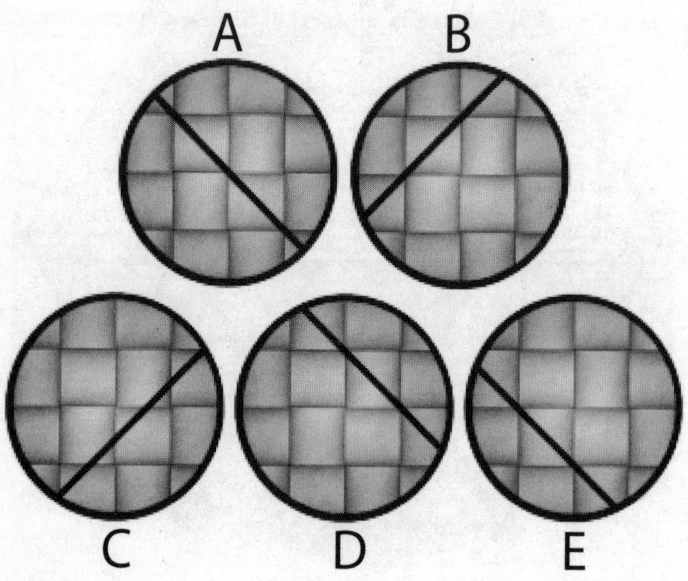

ANSWER:

Puzzle 3.21	Difficulty rating: 2

MISSING PIECES

Given the puzzle piece shown, determine the maximum number of times the piece can fit into the missing areas of the puzzle.

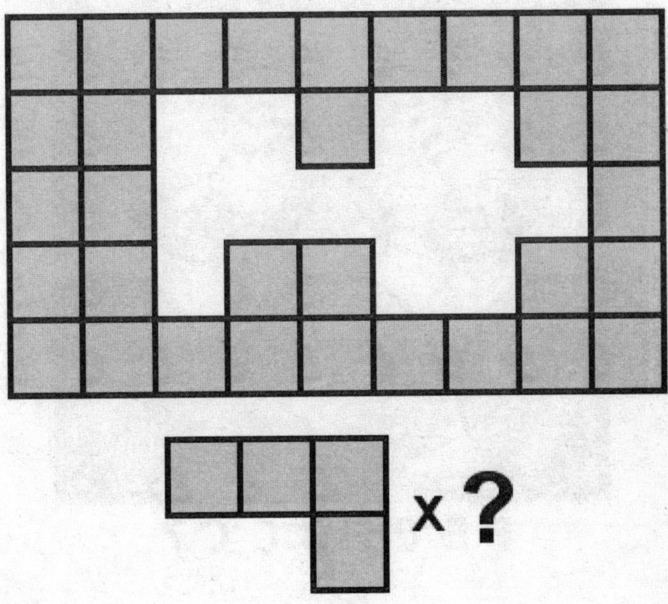

ANSWER:

Puzzle 3.22	**Difficulty rating: 1**

MOLECULAR SEQUENCE

Use the diagram to determine the missing letter in the sequence.

F E C F B C C ?

ANSWER:

Puzzle 3.23	Difficulty rating: 3

STARGAZING

Which item is the best continuation of the sequence?

ANSWER:

Puzzle 3.24	Difficulty rating: 2

CHOOSE A TILE

Which item is the best continuation of the sequence?

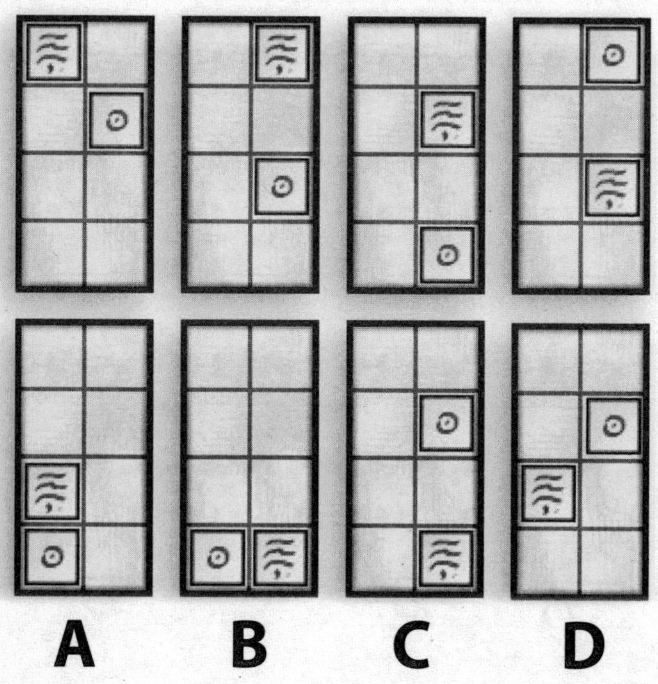

ANSWER:

Puzzle 3.25	Difficulty rating: 2

OVER THE EDGE?

Which item is the best continuation of the sequence?

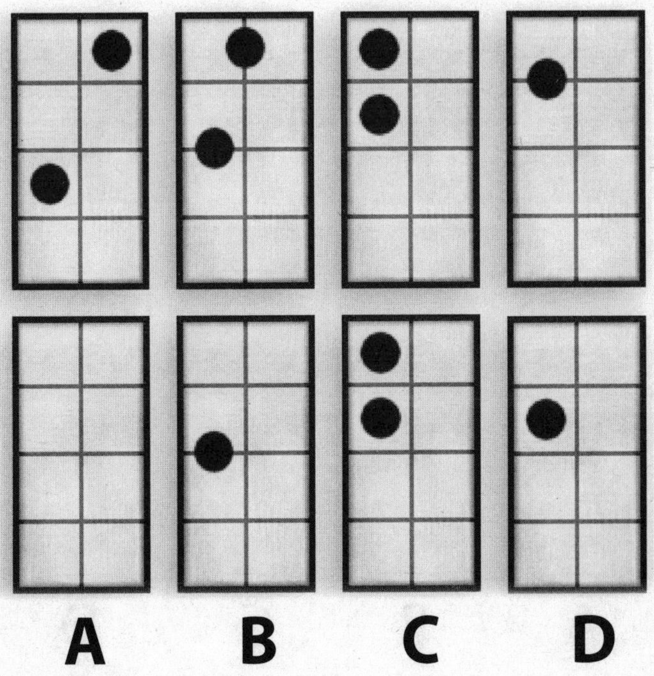

ANSWER:

Puzzle 3.26	Difficulty rating: 2

ANALOGY PUZZLE

Determine the item that best completes the analogy.

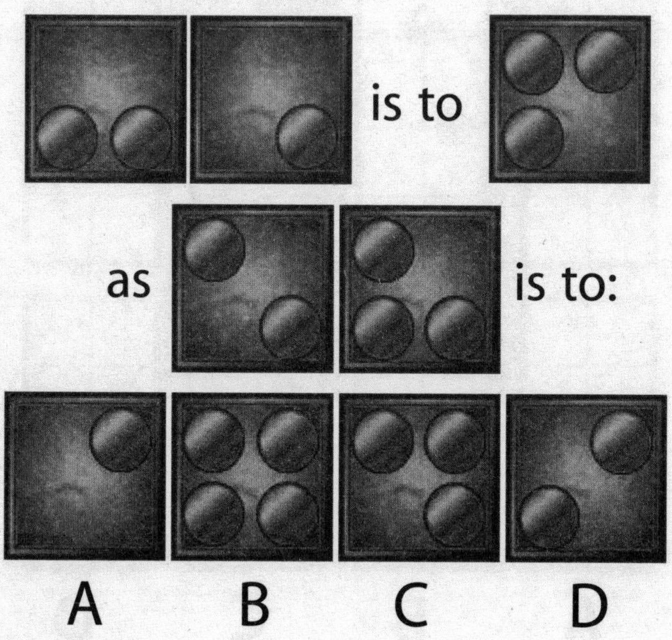

ANSWER:

Puzzle 3.27	**Difficulty rating: 3**

CHILD'S PLAY

Determine the missing item.

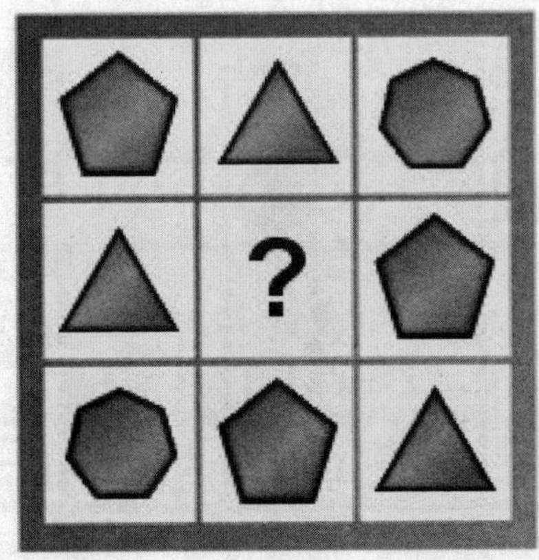

A B C D E

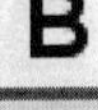

ANSWER:

Puzzle 3.28	**Difficulty rating: 3**

TRELLIS PATTERN

Determine the system used to generate numbers in the grid below, and find the missing value.

ANSWER:

Puzzle 3.29 | **Difficulty rating: 2**

WHEELS WITHIN WHEELS

Determine the system used to generate numbers in the diagram below, and find the missing value.

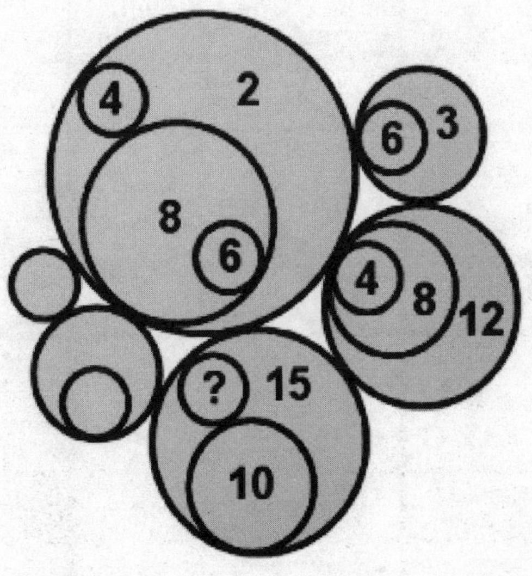

ANSWER:

Puzzle 3.30	**Difficulty rating: 4**

HIDDEN NUMBERS

What is the missing number in the figure below?

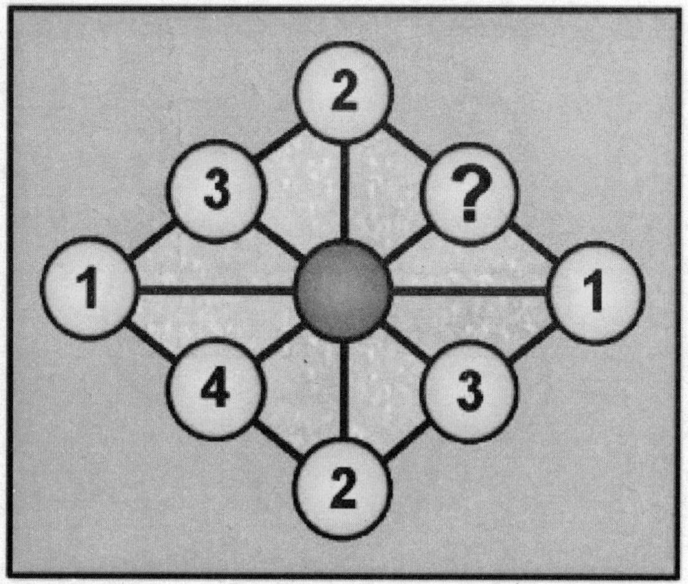

ANSWER:

Puzzle 3.31	**Difficulty rating: 3**

HIDDEN VALUES

Determine the system used to generate numbers in the grid below, and find the missing value.

ANSWER:

Puzzle 3.32	**Difficulty rating: 3**

CIRCUITOUS NUMBERS

Determine the system used to generate numbers in the grid below, and find the missing value.

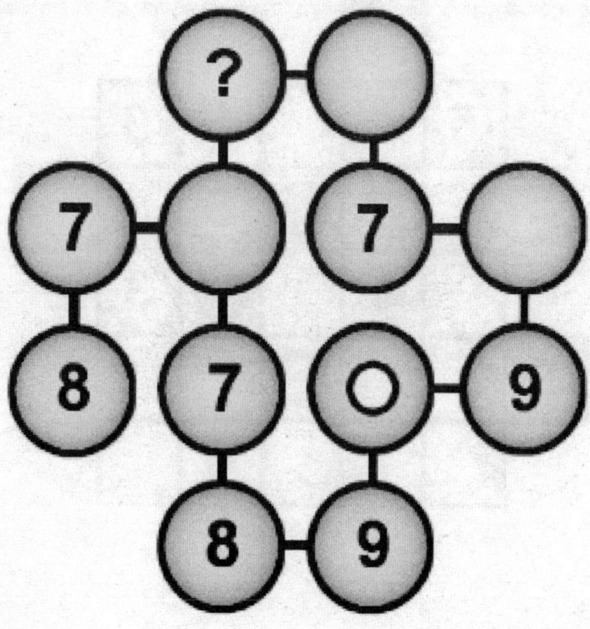

ANSWER:

Puzzle 3.33	**Difficulty rating: 2**

STARBURST

Determine the relationship between the central star and the outer circles, and find the missing value.

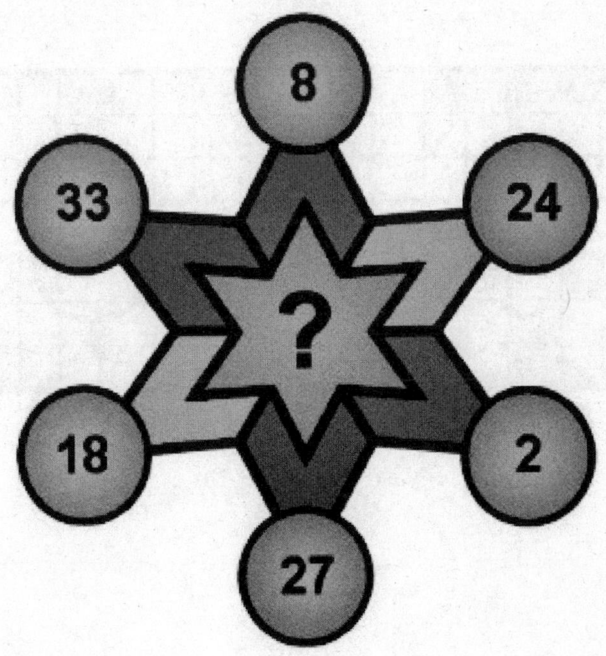

ANSWER:

Puzzle 3.34	**Difficulty rating: 2**

ODD ONE IN

Which item is most like the first five?

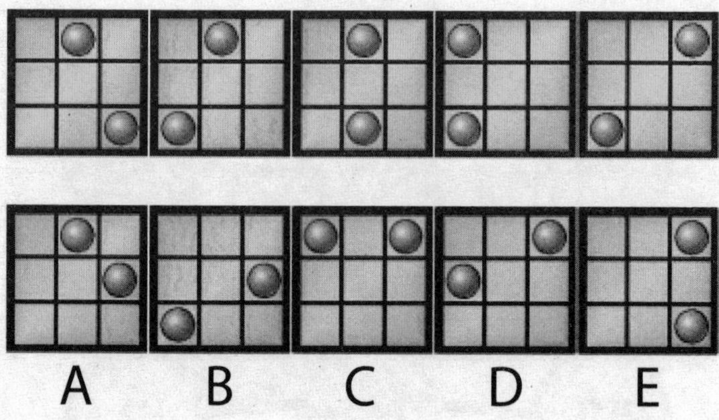

ANSWER:

Puzzle 3.35	Difficulty rating: 2

FAST EXIT

Which of the circles in the maze is nearest to the exit?

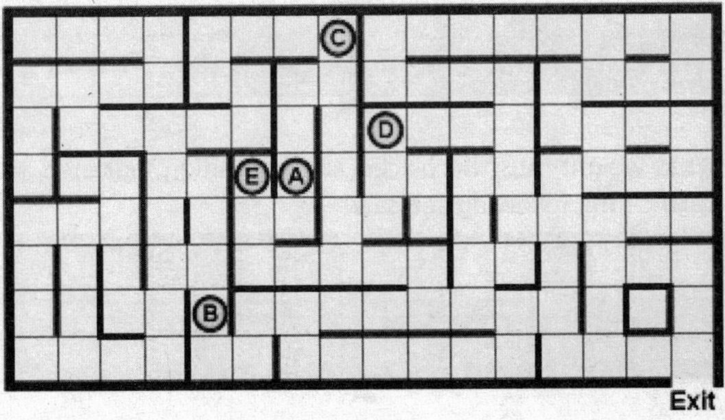

ANSWER:

Puzzle 3.36	**Difficulty rating: 2**

BALANCING ACT

Shown below is the aerial view of a see-saw perfectly balanced by weights on both sides.

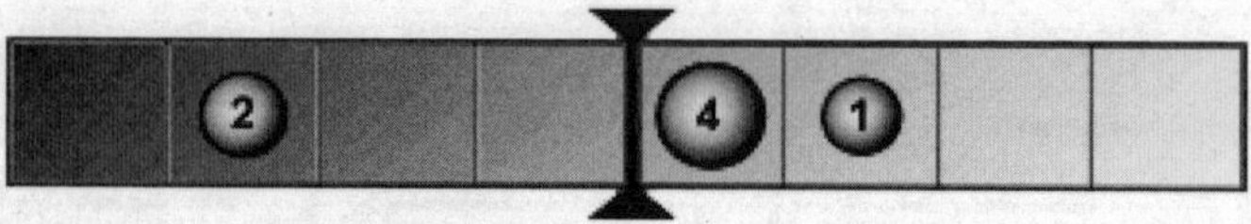

What weight must be placed at the position indicated, to balance the following see-saw?

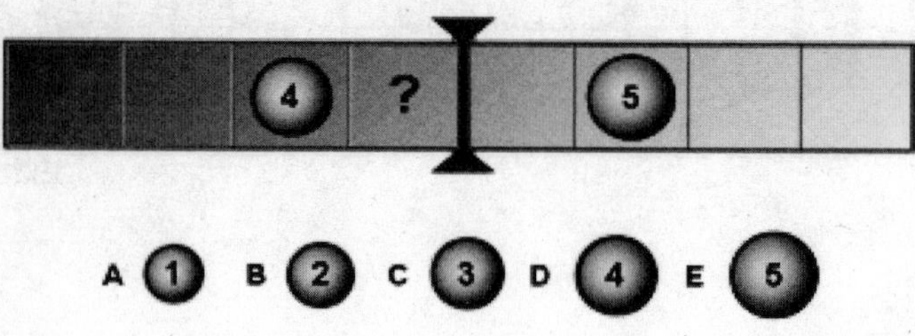

A 1 B 2 C 3 D 4 E 5

ANSWER:

Puzzle 3.37	**Difficulty rating: 2**

TURNING WHEELS

Shown below is a system of wheels connected by belts. The circumference of the outer rim of each wheel is exactly twice that of the inner rim. If wheel A turns at 100 revolutions per minute, how fast will wheel E turn?

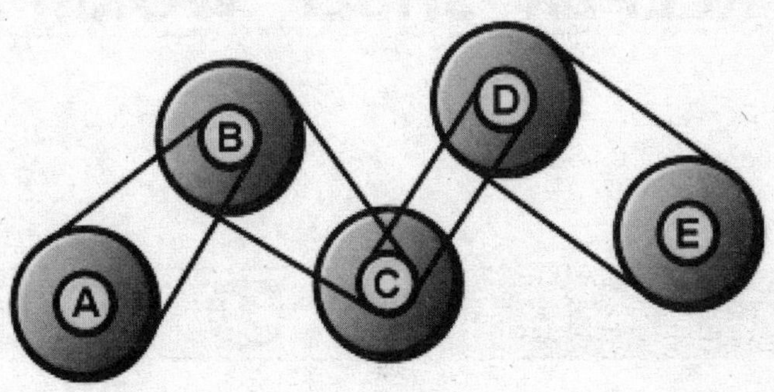

ANSWER:

Puzzle 3.38	**Difficulty rating: 2**

NOVEL IDEA

What word can be added to each of these to create three new words?

KEEPER SHELF WORM

ANSWER:

Puzzle 3.39	**Difficulty rating: 2**

FISHY PRICING

At a local fish store, the owners have a particular way of pricing fish. According to their method, how much should the SALMON cost?

TROUT	**11**
SWORDFISH	**23**
TUNA	**8**
BASS	**10**
BLUEFISH	**18**
HALIBUT	**15**
SALMON	**?**

ANSWER:

Puzzle 3.40	**Difficulty rating: 3**

CHAPTER 3 ANSWERS

3.1. B
3.2. B
3.3. 34
3.4. A
3.5. 6
3.6. 3
3.7. 5
3.8. 6
3.9. 9
3.10. A
3.11. D
3.12. 50 revolutions per minute.
3.13. 458330. 1 x 1 + 1 = 2; 2 x 2 + 1 = 5; 5 x 5 + 1 = 26 . . .
3.14. E. All the others are symmetrical.
3.15. 111
3.16. Slime, Limes, Miles, Smile
3.17. Barn (yard) stick
Camp (fire) place
3.18. A
3.19. C
3.20. 5
3.21. C
3.22. 3
3.23. B
3.24. A
3.25. C
3.26. C
3.27. D
3.28. A
3.29. 3
3.30. 5
3.31. 4
3.32. 3
3.33. 5
3.34. 6
3.35. E
3.36. D
3.37. B
3.38. 400 revolutions per minute.
3.39. BOOK
3.40. 14

DIFFICULTY RATING: 113

FIND THE HIDDEN VALUE

Each of the three different symbols has a different value associated with it. When you add up the value of all the different symbols you get the total value for that row. The objective is to determine the value for each of the three symbols and fill in the missing value.

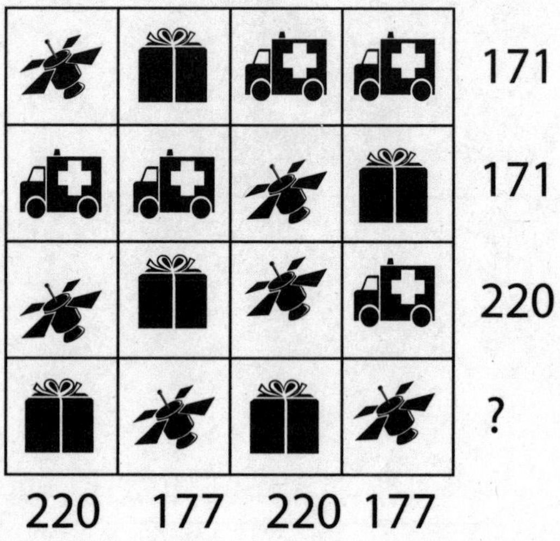

ANSWER:

Puzzle 4.1	**Difficulty rating: 3**

WORD SCRAMBLE

There are five scrambled letters below that can be formed into five English words. You must use all the letters in the word, and they can only be used once. Can you find all five?

S E O R P

ANSWER:

Puzzle 4.2	**Difficulty rating: 3**

WORD ADDITION

What word inserted in the blank space will create two new words? Find at least one word for each set of words. *Example: QUICK <u>sand</u> PAPER*

EAR _____ TONE

HEAD _____ HOUSE

ANSWER:

Puzzle 4.3	**Difficulty rating: 2**

NOUGHTS AND CROSSES

Complete the sequence.

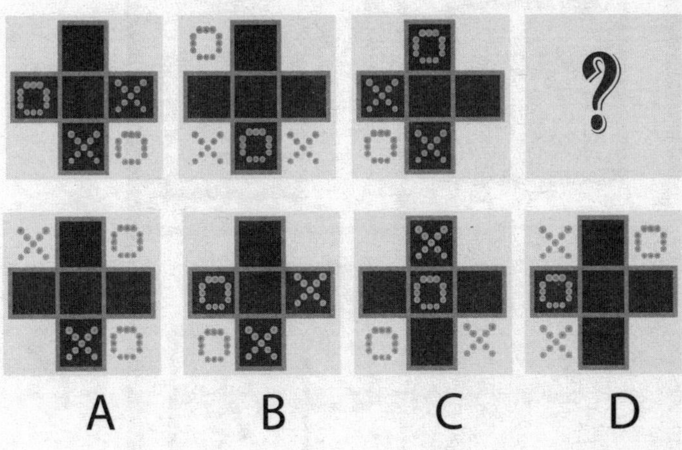

ANSWER:

Puzzle 4.4	**Difficulty rating: 3**

MISSING FIGURE

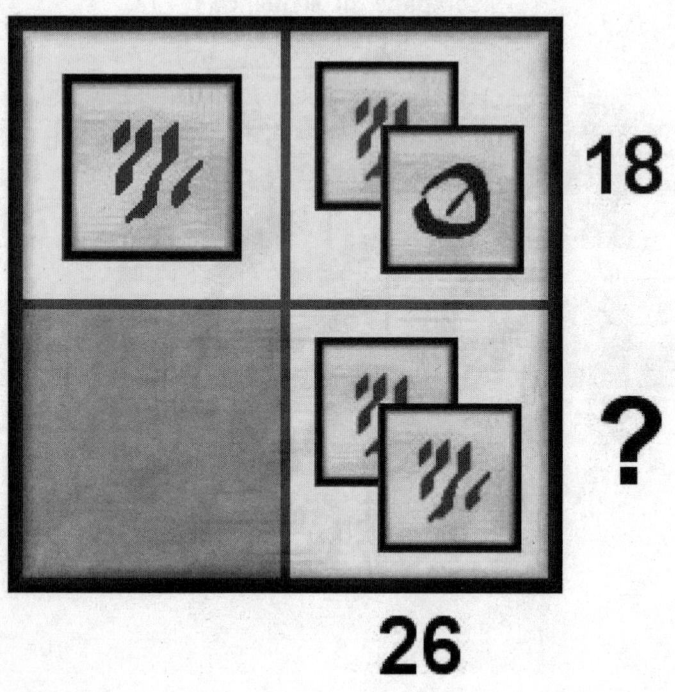

ANSWER:

Puzzle 4.5	Difficulty rating: 4

MISSING NUMBER

ANSWER:

Puzzle 4.6	Difficulty rating: 3

ODD ONE OUT

Which of the following is least like the others?

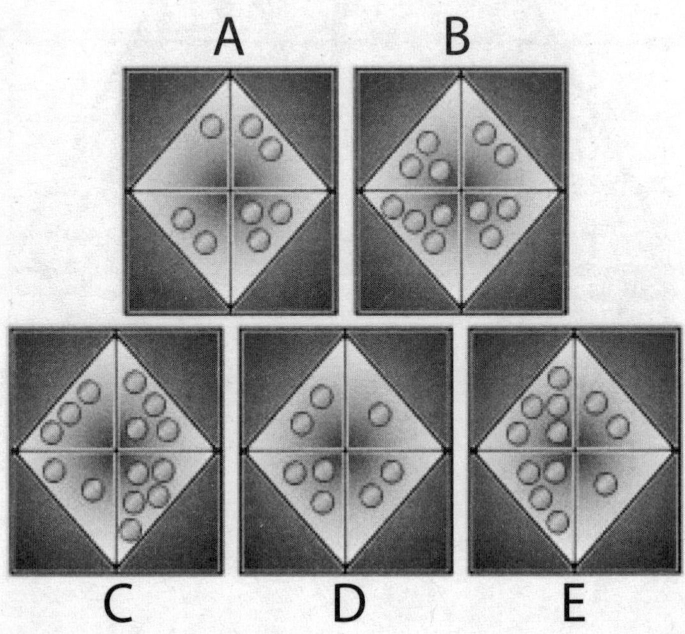

ANSWER:

Puzzle 4.7	Difficulty rating: 2

MISSING PIECES

Given the puzzle piece shown, determine the maximum number of times the piece can fit into the missing areas of the puzzle.

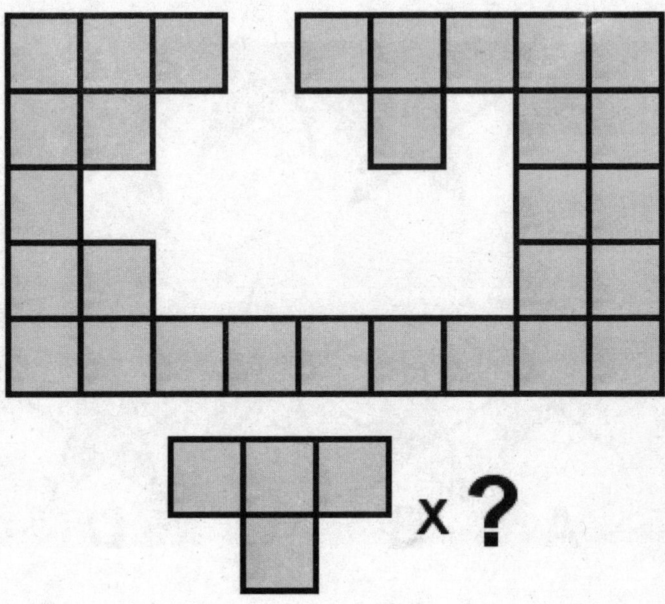

ANSWER:

Puzzle 4.8	**Difficulty rating: 1**

STARGAZING

Which item is the best continuation of the sequence?

ANSWER:

Puzzle 4.9	Difficulty rating: 2

CHOOSE A TILE

Which item is the best continuation of the sequence?

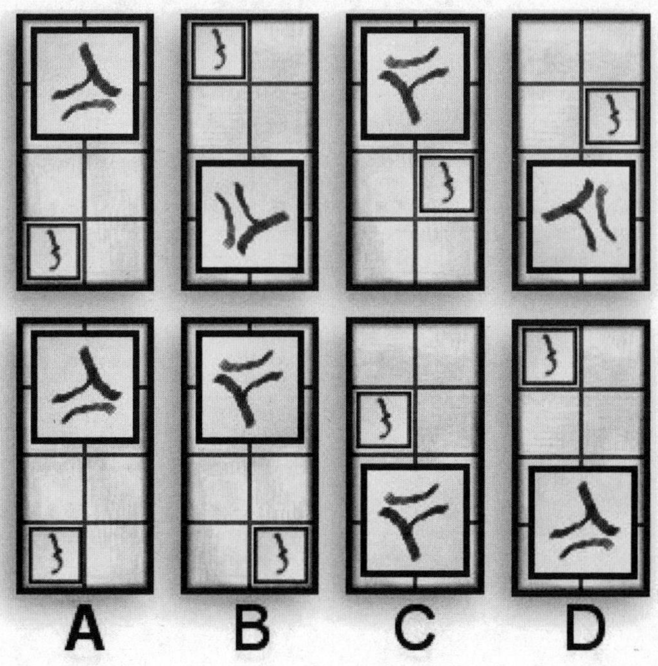

ANSWER:

Puzzle 4.10	**Difficulty rating: 4**

THREE INTO EIGHT

Which item is the best continuation of the sequence?

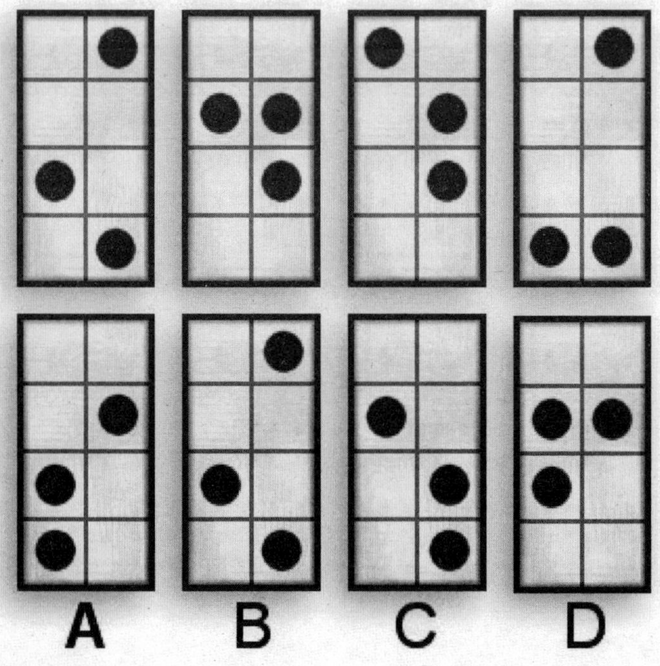

ANSWER:

Puzzle 4.11	**Difficulty rating: 3**

ANALOGY PUZZLE

Determine the item that best completes the analogy.

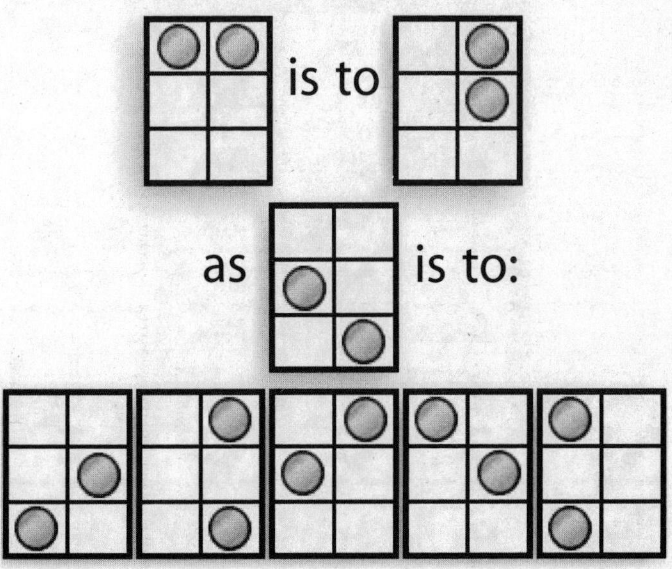

ANSWER:

Puzzle 4.12	**Difficulty rating: 2**

CHILD'S PLAY

Determine the missing item.

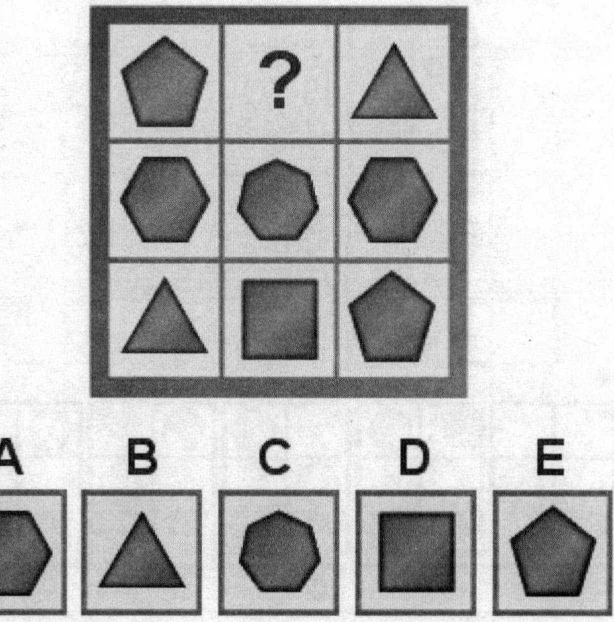

ANSWER:

Puzzle 4.13	Difficulty rating: 2

TRELLIS PATTERN

Determine the system used to generate numbers in the grid below, and find the missing value.

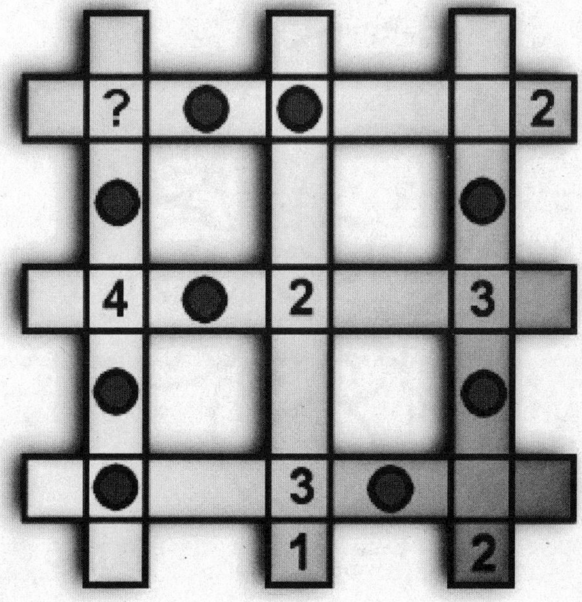

ANSWER:

Puzzle 4.14	**Difficulty rating: 4**

WHEELS WITHIN WHEELS

Determine the system used to generate numbers in the diagram below, and find the missing value.

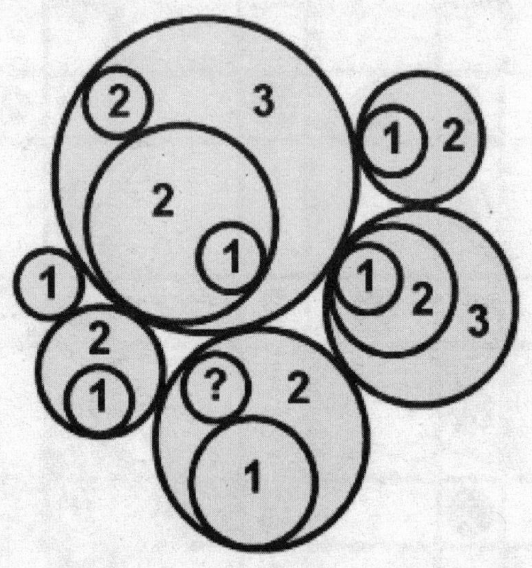

ANSWER:

Puzzle 4.15	Difficulty rating: 4

HIDDEN NUMBERS

What is the missing number in the figure below?

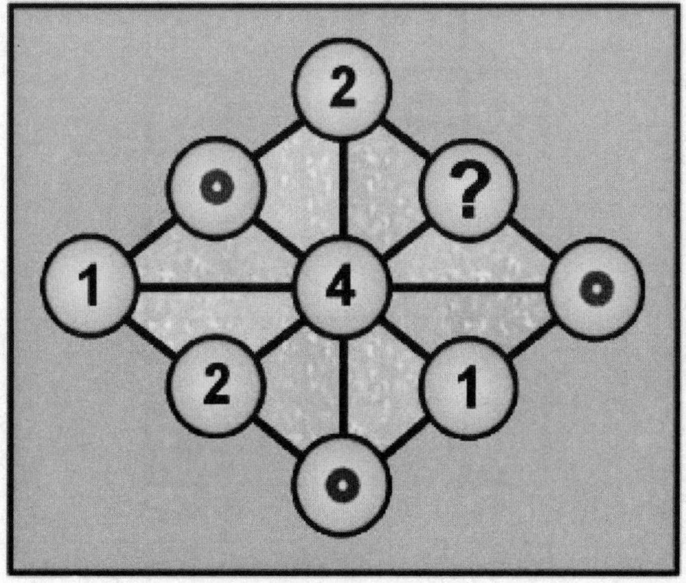

ANSWER:

Puzzle 4.16	**Difficulty rating: 3**

HIDDEN VALUES

Determine the system used to generate numbers in the grid below, and find the missing value.

ANSWER:

Puzzle 4.17	**Difficulty rating: 3**

CIRCUITOUS NUMBERS

Determine the system used to generate numbers in the grid below, and find the missing value.

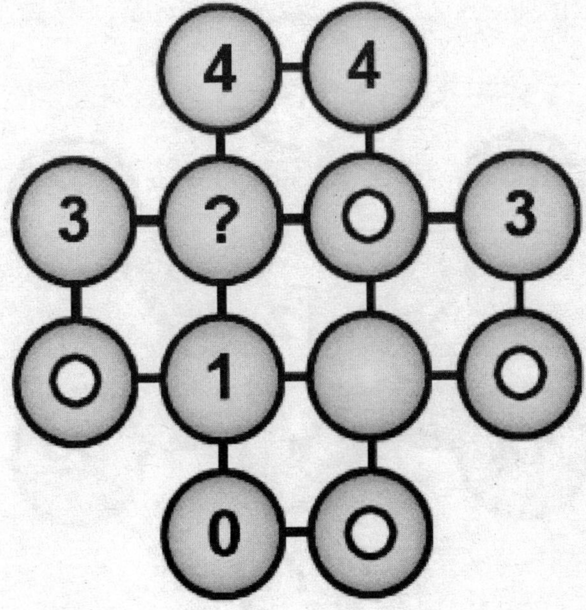

ANSWER:

Puzzle 4.18	**Difficulty rating: 3**

STARBURST

Determine the relationship between the central star and the outer circles, and find the missing value.

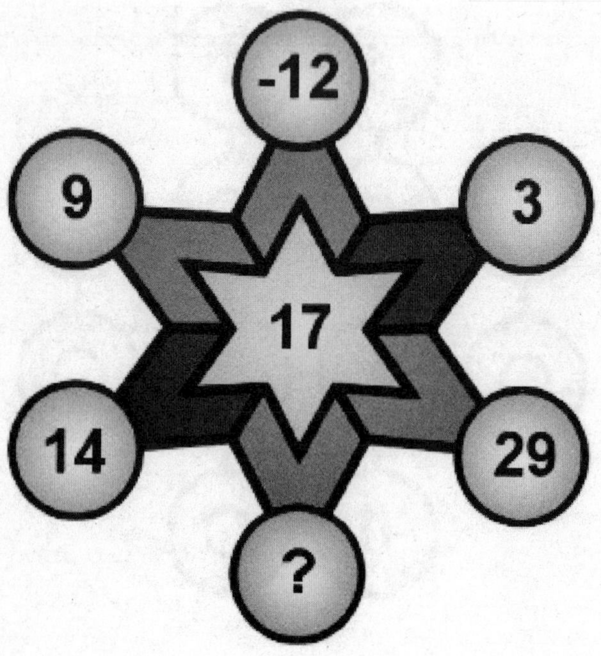

ANSWER:

Puzzle 4.19	**Difficulty rating: 3**

ODD ONE IN

Which item is most like the first five?

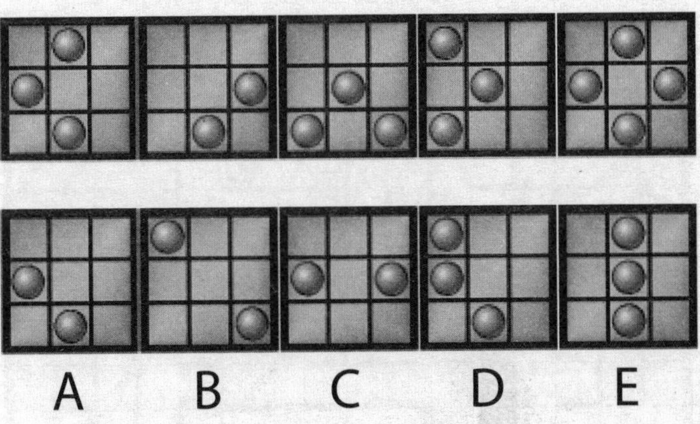

ANSWER:

Puzzle 4.20	**Difficulty rating: 3**

FAST EXIT

Which of the circles in the maze is nearest to the exit?

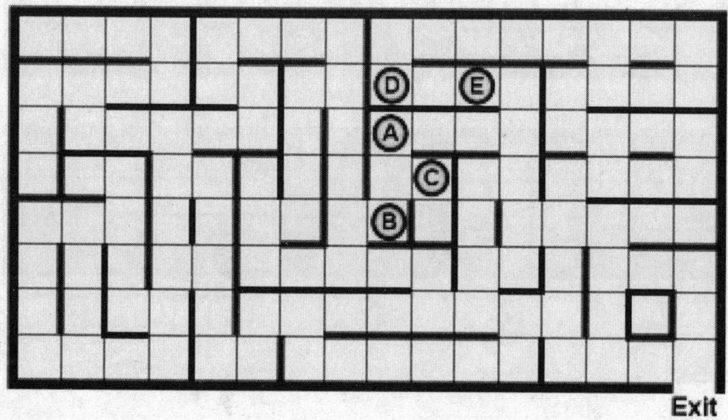

ANSWER:

Puzzle 4.21	**Difficulty rating: 2**

BALANCING ACT

Shown below is the aerial view of a see-saw perfectly balanced by weights on both sides.

What weight must be placed at the position indicated, to balance the following see-saw?

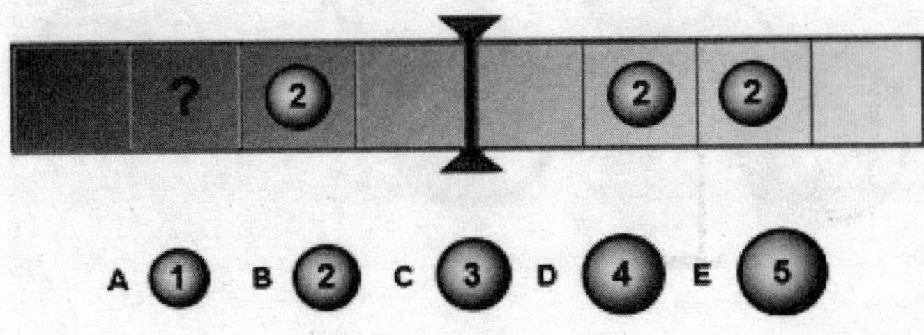

A 1 B 2 C 3 D 4 E 5

ANSWER:

Puzzle 4.22	Difficulty rating: 2

TURNING WHEELS

Shown below is a system of wheels connected by belts. The circumference of the outer rim of each wheel is exactly twice that of the inner rim. If wheel A turns at 100 revolutions per minute, how fast will wheel E turn?

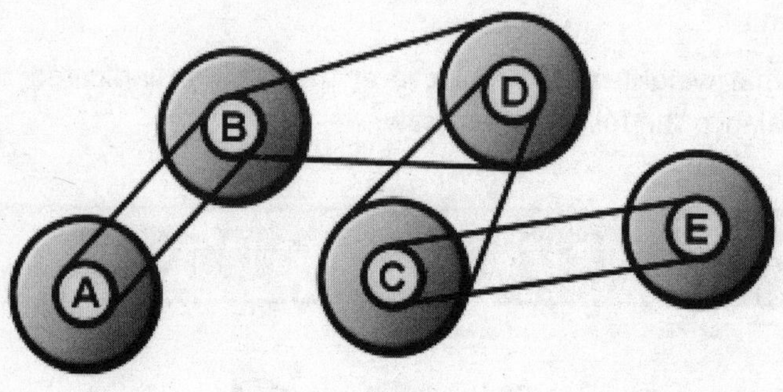

ANSWER:

Puzzle 4.23	**Difficulty rating: 3**

PRIMITIVE PUZZLE

Figure out how the word in parentheses is arrived at and find the word for the second set of parentheses.

TITAN (TAME) POLYMER

BECOME (_ _ _ _) PRIMATE

ANSWER:

Puzzle 4.24	**Difficulty rating: 2**

WORD EXTENSION

What word can be added to each of these to create three new words?

SIDE CHAIR PIT

ANSWER:

Puzzle 4.25	Difficulty rating: 2

WORD SCRAMBLE

There are five scrambled letters below that can be formed into five English words. You must use all the letters in the word, and they can only be used once. Can you find all five?

R C E T A

ANSWER:

Puzzle 4.26	**Difficulty rating: 3**

WORD ADDITION

What word inserted in the blank space will create two new words? Find at least one word for each set of words. *Example: QUICK sand PAPER*

FOOT __ball__ GAME

DOWN _____ LINE

ANSWER:

Puzzle 4.27	**Difficulty rating: 2**

REVOLVING SPHERES

Complete the sequence.

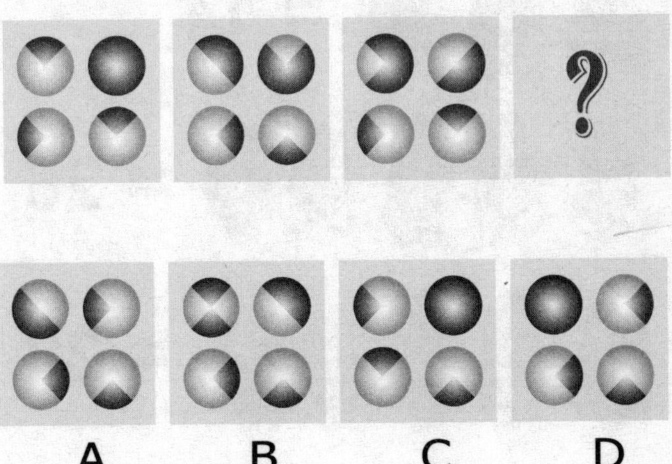

ANSWER:

Puzzle 4.28	Difficulty rating: 3

FIND THE MISSING VALUE

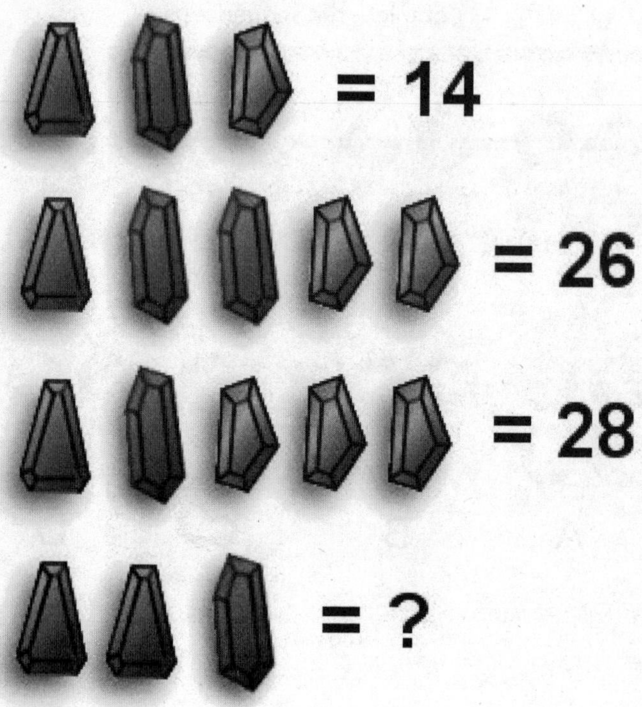

ANSWER:

Puzzle 4.29	Difficulty rating: 3

MISSING FIGURE

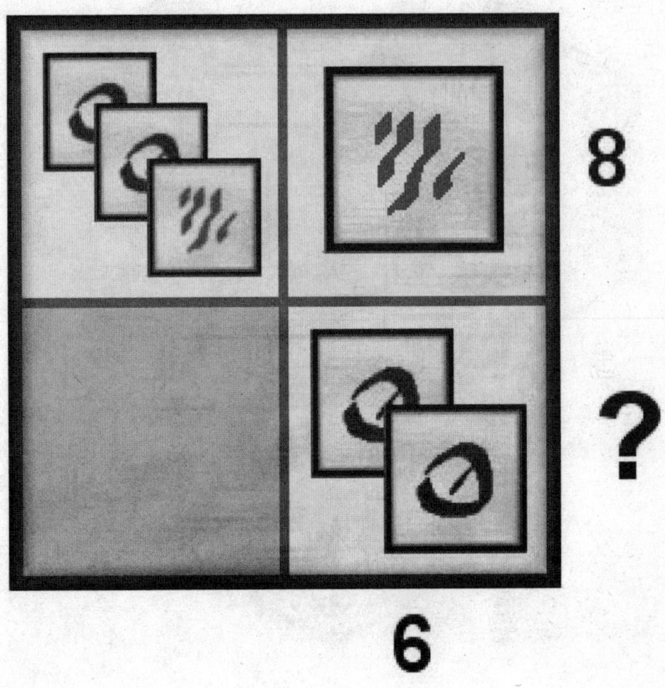

ANSWER:

Puzzle 4.30	Difficulty rating: 3

MISSING VALUE

ANSWER:

Puzzle 4.31	Difficulty rating: 4

ODD ONE OUT

Which of the following is least like the others?

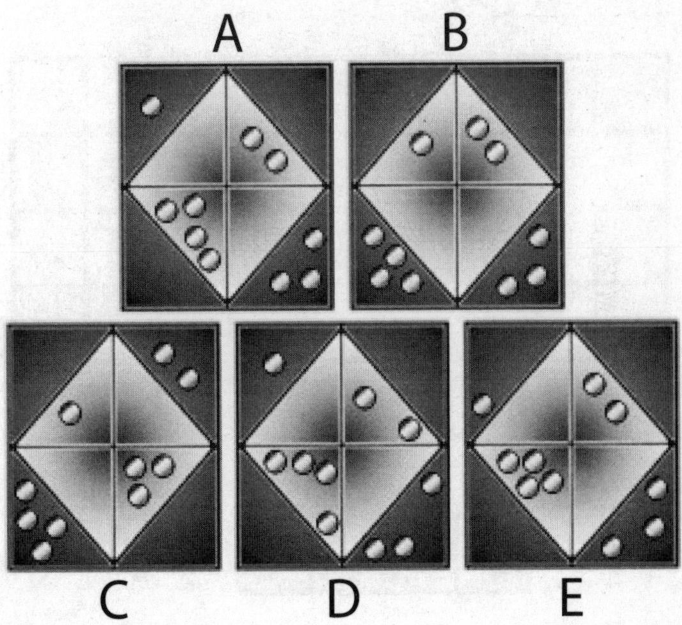

ANSWER:

Puzzle 4.32	**Difficulty rating: 4**

MISSING PIECES

Given the puzzle piece shown, determine the maximum number of times the piece can fit into the missing areas of the puzzle.

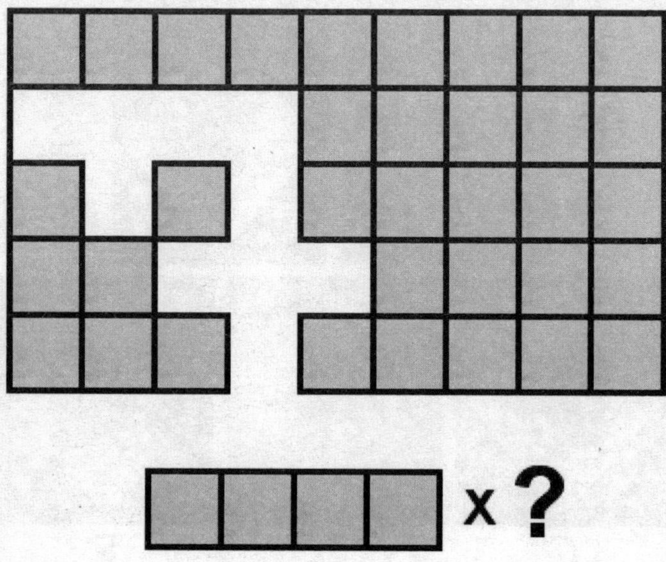

ANSWER:

Puzzle 4.33	**Difficulty rating: 1**

MOLECULAR SEQUENCE

Use the diagram to determine the missing letter in the sequence.

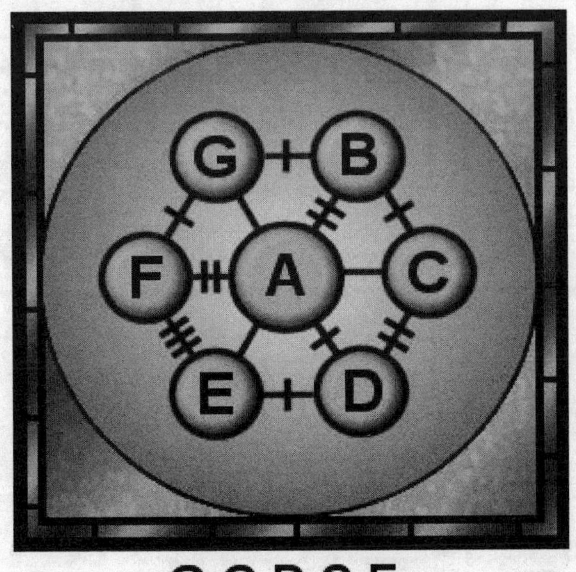

G C D ? F

ANSWER:

Puzzle 4.34	**Difficulty rating: 4**

FIVE INTO EIGHT

Which item is the best continuation of the sequence?

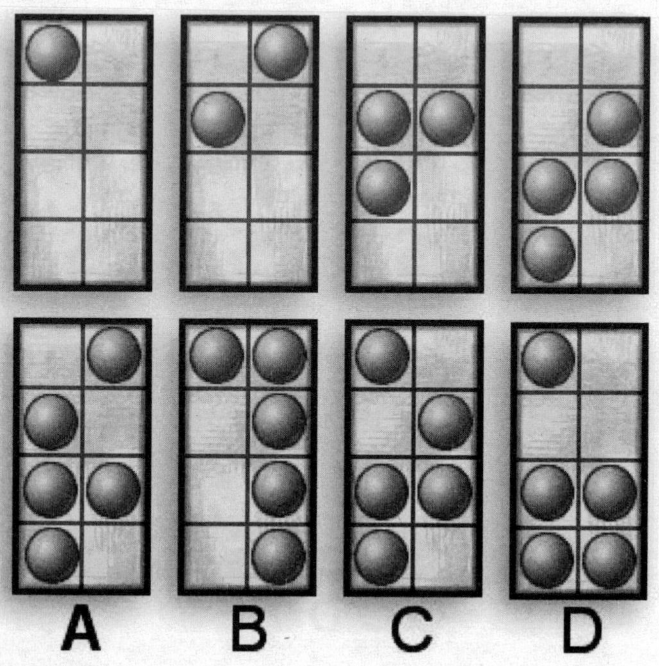

ANSWER:

Puzzle 4.35	Difficulty rating: 3

ONE INTO EIGHT

Which item is the best continuation of the sequence?

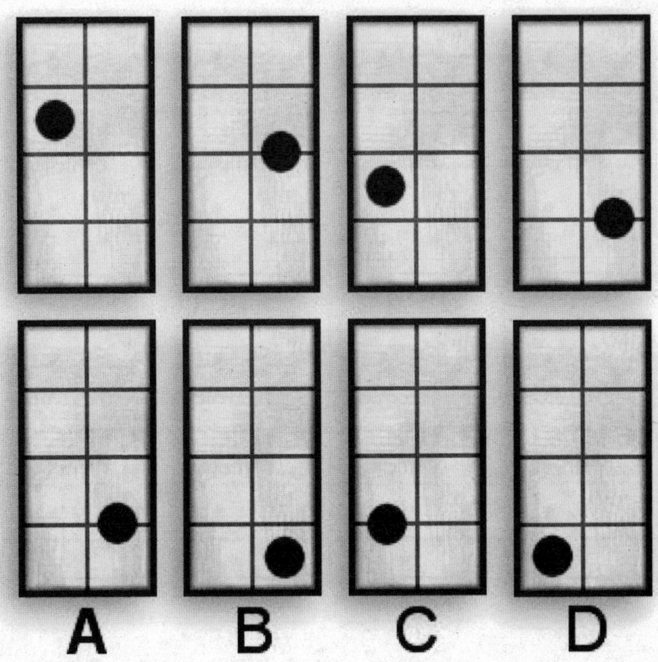

ANSWER:

Puzzle 4.36	Difficulty rating: 2

ANALOGY PUZZLE

Determine the item that best completes the analogy.

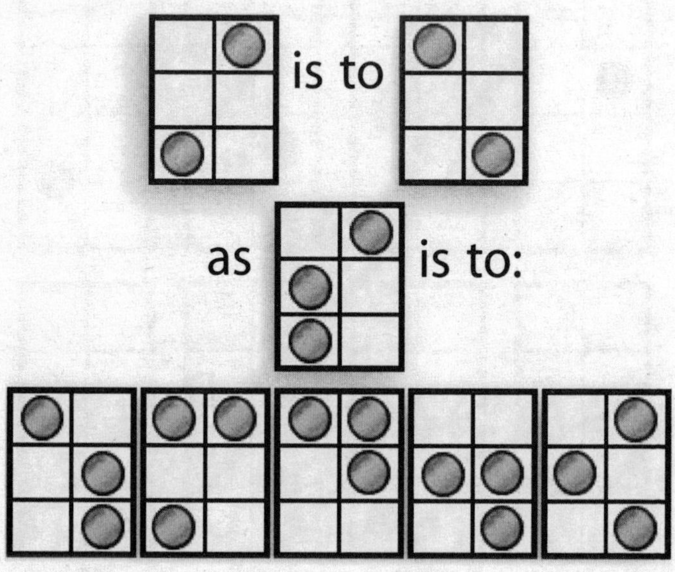

ANSWER:

Puzzle 4.37	Difficulty rating: 3

WINDOW FILLER

Determine the missing square.

A B C D E

ANSWER:

Puzzle 4.38	**Difficulty rating: 3**

TRELLIS PATTERN

Determine the system used to generate numbers in the grid below, and find the missing value.

ANSWER:

Puzzle 4.39	**Difficulty rating: 3**

WHEELS WITHIN WHEELS

Determine the system used to generate numbers in the diagram below, and find the missing value.

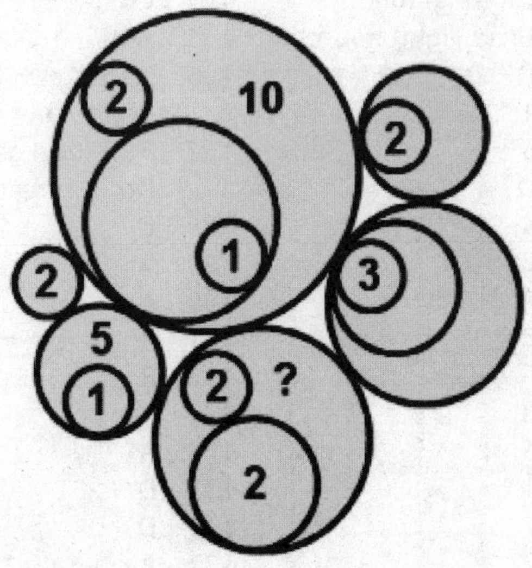

ANSWER:

Puzzle 4.40	**Difficulty rating: 4**

CHAPTER 4 ANSWERS

4.1. 226
4.2. Spore, Pores, Prose, Poser, Ropes
4.3. Ear (ring) tone
Head (light) house
4.4. D
4.5. 16
4.6. 3
4.7. D
4.8. 4
4.9. B
4.10. A
4.11. B
4.12. E
4.13. B
4.14. 5
4.15. 1
4.16. 2
4.17. 2
4.18. 3
4.19. 8
4.20. A
4.21. E
4.22. B
4.23. 25 revolutions per minute.
4.24. COMA
4.25. ARM
4.26. Trace, Cater, Crate, React, Caret
4.27. Foot (ball) game
Down (stream) line
4.28. D
4.29. 9
4.30. 4
4.31. -8
4.32. B
4.33. 1
4.34. A
4.35. D
4.36. D
4.37. A
4.38. A
4.39. 3
4.40. 4

DIFFICULTY RATING: 119

HIDDEN NUMBERS

What is the missing number in the figure below?

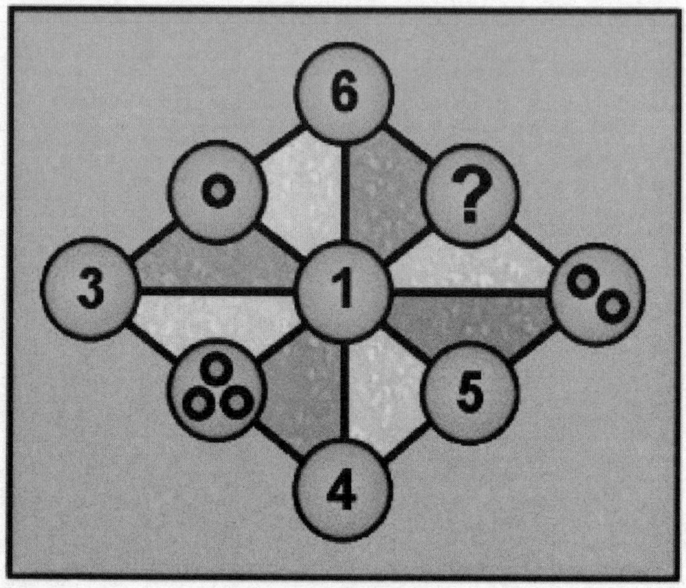

ANSWER:

Puzzle 5.1	**Difficulty rating: 3**

HIDDEN VALUES

Determine the system used to generate numbers in the grid below, and find the missing value.

ANSWER:

Puzzle 5.2	**Difficulty rating: 3**

CIRCUITOUS NUMBERS

Determine the system used to generate numbers in the grid below, and find the missing value.

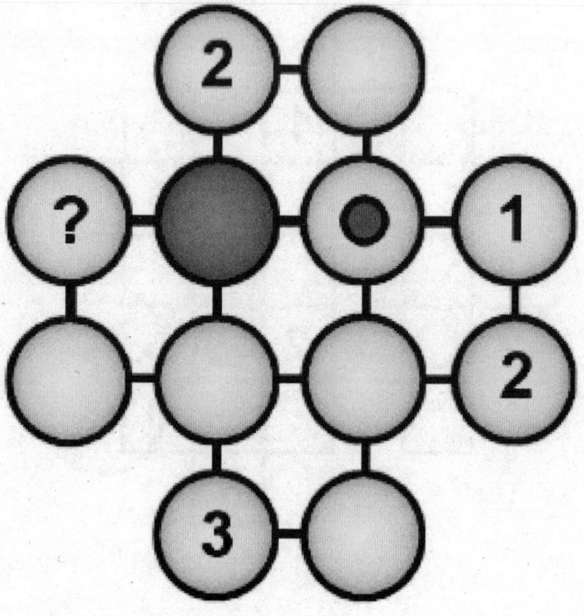

ANSWER:

Puzzle 5.3	**Difficulty rating: 3**

STARBURST

Determine the relationship between the central star and the outer circles, and find the missing value.

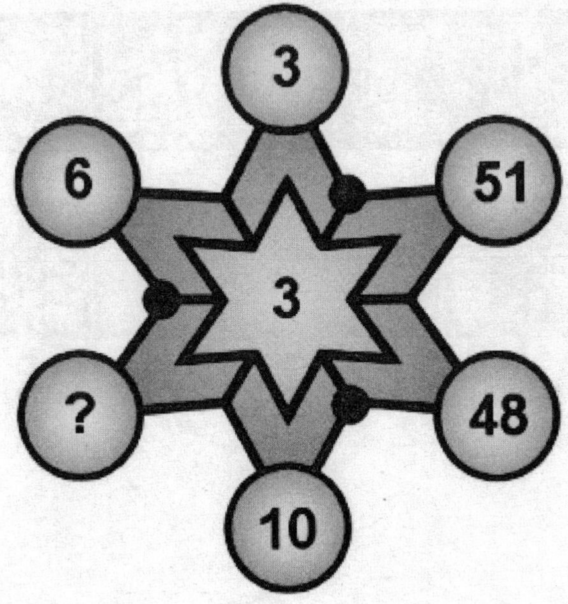

ANSWER:

Puzzle 5.4	Difficulty rating: 3

ODD ONE IN

Which square is most like the first five?

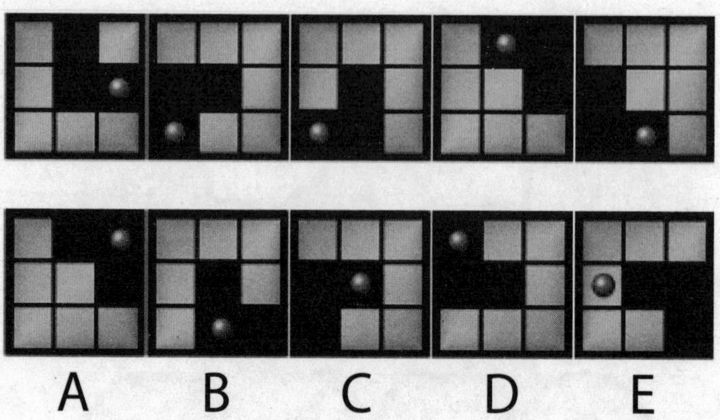

ANSWER:

Puzzle 5.5	**Difficulty rating: 3**

FAST EXIT

Which of the circles in the maze is nearest to the exit?

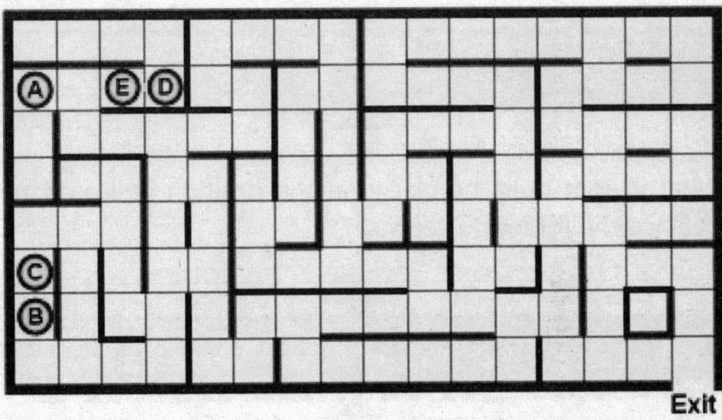

ANSWER:

Puzzle 5.6	Difficulty rating: 2

BALANCING ACT

Shown below is the aerial view of a see-saw perfectly balanced by weights on both sides.

What weight must be placed at the position indicated, to balance the following see-saw?

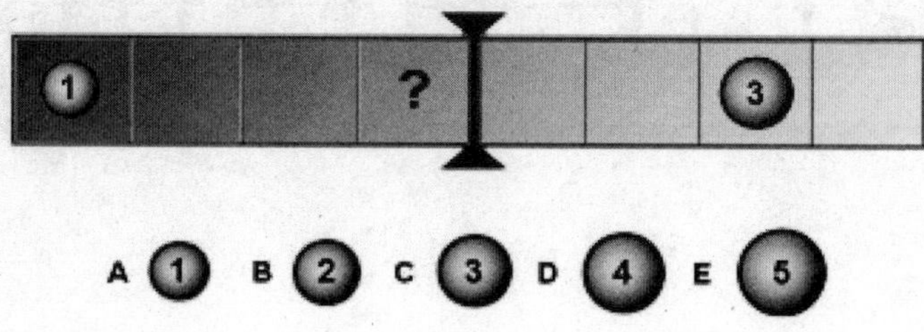

A 1 B 2 C 3 D 4 E 5

ANSWER:

Puzzle 5.7	Difficulty rating: 2

TURNING WHEELS

Shown below is a system of wheels connected by belts. The circumference of the outer rim of each wheel is exactly twice that of the inner rim. If wheel A turns at 100 revolutions per minute, how fast will wheel E turn?

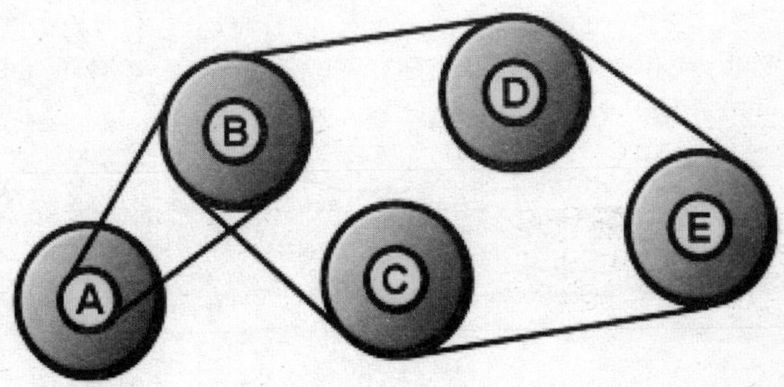

ANSWER:

Puzzle 5.8	Difficulty rating: 3

WORD EXTENSION

What word can be added to each of these to create three new words?

FILM WAVE SCOPE

ANSWER:

Puzzle 5.9	**Difficulty rating: 2**

WORD SCRAMBLE

There are four scrambled letters below that can be formed into three English words. You must use all the letters in the word, and they can only be used once. Can you find all three?

S N K I

ANSWER:

Puzzle 5.10	**Difficulty rating: 3**

WORD ADDITION

What word inserted in the blank space will create two new words? Find at least one word for each set of words. *Example: QUICK sand PAPER*

CARD _____ GAME

GUIDE _____ WORM

ANSWER:

Puzzle 5.11	**Difficulty rating: 2**

COMPLETE THE SEQUENCE

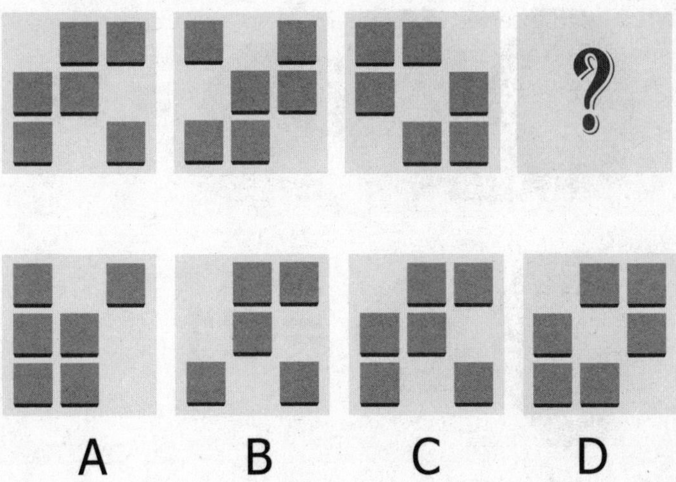

ANSWER:

Puzzle 5.12	**Difficulty rating: 3**

FIND THE MISSING VALUE

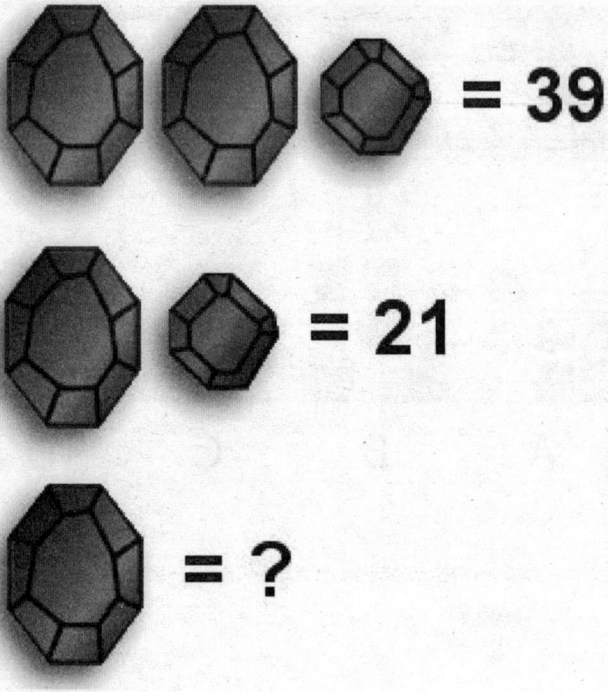

= 39

= 21

= ?

ANSWER:

Puzzle 5.13	Difficulty rating: 3

MISSING FIGURE

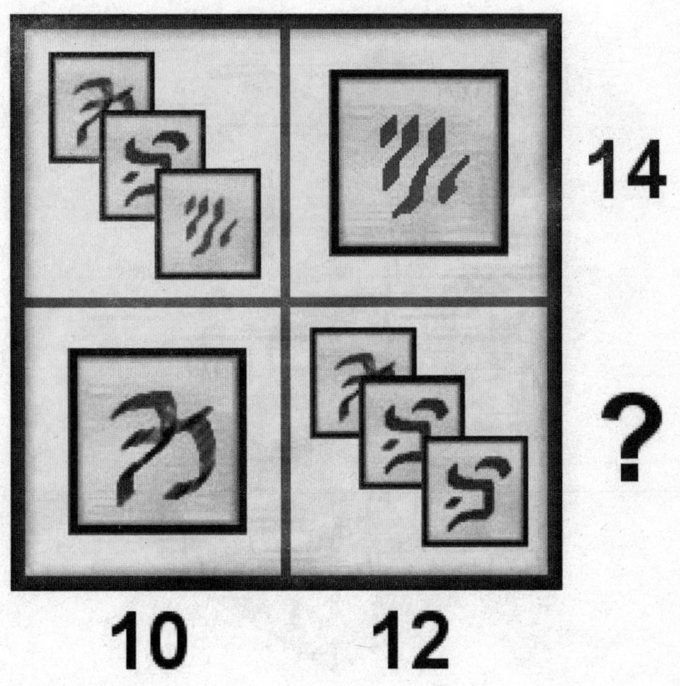

ANSWER:

Puzzle 5.14	**Difficulty rating: 4**

MISSING VALUE

ANSWER:

Puzzle 5.15	Difficulty rating: 4

ODD ONE OUT

Which of the following is least like the others?

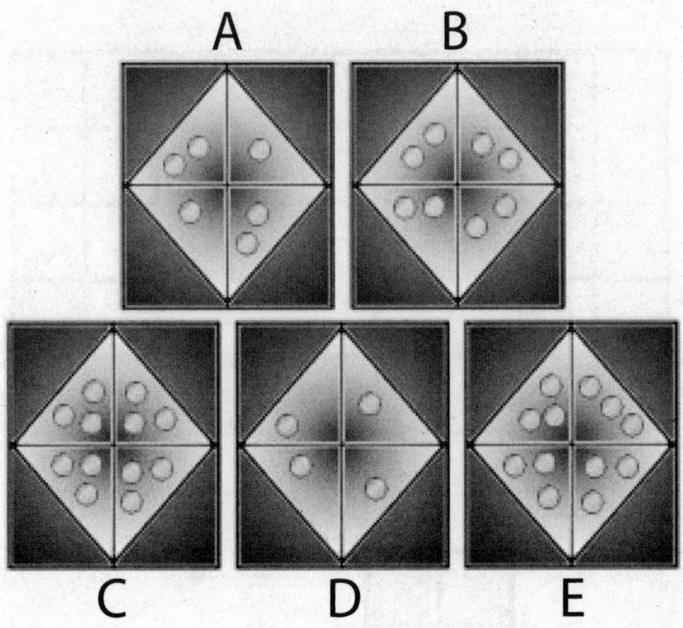

ANSWER:

Puzzle 5.16	**Difficulty rating: 3**

MISSING PIECES

Given the puzzle piece shown, determine the maximum number of times the piece can fit into the missing areas of the puzzle.

ANSWER:

Puzzle 5.17	Difficulty rating: 1

MOLECULAR SEQUENCE

Use the diagram to determine the missing letter in the sequence.

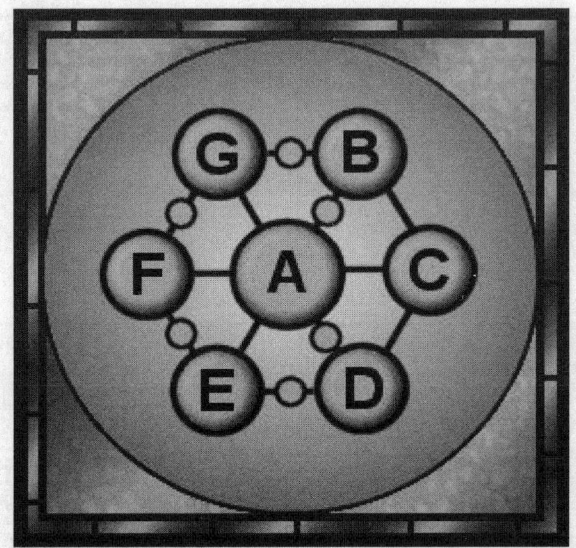

A C B C G C F C E C ? C A

ANSWER:

Puzzle 5.18	Difficulty rating: 4

CHOOSE A TILE

Which item is the best continuation of the sequence?

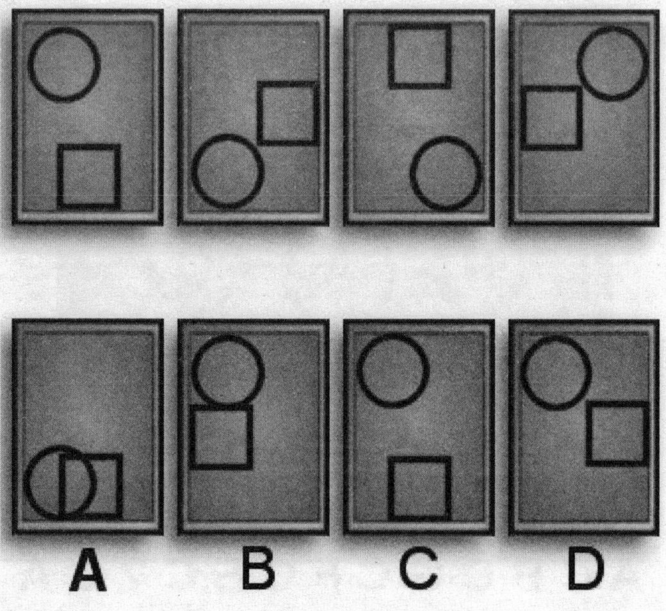

ANSWER:

Puzzle 5.19	**Difficulty rating: 3**

ANALOGY PUZZLE

Determine the item that best completes the analogy.

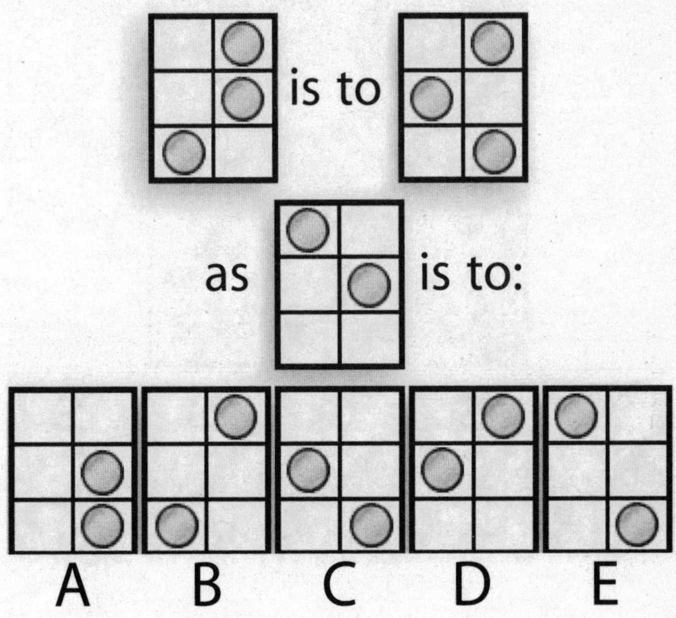

ANSWER:

Puzzle 5.20	**Difficulty rating: 3**

WINDOW FILLER

Determine the missing square.

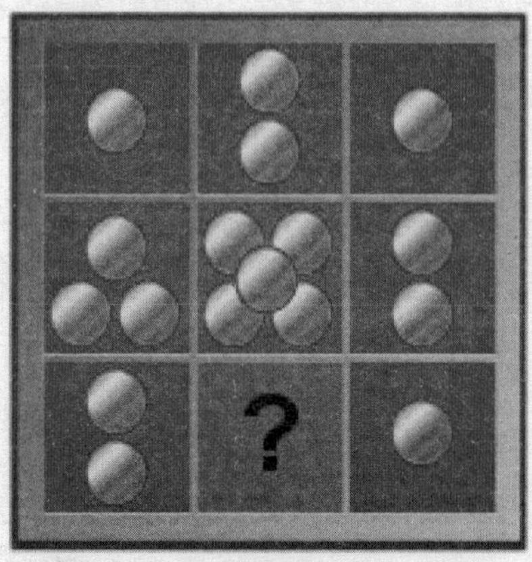

A B C D E

ANSWER:

Puzzle 5.21 | **Difficulty rating: 3**

TRELLIS PATTERN

Determine the system used to generate numbers in the grid below, and find the missing value.

ANSWER:

Puzzle 5.22	**Difficulty rating: 4**

WHEELS WITHIN WHEELS

Determine the system used to generate numbers in the diagram below, and find the missing value.

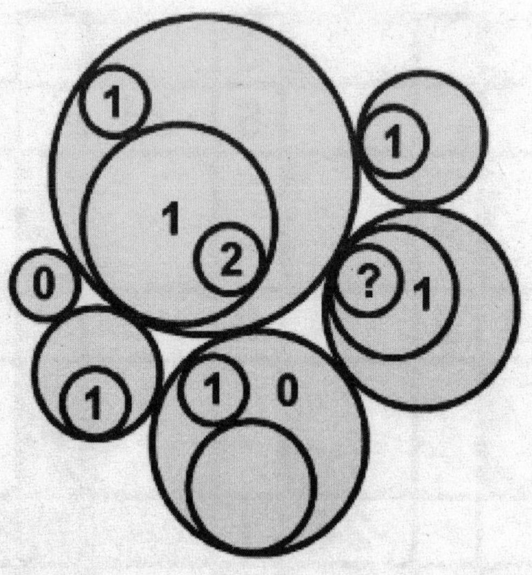

ANSWER:

Puzzle 5.23	**Difficulty rating: 4**

HIDDEN VALUES

Determine the system used to generate numbers in the grid below, and find the missing value.

ANSWER:

Puzzle 5.24	Difficulty rating: 3

CIRCUITOUS NUMBERS

Determine the system used to generate numbers in the grid below, and find the missing value.

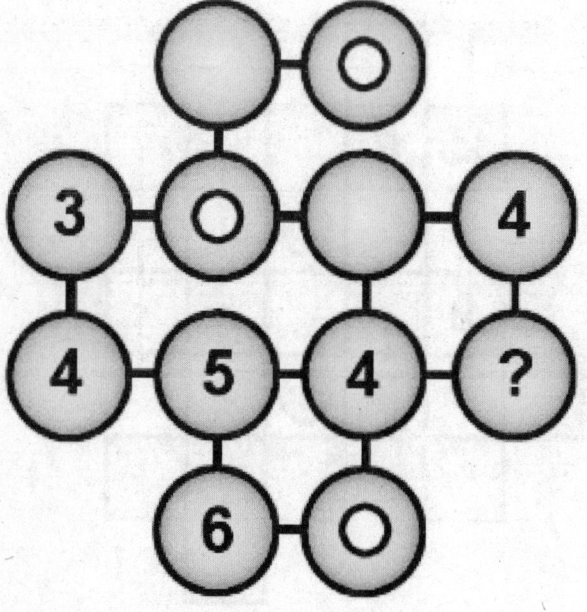

ANSWER:

Puzzle 5.25	Difficulty rating: 3

FAST EXIT

Which of the circles in the maze is nearest to the exit?

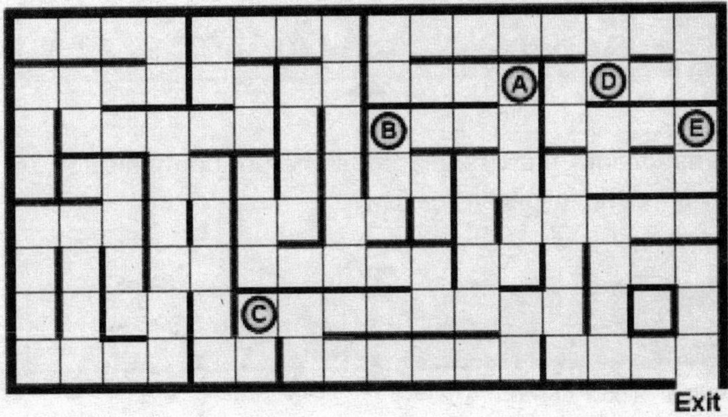

ANSWER:

Puzzle 5.26	**Difficulty rating: 2**

BALANCING ACT

Shown below is the aerial view of a see-saw perfectly balanced by weights on both sides.

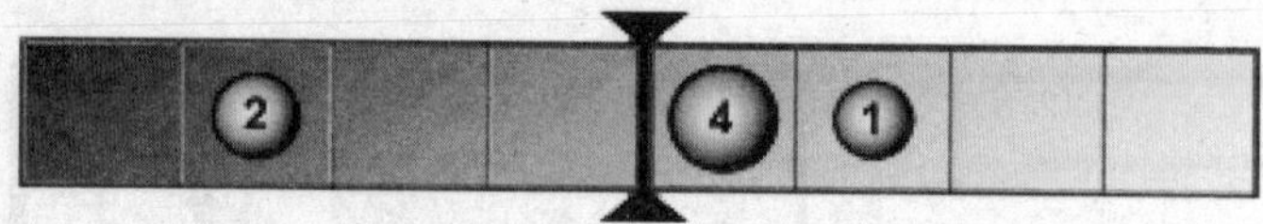

What weight must be placed at the position indicated, to balance the following see-saw?

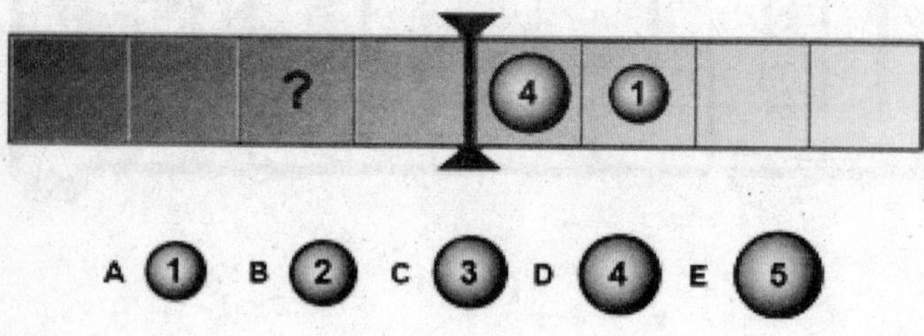

ANSWER:

Puzzle 5.27	Difficulty rating: 2

TURNING WHEELS

Shown below is a system of wheels connected by belts. The circumference of the outer rim of each wheel is exactly twice that of the inner rim. If wheel A turns at 100 revolutions per minute, how fast will wheel E turn?

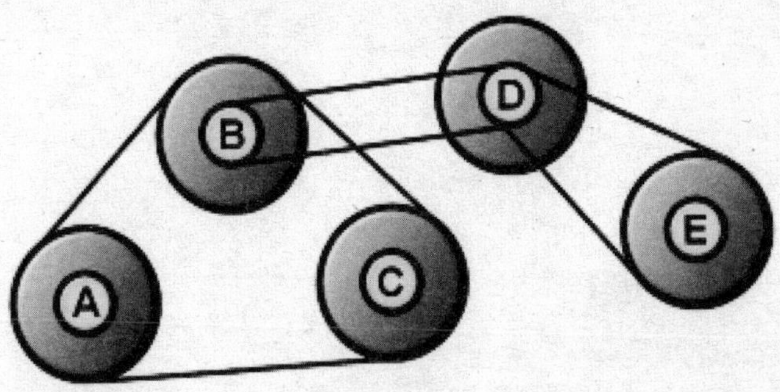

ANSWER:

Puzzle 5.28	**Difficulty rating: 3**

WORD EXTENSION

What word can be added to each of these to create three new words?

TOOL MAIL LUNCH

ANSWER:

Puzzle 5.29	**Difficulty rating: 2**

WORD SCRAMBLE

There are four scrambled letters below that can be formed into five English words. You must use all the letters in the word, and they can only be used once. Can you find all five?

T E M A

ANSWER:

Puzzle 5.30	**Difficulty rating: 3**

WORD ADDITION

What word inserted in the blank space will create two new words? Find at least one word for each set of words. *Example: QUICK* *sand* *PAPER*

GUN _____ FLY

COUNTRY _____ CAR

ANSWER:

Puzzle 5.31	**Difficulty rating: 2**

THE X-FACTOR

Complete the sequence.

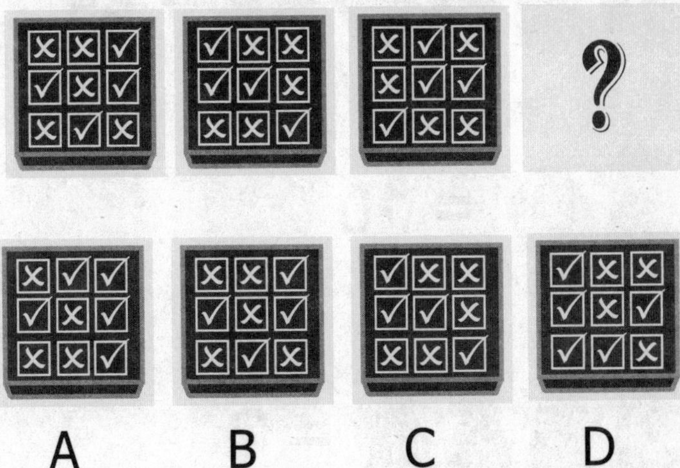

ANSWER:

Puzzle 5.32	Difficulty rating: 4

FIND THE MISSING VALUE

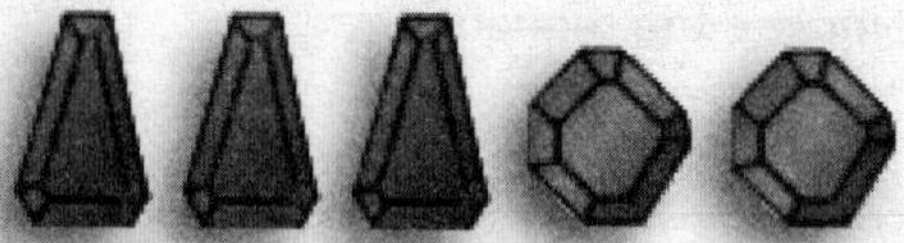

= 24

= 10

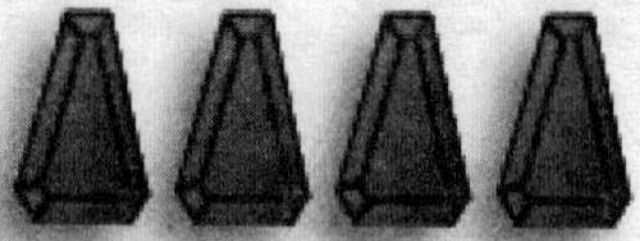

= ?

ANSWER:

Puzzle 5.33	Difficulty rating: 3

MISSING FIGURE

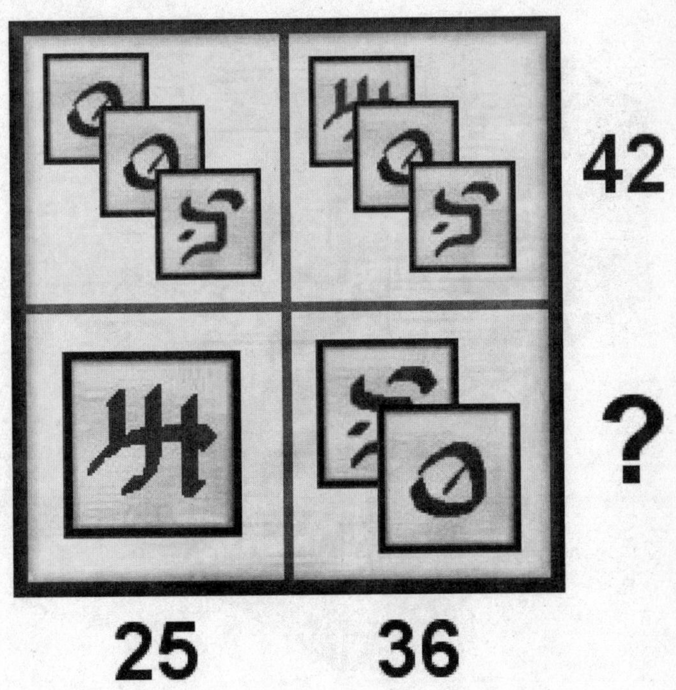

ANSWER:

Puzzle 5.34	Difficulty rating: 4

MISSING VALUE

ANSWER:

Puzzle 5.35	**Difficulty rating: 4**

ODD ONE OUT

Which of the following is least like the others?

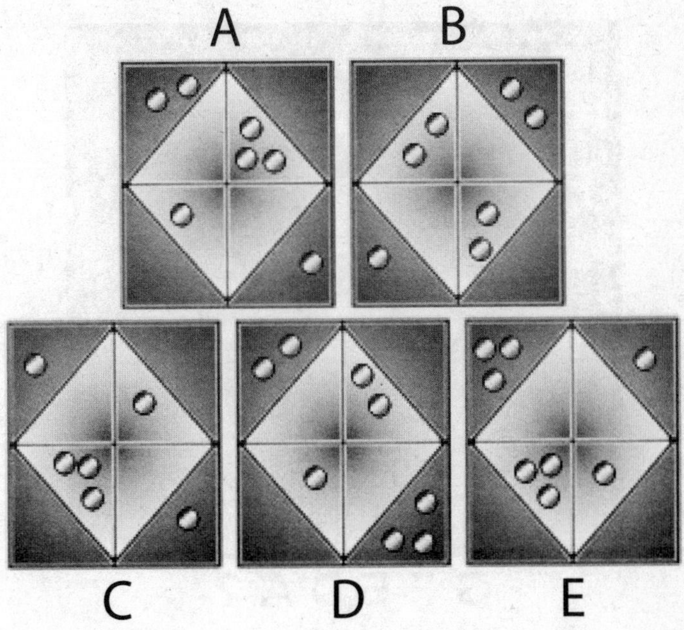

ANSWER:

Puzzle 5.36	Difficulty rating: 3

MOLECULAR SEQUENCE

Use the diagram to determine the missing letter in the sequence.

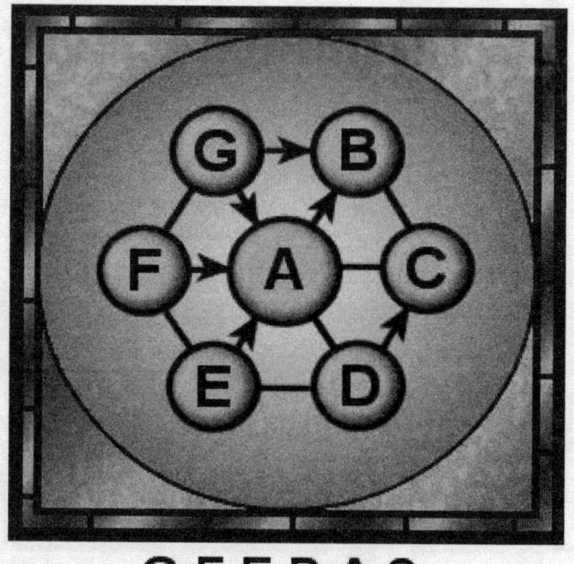

G F E D A ?

ANSWER:

Puzzle 5.37	**Difficulty rating: 3**

ALL BOXED IN

Which item is the best continuation of the sequence?

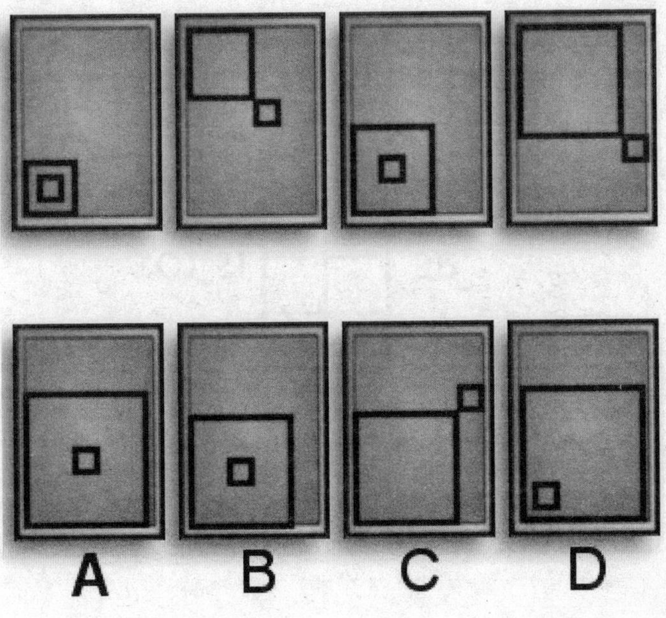

ANSWER:

Puzzle 5.38	Difficulty rating: 3

ANALOGY PUZZLE

Determine the item that best completes the analogy.

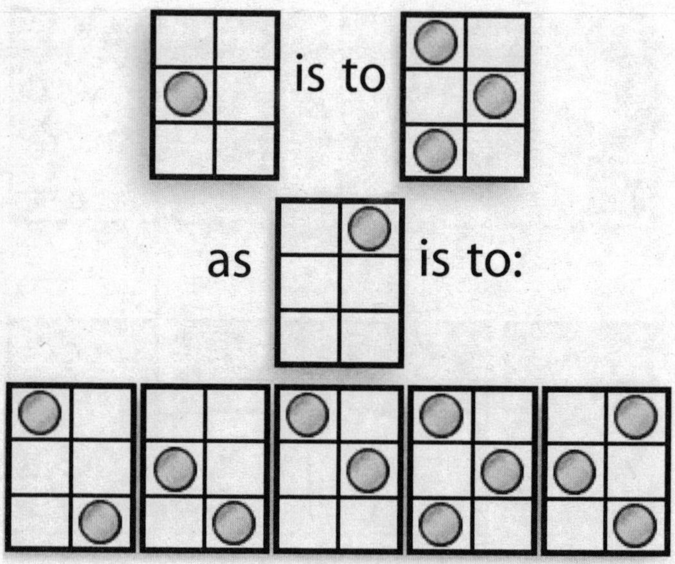

ANSWER:

Puzzle 5.39	Difficulty rating: 3

WINDOW FILLER

Determine the missing square.

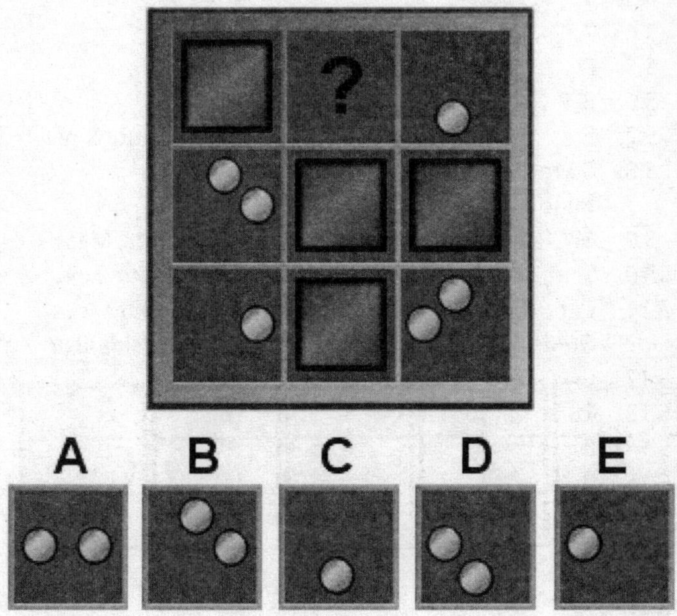

ANSWER:

Puzzle 5.40	**Difficulty rating: 4**

CHAPTER 5 ANSWERS

5.1. 5
5.2. 2
5.3. 4
5.4. 7
5.5. D
5.6. B
5.7. E
5.8. 50 revolutions per minute.
5.9. MICRO
5.10. Skin, Sink, Inks
5.11. Card (board) game
Guide (book) worm
5.12. C
5.13. 18
5.14. 8
5.15. 0
5.16. A
5.17. 2
5.18. D
5.19. C
5.20. B
5.21. E
5.22. 4
5.23. 2
5.24. 3
5.25. 5
5.26. A
5.27. C
5.28. 50 revolutions per minute.
5.29. BOX
5.30. Mate, Meta, Meat, Tame, Team
5.31. Gun (fire) fly
Country (side) car
5.32. B
5.33. 16
5.34. 19
5.35. 11
5.36. E
5.37. C
5.38. A
5.39. C
5.40. D

DIFFICULTY RATING: 120

TRELLIS PATTERN

Determine the system used to generate numbers in the grid below, and find the missing value.

ANSWER:

Puzzle 6.1	**Difficulty rating: 3**

WHEELS WITHIN WHEELS

Determine the system used to generate numbers in the diagram below, and find the missing value.

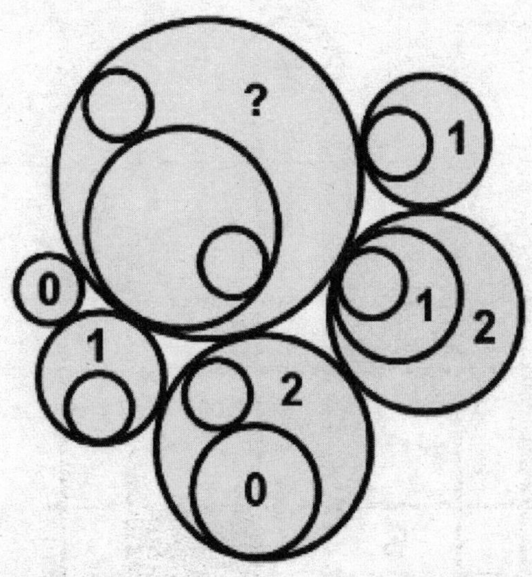

ANSWER:

Puzzle 6.2	**Difficulty rating: 3**

HIDDEN NUMBERS

What is the missing number in the figure below?

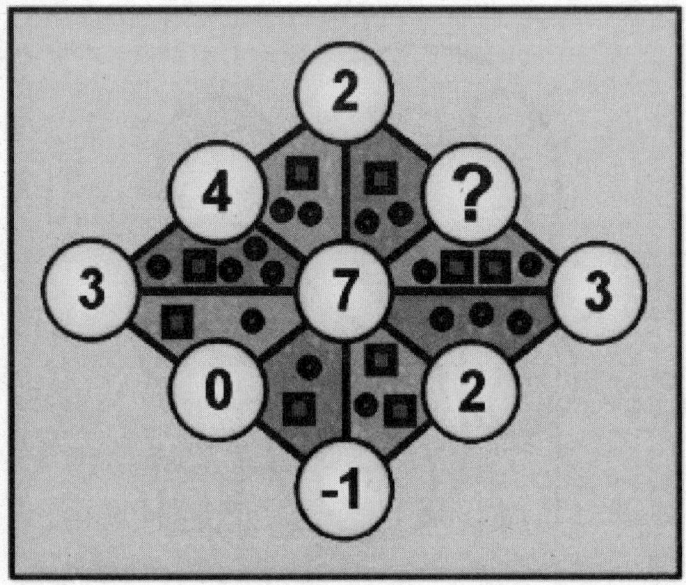

ANSWER:

Puzzle 6.3	**Difficulty rating: 3**

HIDDEN VALUES

Determine the system used to generate numbers in the grid below, and find the missing value.

ANSWER:

Puzzle 6.4	Difficulty rating: 3

CIRCUITOUS NUMBERS

Determine the system used to generate numbers in the grid below, and find the missing number.

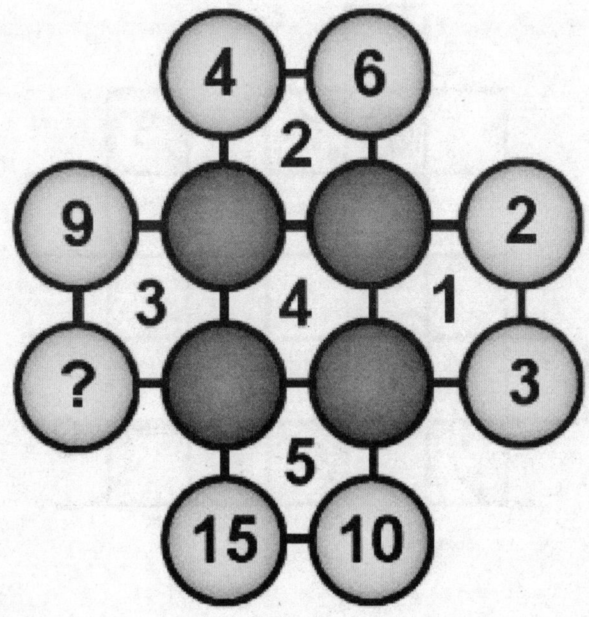

ANSWER:

Puzzle 6.5	**Difficulty rating: 3**

STARBURST

Determine the relationship between the central star and the outer circles, and find the missing value.

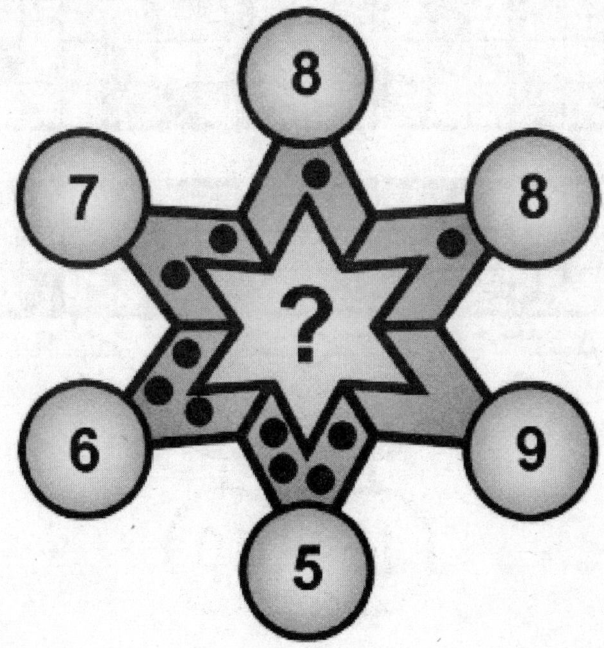

ANSWER:

Puzzle 6.6	**Difficulty rating: 4**

ODD ONE IN

Which square is most like the first five?

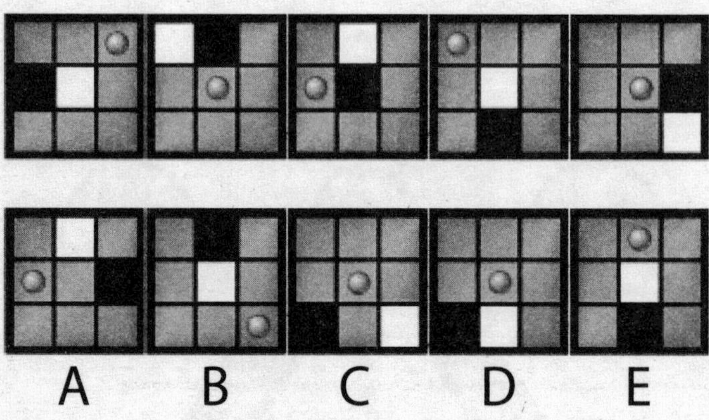

ANSWER:

Puzzle 6.7	**Difficulty rating: 3**

FAST EXIT

Which of the circles in the maze is nearest to the exit?

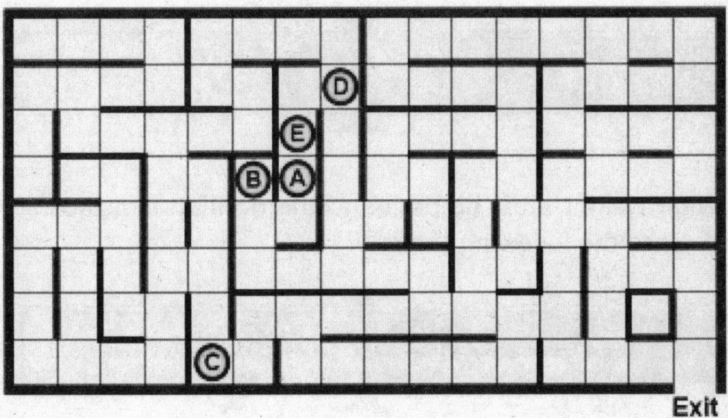

ANSWER:

Puzzle 6.8	**Difficulty rating: 2**

BALANCING ACT

Shown below is the aerial view of a see-saw perfectly balanced by weights on both sides.

What weight must be placed at the position indicated, to balance the following see-saw?

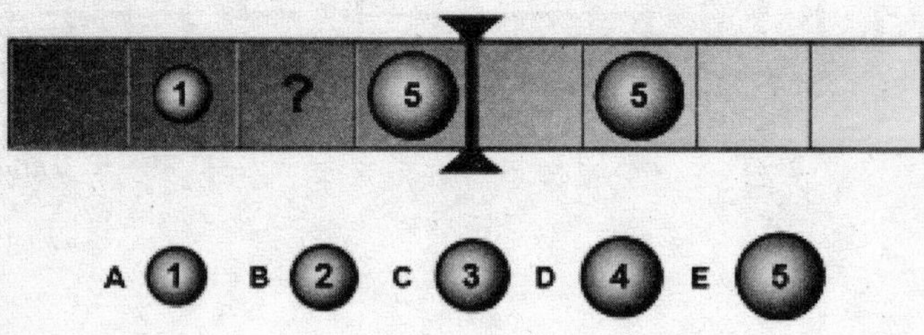

ANSWER:

Puzzle 6.9	**Difficulty rating: 2**

TURNING WHEELS

Shown below is a system of wheels connected by belts. The circumference of the outer rim of each wheel is exactly twice that of the inner rim. If wheel A turns at 100 revolutions per minute, how fast will wheel E turn?

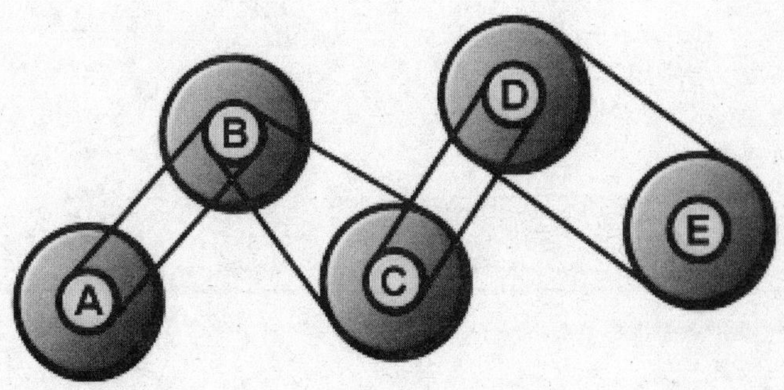

ANSWER:

Puzzle 6.10	**Difficulty rating: 3**

WORD EXTENSION

What word can be added to each of these to create three new words?

DAY OUT FAST

ANSWER:

Puzzle 6.11	**Difficulty rating: 2**

WORD SCRAMBLE

There are four scrambled letters below that can be formed into five English words. You must use all the letters in the word, and they can only be used once. Can you find all five?

S R T A

ANSWER:

Puzzle 6.12	**Difficulty rating: 3**

WORD ADDITION

What word inserted in the blank space will create two new words? Find at least one word for each set of words. *Example: QUICK* *sand* *PAPER*

CROSS ____ HOUSE

DOWN ____ TOP

ANSWER:

Puzzle 6.13	**Difficulty rating: 2**

PHONE A FRIEND

Complete the sequence.

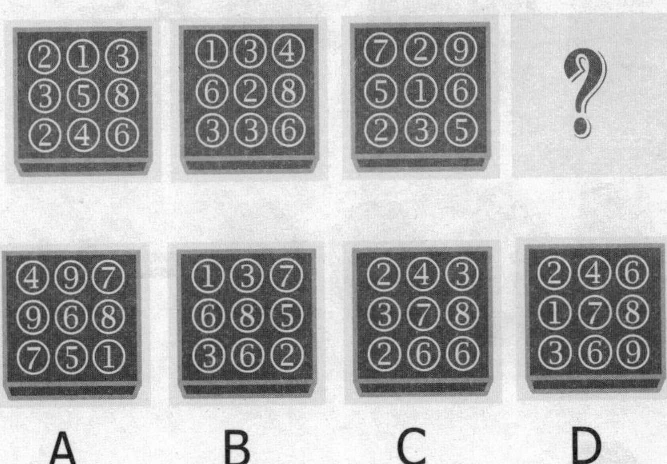

ANSWER:

Puzzle 6.14	**Difficulty rating: 4**

FIND THE MISSING VALUE

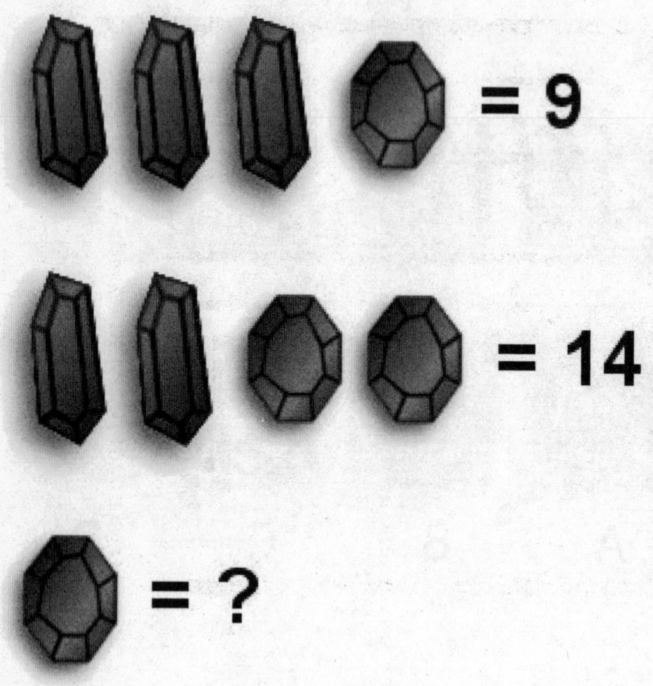

ANSWER:

Puzzle 6.15	**Difficulty rating: 2**

MISSING FIGURE

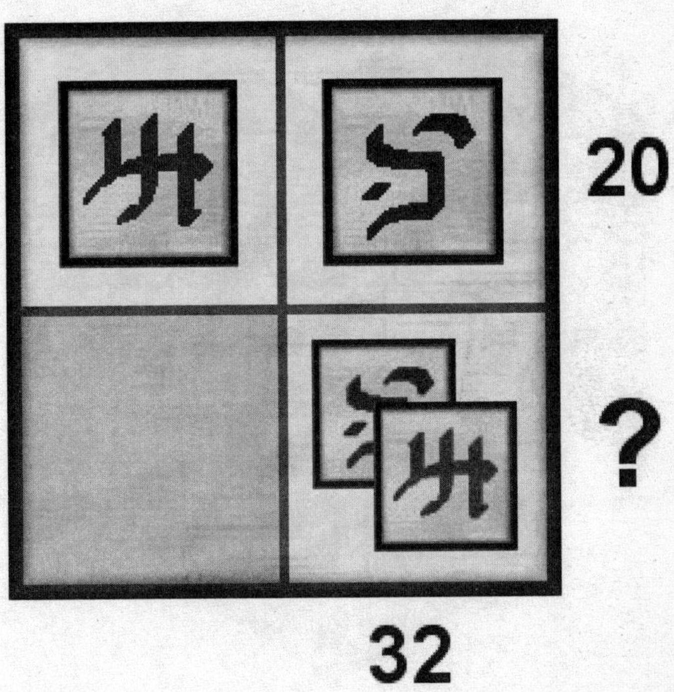

ANSWER:

Puzzle 6.16	Difficulty rating: 3

MISSING VALUE

ANSWER:

Puzzle 6.17	**Difficulty rating: 4**

ODD ONE OUT

Which of the following is least like the others?

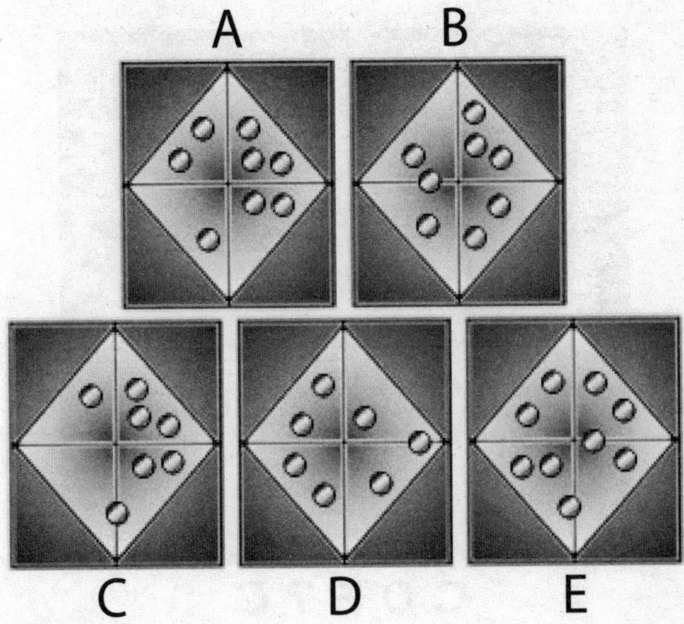

ANSWER:

Puzzle 6.18	Difficulty rating: 3

MOLECULAR SEQUENCE

Use the diagram to determine the missing letter in the sequence.

C D E ? G

ANSWER:

Puzzle 6.19	**Difficulty rating: 4**

CHOOSE A TILE

Which item is the best continuation of the sequence?

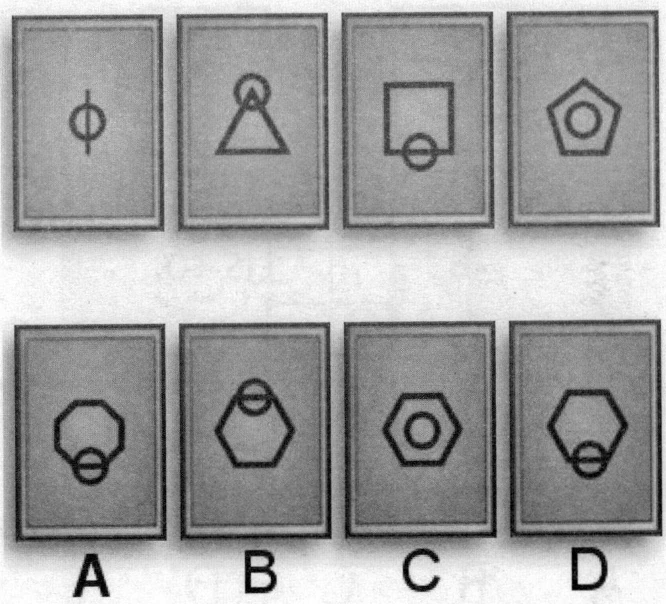

ANSWER:

Puzzle 6.20	Difficulty rating: 3

ANALOGY PUZZLE

Determine the item that best completes the analogy.

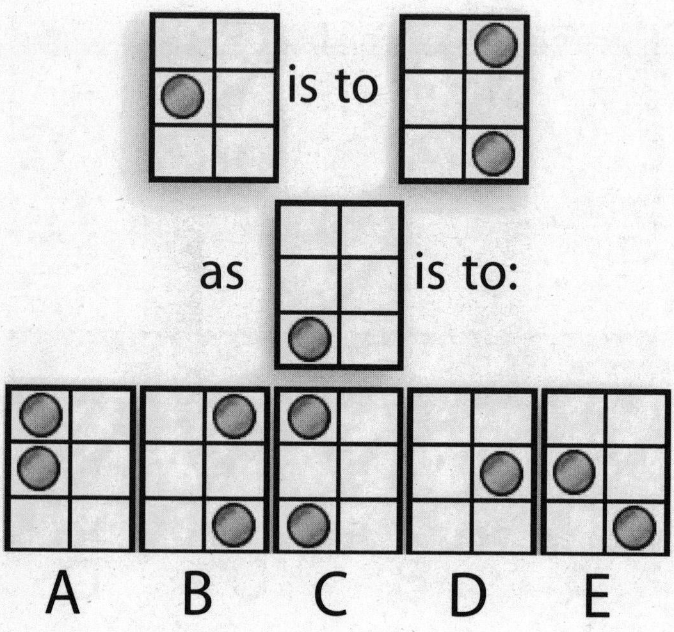

ANSWER:

Puzzle 6.21	**Difficulty rating: 3**

WINDOW FILLER

Determine the missing square.

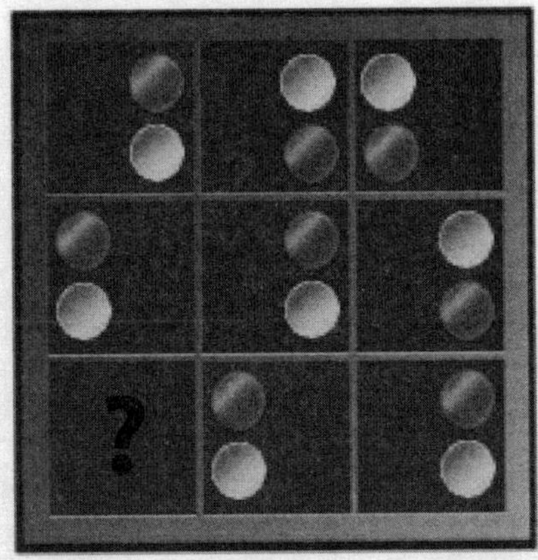

A B C D E

ANSWER:

Puzzle 6.22 | **Difficulty rating: 3**

TRELLIS PATTERN

Determine the system used to generate numbers in the grid below, and find the missing value.

ANSWER:

Puzzle 6.23	Difficulty rating: 4

WHEELS WITHIN WHEELS

Determine the system used to generate numbers in the diagram below, and find the missing value.

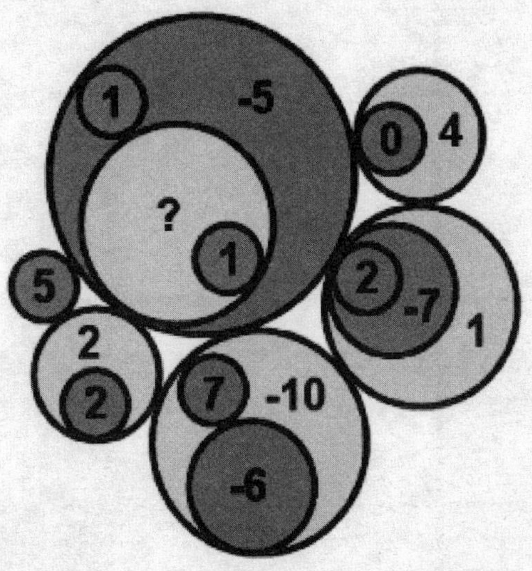

ANSWER:

Puzzle 6.24	Difficulty rating: 4

HIDDEN NUMBERS

What is the missing number in the figure below?

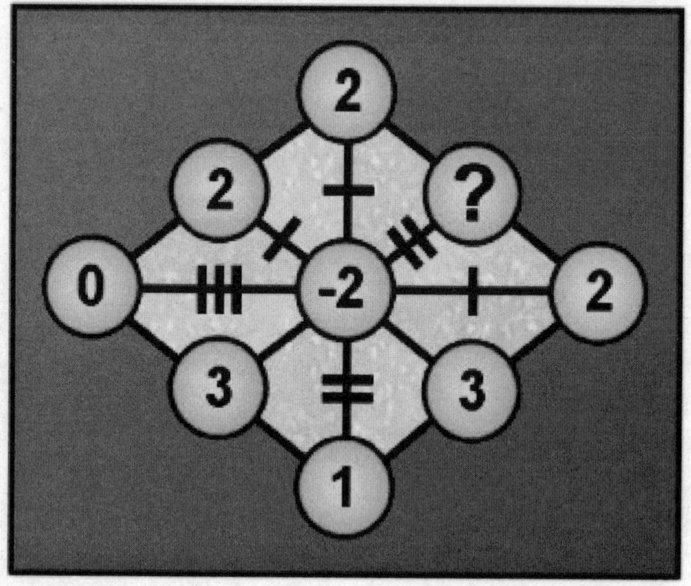

ANSWER:

Puzzle 6.25	**Difficulty rating: 4**

HIDDEN VALUES

Determine the system used to generate numbers in the grid below, and find the missing value.

ANSWER:

Puzzle 6.26	**Difficulty rating: 3**

STARBURST

Determine the relationship between the central star and the outer circles, and find the missing number.

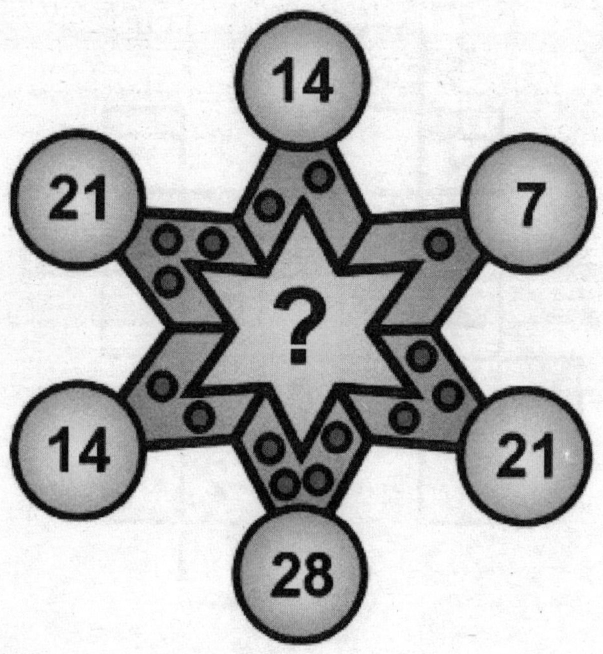

ANSWER:

Puzzle 6.27	Difficulty rating: 4

ODD ONE IN

Which square is most like the first five?

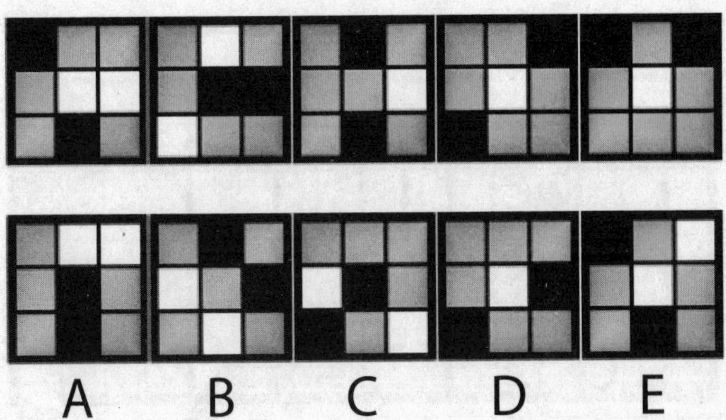

ANSWER:

Puzzle 6.28	**Difficulty rating: 3**

FAST EXIT

Which of the circles in the maze is nearest to the exit?

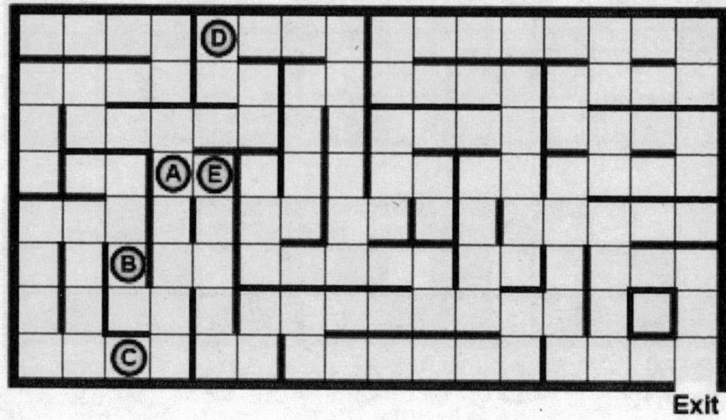

ANSWER:

Puzzle 6.29	**Difficulty rating: 2**

BALANCING ACT

Shown below is the aerial view of a see-saw perfectly balanced by weights on both sides.

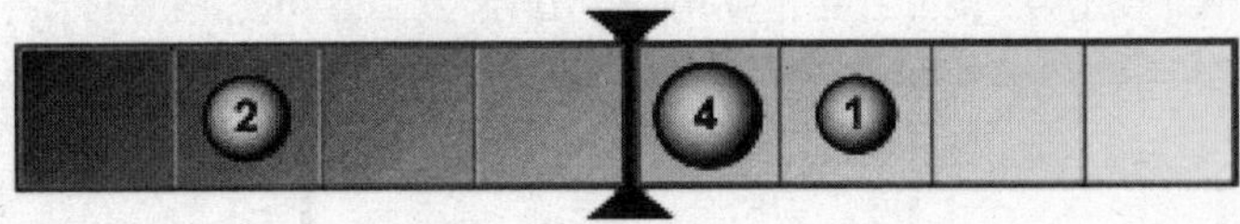

What weight must be placed at the position indicated, to balance the following see-saw?

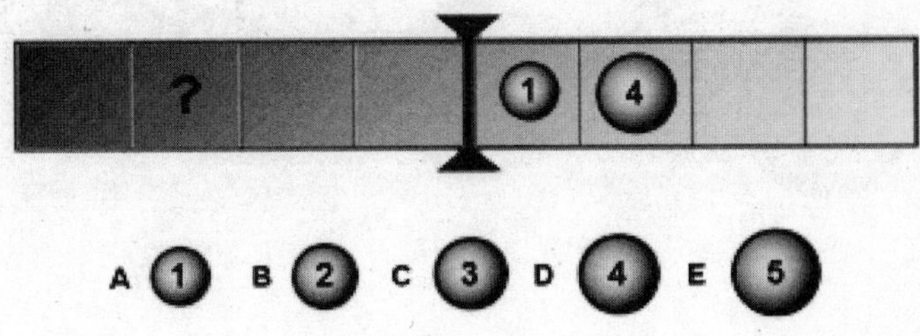

ANSWER:

Puzzle 6.30	Difficulty rating: 2

TURNING WHEELS

Shown below is a system of wheels connected by belts. The circumference of the outer rim of each wheel is exactly twice that of the inner rim. If wheel A turns at 100 revolutions per minute, how fast will wheel E turn?

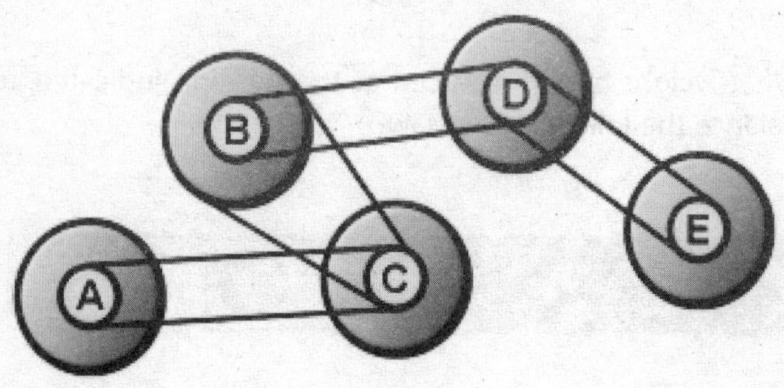

ANSWER:

Puzzle 6.31	Difficulty rating: 3

WORD EXTENSION

What word can be added to each of these to create three new words?

BAR SHED BOX

ANSWER:

Puzzle 6.32	**Difficulty rating: 2**

WORD SCRAMBLE

There are five scrambled letters below that can be formed into three English words. You must use all the letters in the word, and they can only be used once. Can you find all three?

E B W O L

ANSWER:

Puzzle 6.33	**Difficulty rating: 3**

WORD ADDITION

What word inserted in the blank space will create two new words? Find at least one word for each set of words. *Example: QUICK sand PAPER*

DRIVE _____ SIDE

FIRE _____ MAT

ANSWER:

Puzzle 6.34	**Difficulty rating: 2**

REVOLVING SPHERES

Complete the sequence.

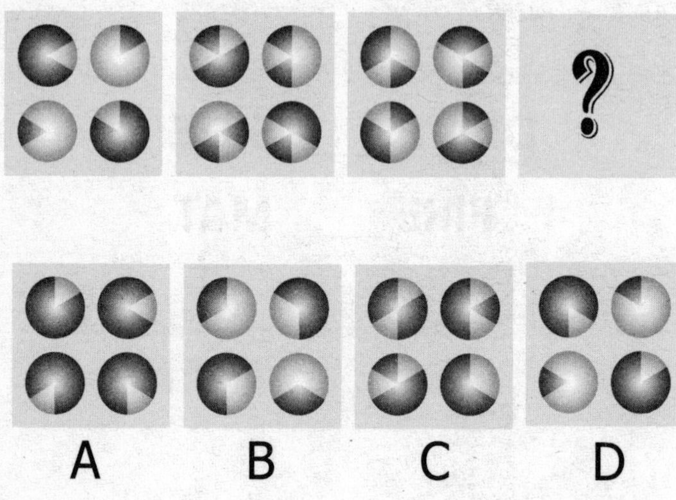

ANSWER:

Puzzle 6.35	**Difficulty rating: 3**

FIND THE MISSING VALUE

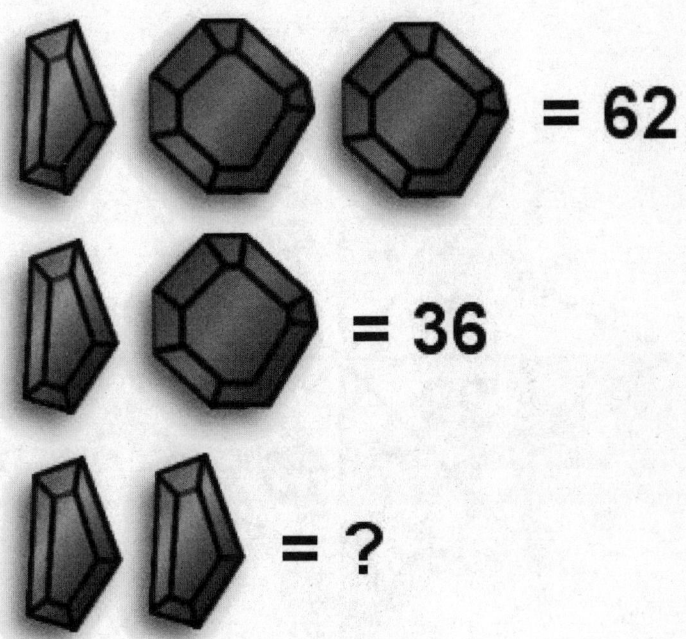

ANSWER:

Puzzle 6.36	**Difficulty rating: 3**

MISSING SEGMENT

ANSWER:

Puzzle 6.37	Difficulty rating: 3

ODD ONE OUT

Which of the following is least like the others?

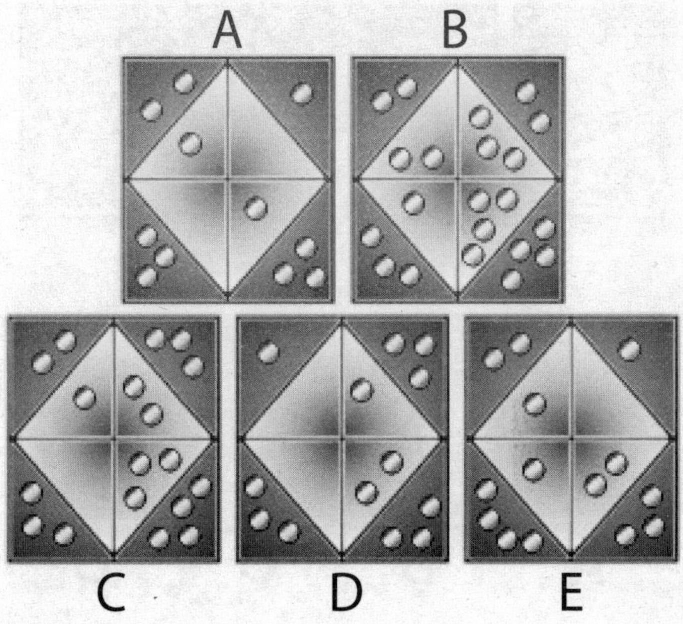

ANSWER:

Puzzle 6.38	Difficulty rating: 3

COMPLETE THE SEQUENCE

Which item is the best continuation of the sequence?

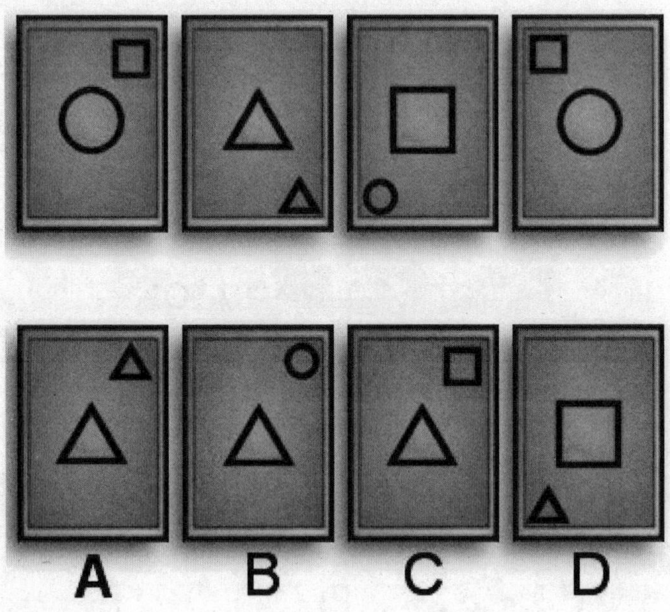

ANSWER:

Puzzle 6.39	**Difficulty rating: 3**

ANALOGY PUZZLE

Determine the item that best completes the analogy.

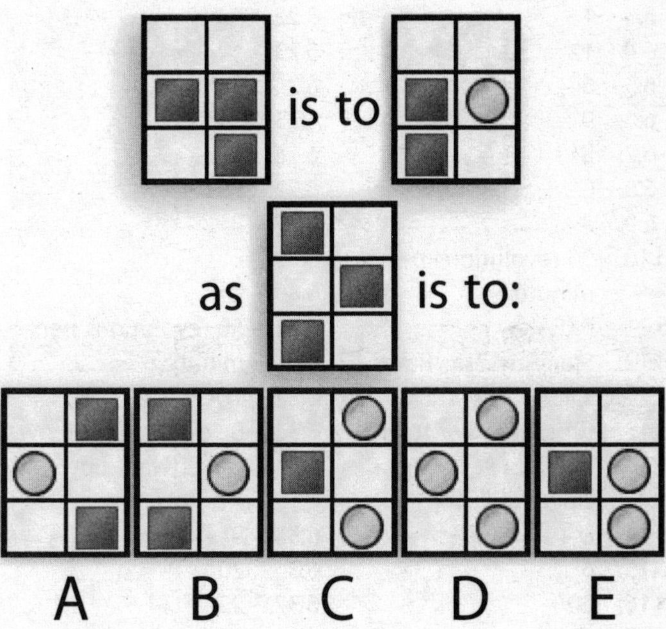

ANSWER:

Puzzle 6.40	**Difficulty rating: 4**

CHAPTER 6 ANSWERS

6.1. 3
6.2. 3
6.3. 1
6.4. 1
6.5. 6
6.6. 9
6.7. B
6.8. C
6.9. A
6.10. 50 revolutions per minute.
6.11. BREAK
6.12. Star, Arts, Tsar, Rats, Tars
6.13. Cross (road *or* town) house
Down (hill) top
6.14. D
6.15. 6
6.16. 20
6.17. -5
6.18. A
6.19. B
6.20. B
6.21. D
6.22. A
6.23. 4
6.24. 3
6.25. 1
6.26. 2
6.27. 7
6.28. B
6.29. E
6.30. C
6.31. 50 revolutions per minute.
6.32. TOOL
6.33. Below, Bowel, Elbow
6.34. Drive (way) side
Fire (place) mat
6.35. B
6.36. 20
6.37. 22
6.38. B
6.39. A
6.40. C

DIFFICULTY RATING: 122

WINDOW FILLER

Determine the missing square.

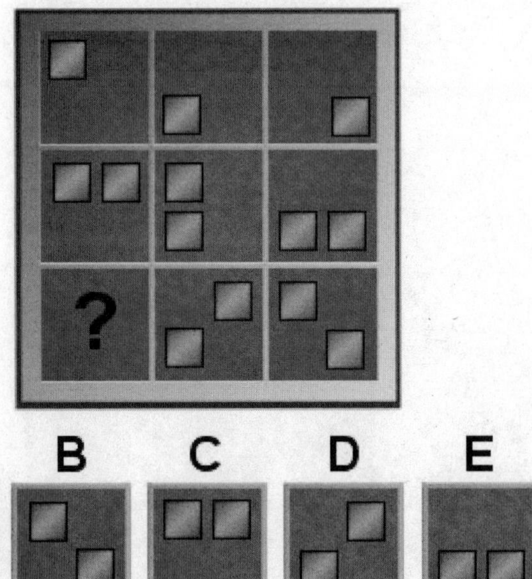

ANSWER:

Puzzle 7.1	Difficulty rating: 3

TRELLIS PATTERN

Determine the system used to generate numbers in the grid below, and find the missing number.

ANSWER:

Puzzle 7.2	Difficulty rating: 3

WHEELS WITHIN WHEELS

Determine the system used to generate numbers in the diagram below, and find the missing value.

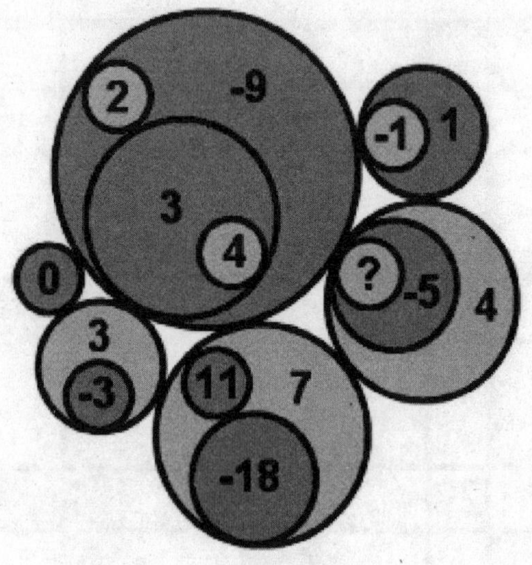

ANSWER:

Puzzle 7.3	**Difficulty rating: 4**

HIDDEN NUMBERS

What is the missing number in the figure below?

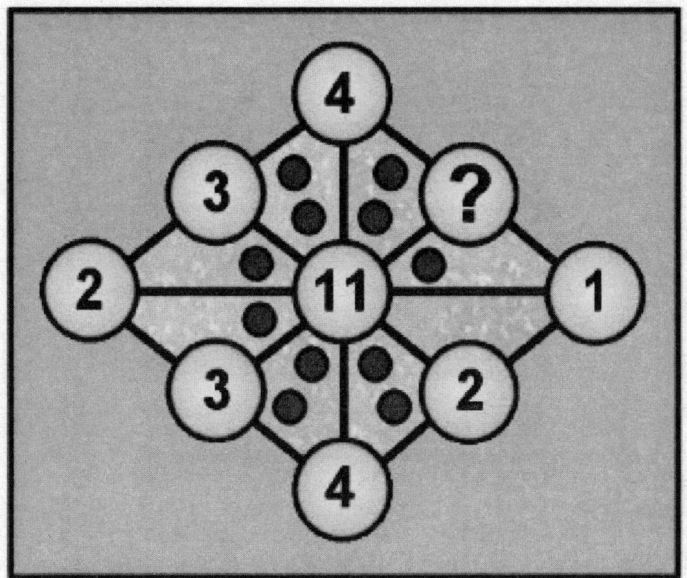

ANSWER:

Puzzle 7.4	**Difficulty rating: 4**

HIDDEN VALUES

Determine the system used to generate numbers in the grid below, and find the missing value.

ANSWER:

Puzzle 7.5	**Difficulty rating: 3**

STARBURST

Determine the relationship between the central star and the outer circles, and find the missing value.

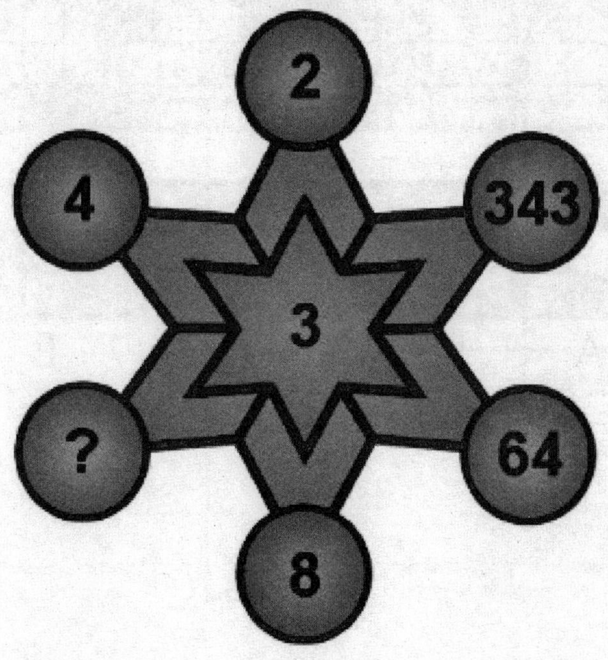

ANSWER:

Puzzle 7.6	Difficulty rating: 3

ODD ONE IN

Which square is most like the first five?

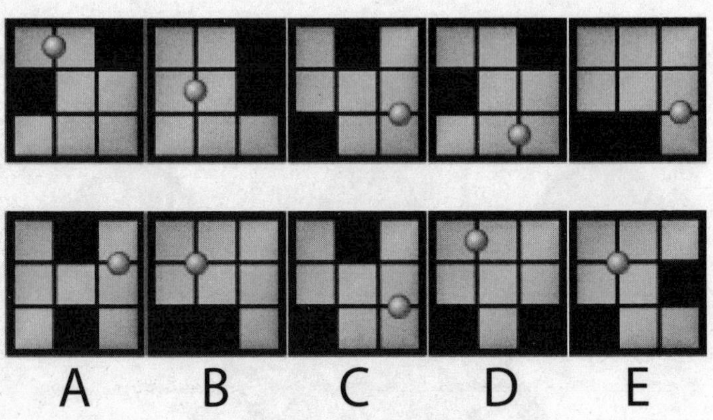

ANSWER:

Puzzle 7.7	**Difficulty rating: 3**

FAST EXIT

Which of the circles in the maze is nearest to the exit?

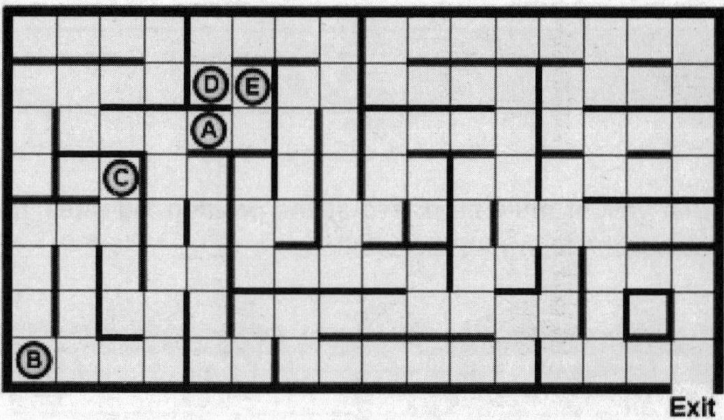

ANSWER:

Puzzle 7.8	Difficulty rating: 2

BALANCING ACT

Shown below is the aerial view of a see-saw perfectly balanced by weights on both sides.

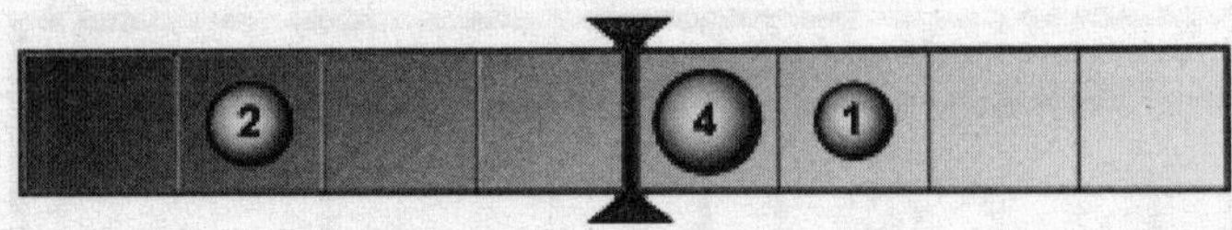

What weight must be placed at the position indicated, to balance the following see-saw?

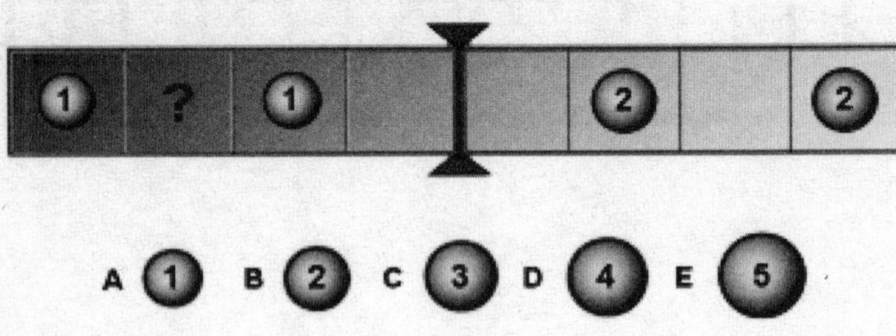

ANSWER:

Puzzle 7.9	Difficulty rating: 2

TURNING WHEELS

Shown below is a system of wheels connected by belts. The circumference of the outer rim of each wheel is exactly twice that of the inner rim. If wheel A turns at 100 revolutions per minute, how fast will wheel E turn?

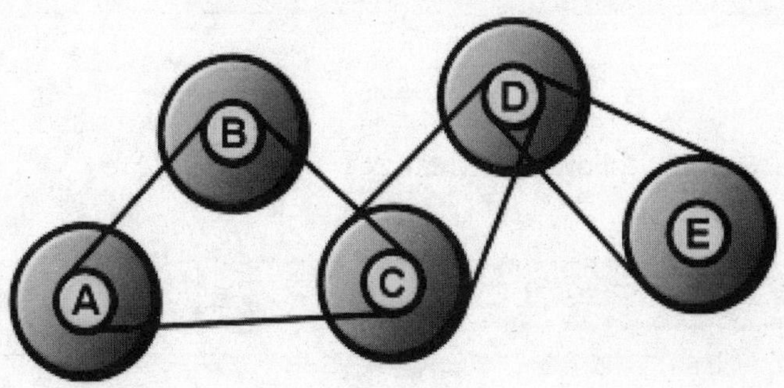

ANSWER:

Puzzle 7.10	**Difficulty rating: 3**

WORD EXTENSION

What word can be added to each of these to create three new words?

TOE CURRENT HAND

ANSWER:

Puzzle 7.11	Difficulty rating: 2

WORD SCRAMBLE

There are five scrambled letters below that can be formed into three English words. You must use all the letters in the word, and they can only be used once. Can you find all three?

E Y R A L

ANSWER:

Puzzle 7.12	**Difficulty rating: 3**

WORD ADDITION

What word inserted in the blank space will create two new words? Find at least one word for each set of words. *Example: QUICK sand PAPER*

GUN ____ KEG

HORSE ____ TRACK

ANSWER:

Puzzle 7.13	**Difficulty rating: 2**

REVOLVING SPHERES

Complete the sequence.

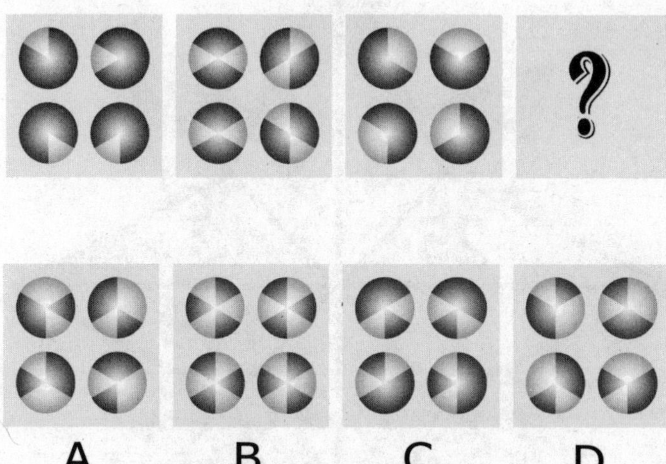

ANSWER:

Puzzle 7.14	**Difficulty rating: 3**

MISSING SEGMENT

ANSWER:

Puzzle 7.15	Difficulty rating: 3

ODD ONE OUT

Which of the following is least like the others?

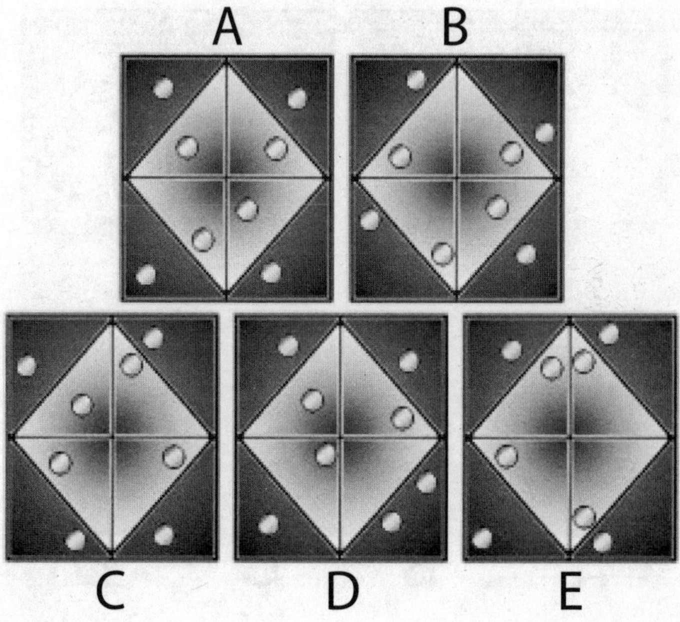

ANSWER:

Puzzle 7.16	Difficulty rating: 3

CHOOSE A TILE

Which item is the best continuation of the sequence?

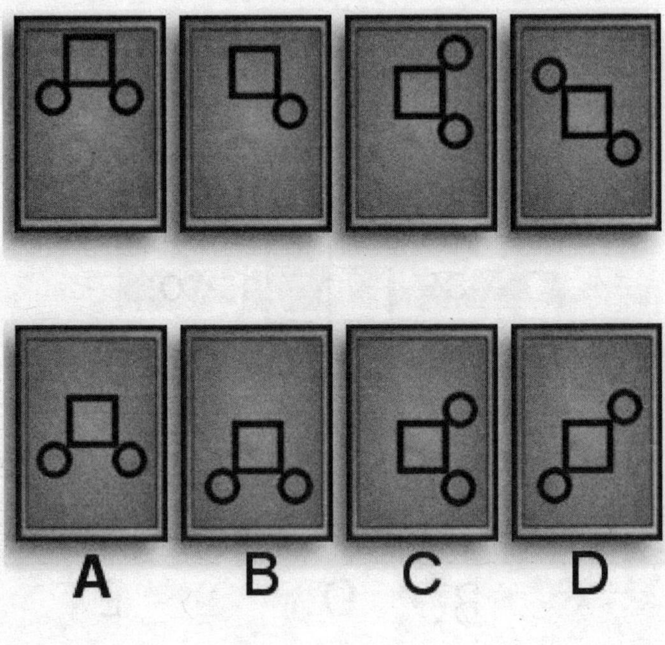

ANSWER:

Puzzle 7.17	Difficulty rating: 3

ANALOGY PUZZLE

Determine the item that best completes the analogy.

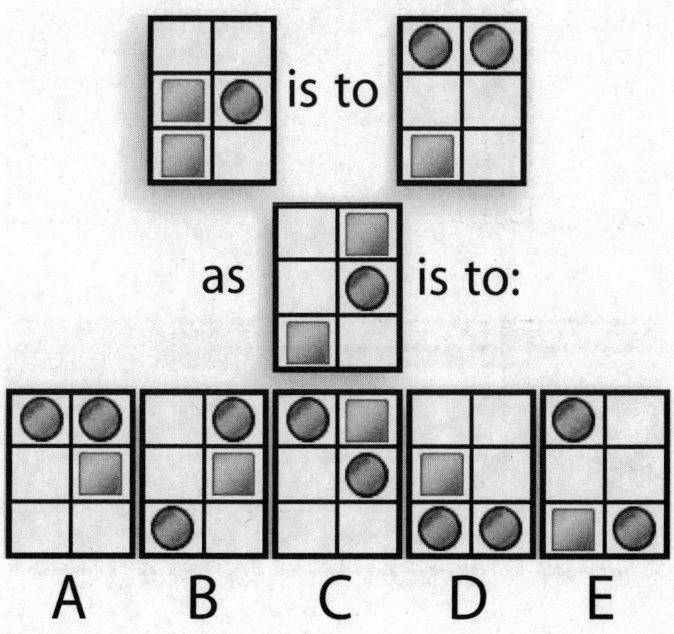

ANSWER:

Puzzle 7.18	Difficulty rating: 4

ARABESQUE

Determine the missing square.

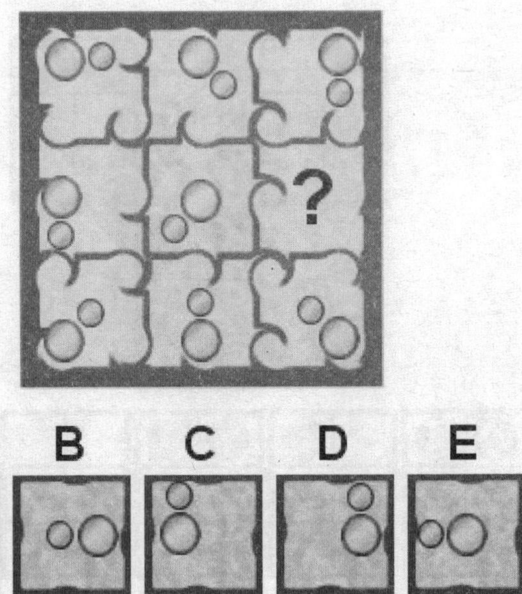

ANSWER:

Puzzle 7.19	Difficulty rating: 3

TRELLIS PATTERN

Determine the system used to generate numbers in the grid below, and find the missing number.

ANSWER:

Puzzle 7.20	**Difficulty rating: 4**

WHEELS WITHIN WHEELS

Determine the system used to generate numbers in the diagram below, and find the missing value.

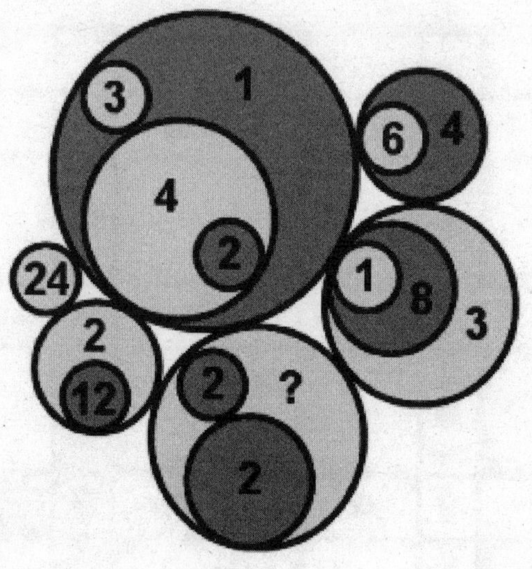

ANSWER:

Puzzle 7.21	**Difficulty rating: 4**

HIDDEN NUMBERS

What is the missing number in the figure below?

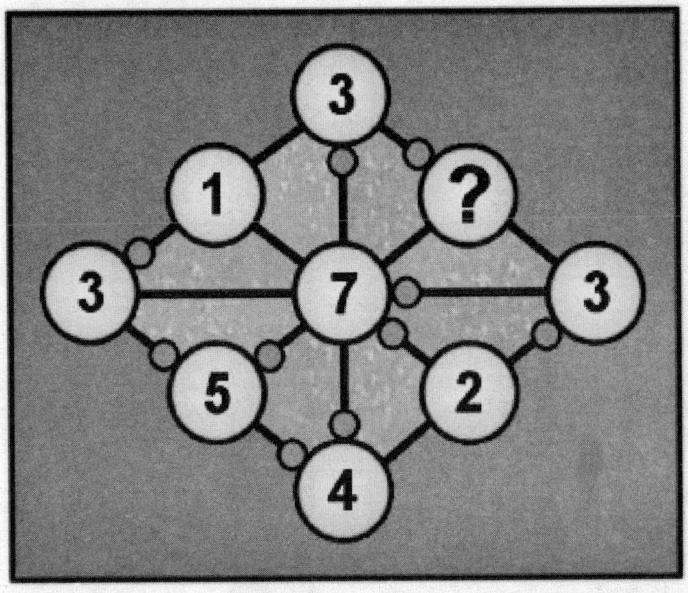

ANSWER:

Puzzle 7.22	Difficulty rating: 4

HIDDEN VALUES

Determine the system used to generate numbers in the grid below, and find the missing value.

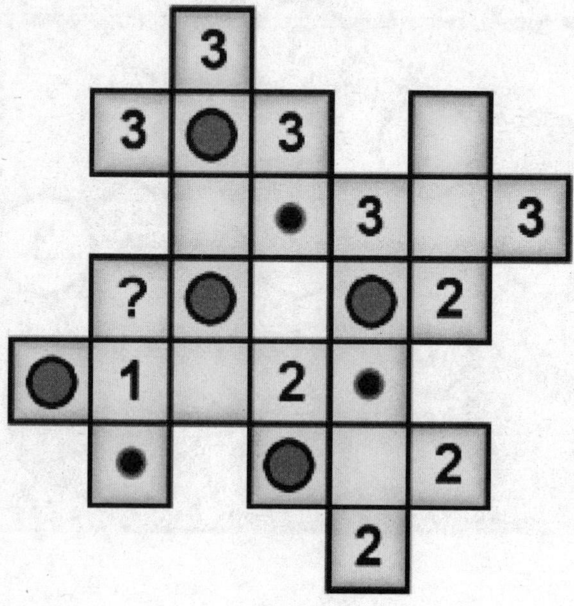

ANSWER:

Puzzle 7.23	**Difficulty rating: 4**

STARBURST

Determine the relationship between the central star and the outer circles, and find the missing value.

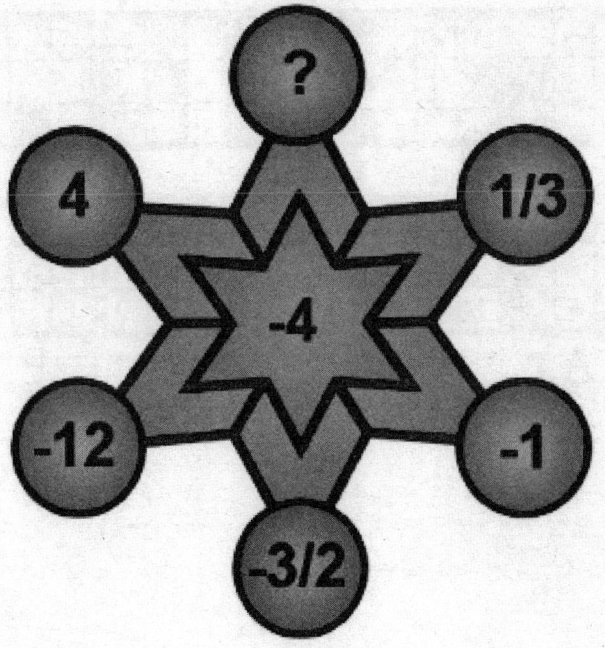

ANSWER:

Puzzle 7.24	Difficulty rating: 3

ODD ONE IN

Which square is most like the first five?

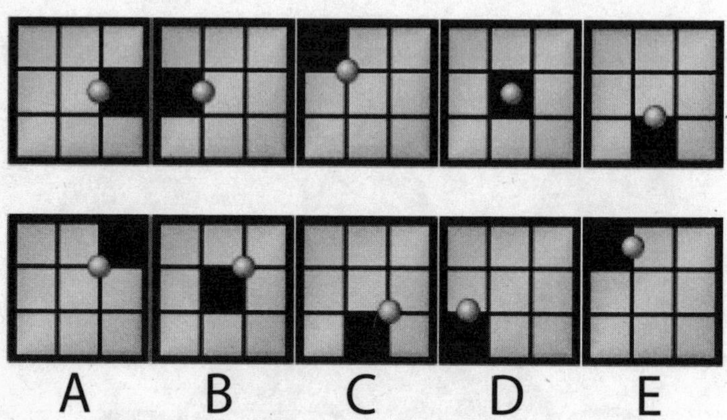

ANSWER:

Puzzle 7.25	**Difficulty rating: 3**

MAZE

Discover the logic behind the placement of the circles within the maze and choose the best location for the last circle.

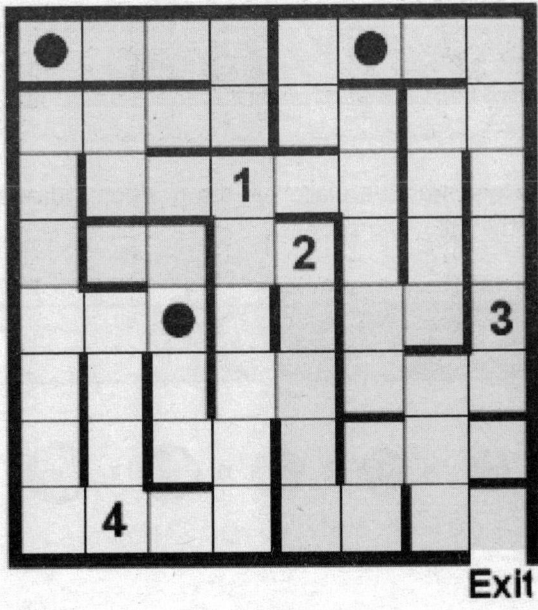

ANSWER:

Puzzle 7.26	Difficulty rating: 3

BALANCING ACT

Shown below is the aerial view of a see-saw perfectly balanced by weights on both sides.

What weight must be placed at the position indicated, to balance the following see-saw?

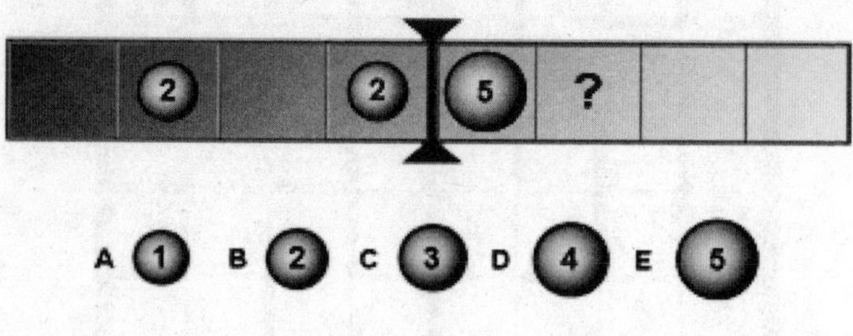

ANSWER:

Puzzle 7.27	**Difficulty rating: 2**

TURNING WHEELS

Shown below is a system of wheels connected by belts. The circumference of the outer rim of each wheel is exactly twice that of the inner rim. If wheel A turns at 100 revolutions per minute, how fast will wheel E turn?

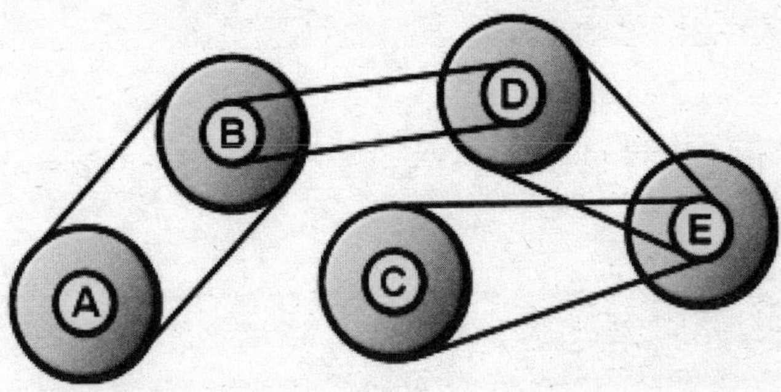

ANSWER:

Puzzle 7.28	**Difficulty rating: 3**

WORD EXTENSION

What word can be added to each of these to create three new words?

SIGHT HANG SEE

ANSWER:

Puzzle 7.29	**Difficulty rating: 2**

WORD SCRAMBLE

There are five scrambled letters below that can be formed into three English words. You must use all the letters in the word, and they can only be used once. Can you find all three?

I N T A S

ANSWER:

Puzzle 7.30	Difficulty rating: 3

WORD ADDITION

What word inserted in the blank space will create two new words? Find at least one word for each set of words. *Example: QUICK sand PAPER*

MASTER ____ MEAL

MOUNTAIN ____ HEAVY

ANSWER:

Puzzle 7.31	Difficulty rating: 2

COMPLETE THE SEQUENCE

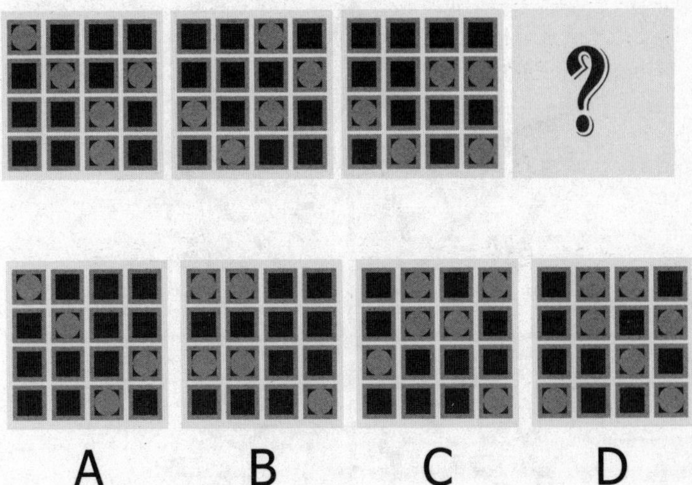

ANSWER:

Puzzle 7.32	**Difficulty rating: 3**

MISSING LETTER

ANSWER:

Puzzle 7.33	Difficulty rating: 3

ODD ONE OUT

Which of the following is least like the others?

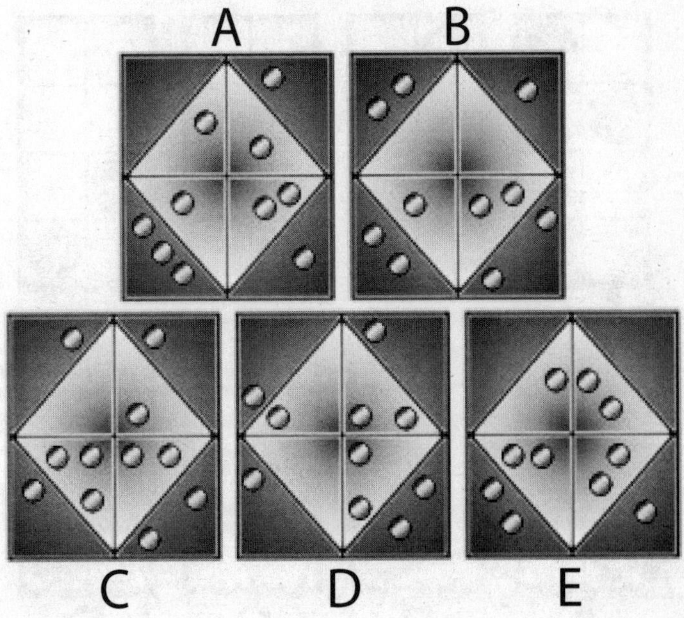

ANSWER:

Puzzle 7.34	Difficulty rating: 3

TWO INTO EIGHT

Which item is the best continuation of the sequence?

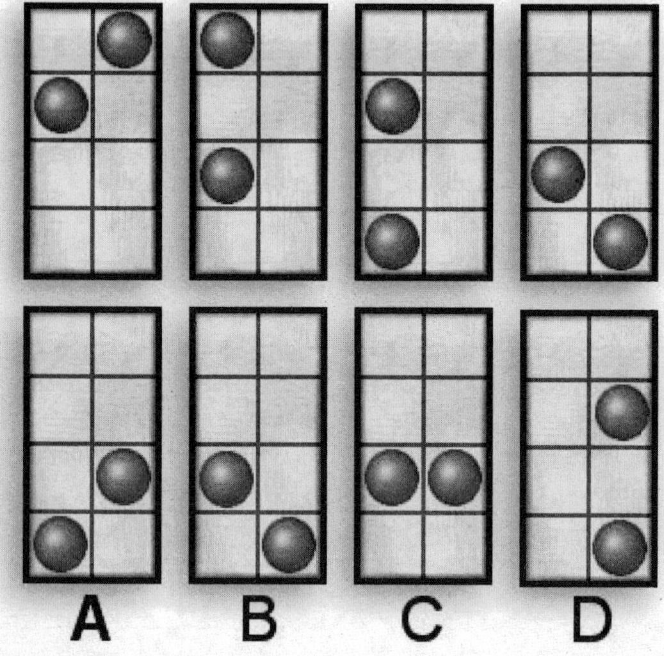

ANSWER:

Puzzle 7.35	**Difficulty rating: 3**

ANALOGY PUZZLE

Determine the item that best completes the analogy.

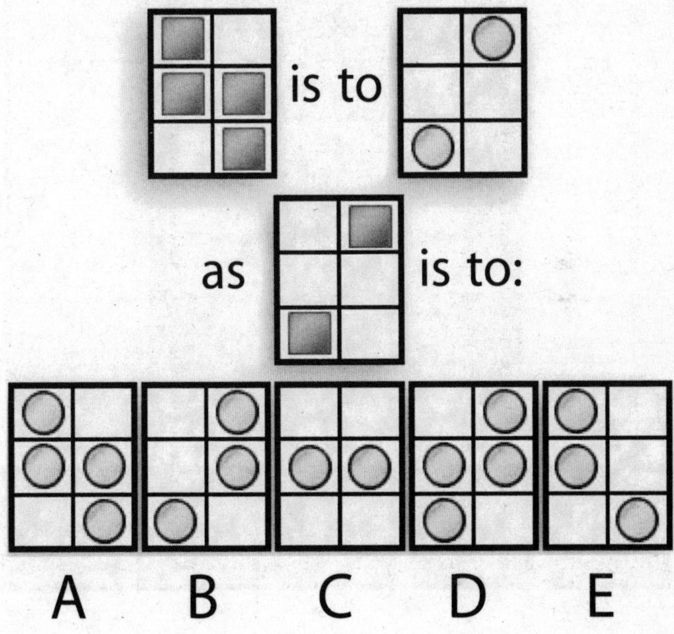

ANSWER:

Puzzle 7.36	Difficulty rating: 4

ARABESQUE

Determine the missing square.

A B C D E

ANSWER:

Puzzle 7.37	**Difficulty rating: 3**

TRELLIS PATTERN

Determine the system used to generate numbers in the grid below, and find the missing number.

ANSWER:

Puzzle 7.38	**Difficulty rating: 3**

WHEELS WITHIN WHEELS

Determine the system used to generate numbers in the diagram below, and find the missing value.

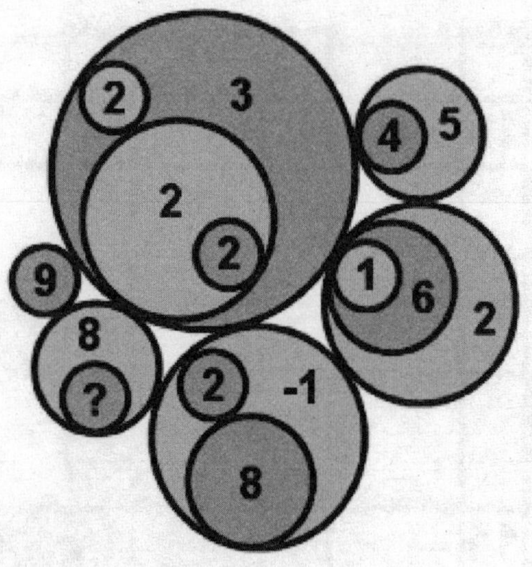

ANSWER:

Puzzle 7.39	Difficulty rating: 4

HIDDEN VALUES

Determine the system used to generate numbers in the grid below, and find the missing value.

ANSWER:

Puzzle 7.40	Difficulty rating: 3

CHAPTER 7 ANSWERS

7.1. B
7.2. 4
7.3. 1
7.4. 3
7.5. 6
7.6. 7
7.7. C
7.8. D
7.9. B
7.10. 100 revolutions per minute.
7.11. UNDER
7.12. Layer, Early, Relay
7.13. Gun (powder) keg
Horse (back) track
7.14. D
7.15. 121
7.16. D
7.17. B
7.18. E
7.19. B
7.20. 6
7.21. 6
7.22. 2
7.23. 1
7.24. 6
7.25. A
7.26. 3
7.27. C
7.28. 200 revolutions per minute.
7.29. OVER
7.30. Saint, Satin, Stain
7.31. Master (piece) meal
Mountain (top) heavy
7.32. B
7.33. x
7.34. C
7.35. A
7.36. A
7.37. C
7.38. 2
7.39. 1
7.40. 4

DIFFICULTY RATING: 127

STARBURST

Determine the relationship between the central star and the outer circles, and find the missing value.

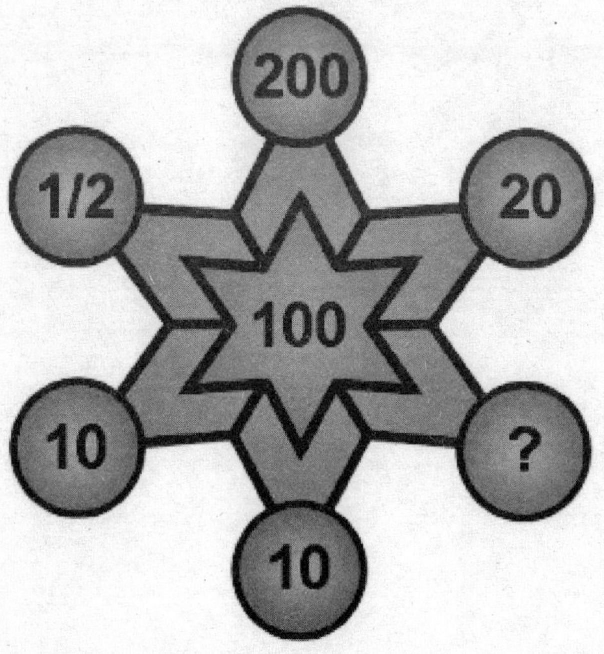

ANSWER:

Puzzle 8.1	**Difficulty rating: 3**

ODD ONE IN

Which square is most like the first five?

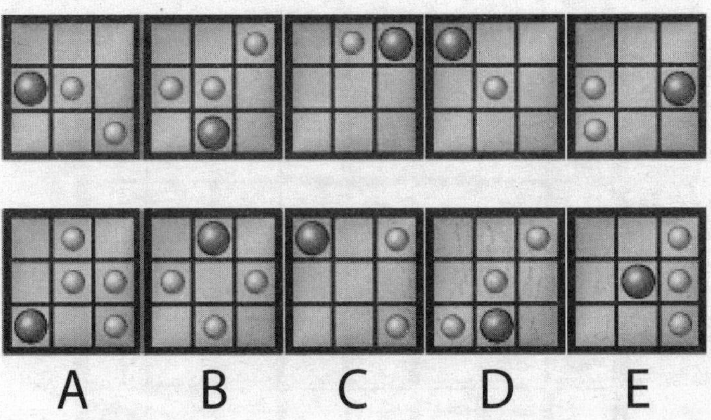

ANSWER:

Puzzle 8.2	**Difficulty rating: 3**

MAZE

Discover the logic behind the placement of the circles within the maze and choose the best location for the last circle.

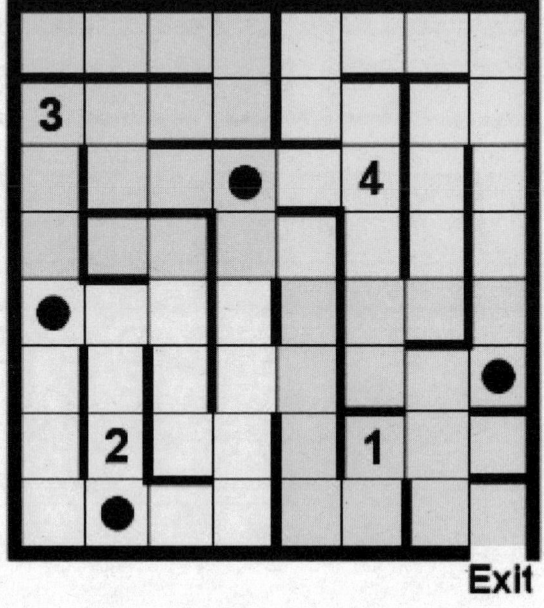

ANSWER:

Puzzle 8.3	Difficulty rating: 3

BALANCING ACT

Shown below is the aerial view of a see-saw perfectly balanced by weights on both sides.

What weight must be placed at the position indicated, to balance the following see-saw?

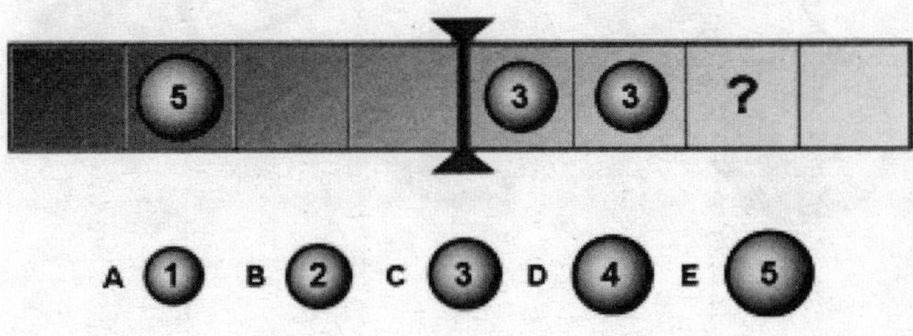

ANSWER:

Puzzle 8.4	**Difficulty rating: 2**

TURNING WHEELS

Shown below is a system of wheels connected by belts. The circumference of the outer rim of each wheel is exactly twice that of the inner rim. If wheel A turns at 100 revolutions per minute, how fast will wheel E turn?

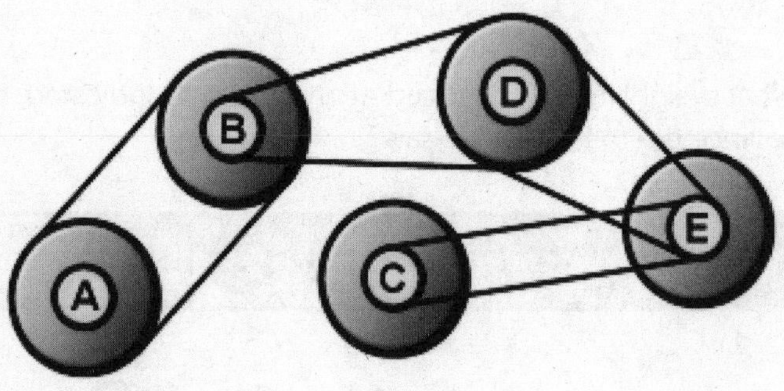

ANSWER:

Puzzle 8.5	Difficulty rating: 3

WORD EXTENSION

What word can be added to each of these to create three new words?

THOUGHT WARN HAND

ANSWER:

Puzzle 8.6	**Difficulty rating: 2**

WORD SCRAMBLE

There are seven scrambled letters below that can be formed into three English words. You must use all the letters in the word, and they can only be used once. Can you find all three?

E R T P S N E

ANSWER:

Puzzle 8.7	Difficulty rating: 3

WORD ADDITION

What word inserted in the blank space will create two new words? Find at least one word for each set of words. *Example: QUICK* <u>*sand*</u> *PAPER*

HORSE ____ CAR

LAMP ____ MAN

ANSWER:

Puzzle 8.8	**Difficulty rating: 2**

THE X-FACTOR

Complete the sequence.

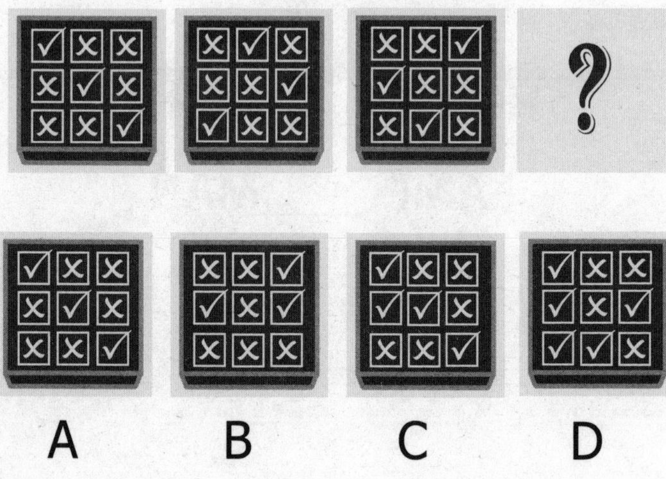

ANSWER:

Puzzle 8.9	Difficulty rating: 4

MISSING VALUE

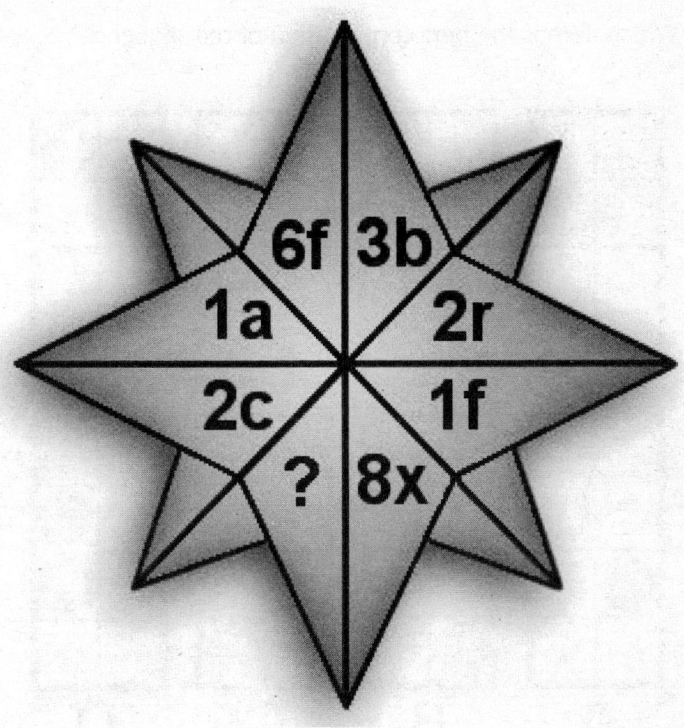

ANSWER:

Puzzle 8.10	**Difficulty rating: 4**

TWO INTO EIGHT

Which item is the best continuation of the sequence?

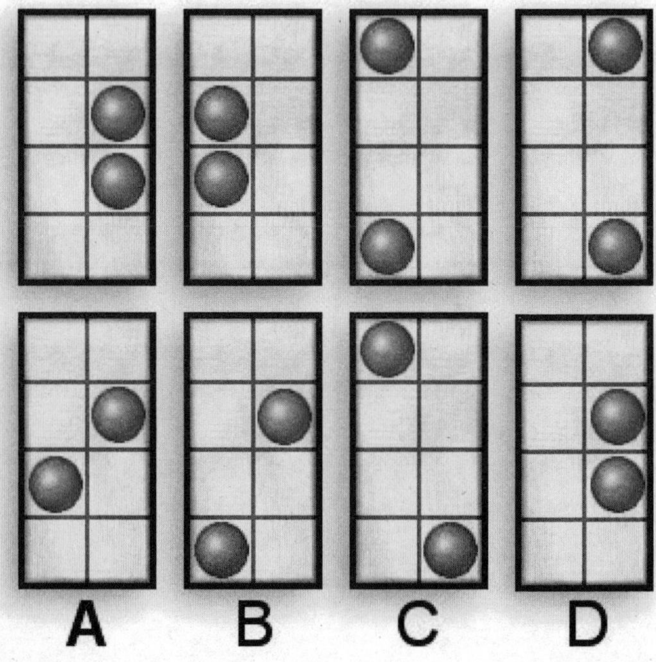

ANSWER:

Puzzle 8.11	**Difficulty rating: 3**

ANALOGY PUZZLE

Determine the item that best completes the analogy.

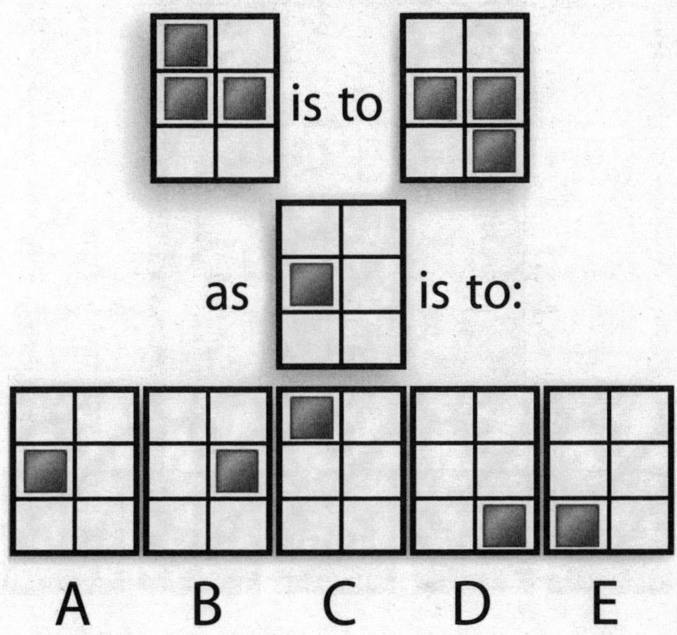

ANSWER:

Puzzle 8.12	**Difficulty rating: 3**

ARABESQUE

Determine the missing square.

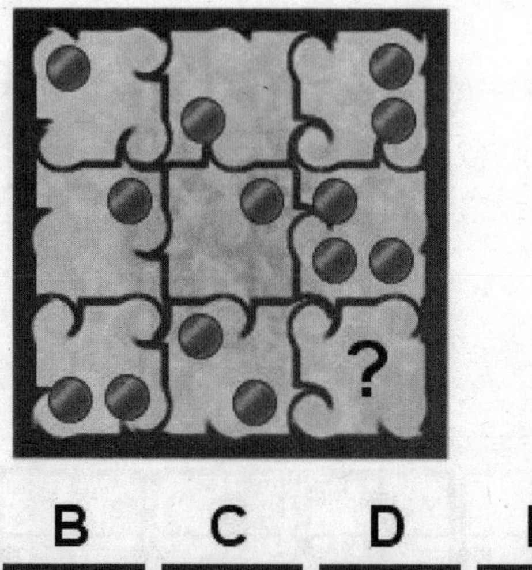

A B C D E

ANSWER:

Puzzle 8.13	**Difficulty rating: 3**

TRELLIS PATTERN

Determine the system used to generate numbers in the grid below, and find the missing number.

ANSWER:

Puzzle 8.14	Difficulty rating: 4

WHEELS WITHIN WHEELS

Determine the system used to generate numbers in the diagram below, and find the missing value.

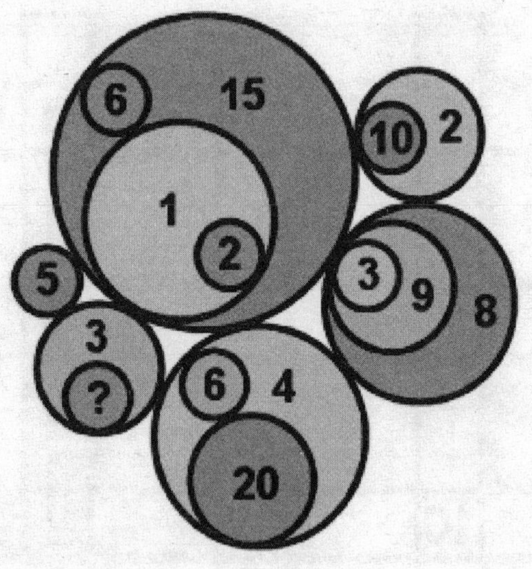

ANSWER:

Puzzle 8.15	Difficulty rating: 4

HIDDEN VALUES

Determine the system used to generate numbers in the grid below, and find the missing value.

ANSWER:

Puzzle 8.16	**Difficulty rating: 4**

STARBURST

Determine the relationship between the central star and the outer circles, and find the missing value.

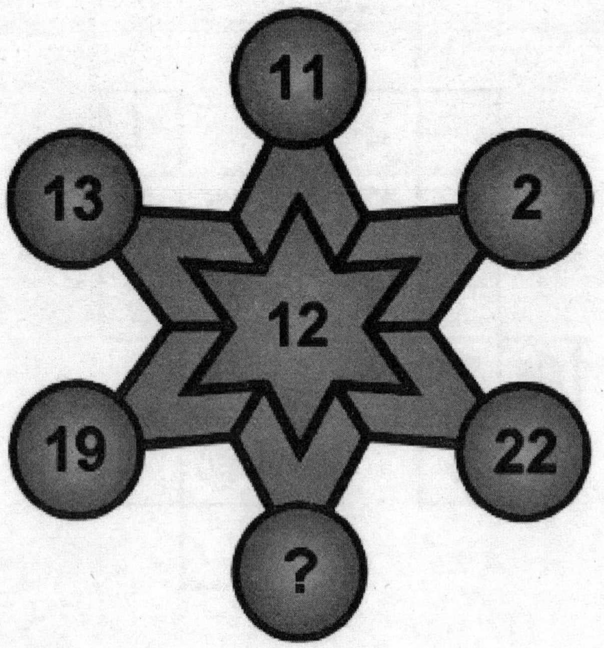

ANSWER:

Puzzle 8.17	Difficulty rating: 3

ODD ONE IN

Which item is most like the first five?

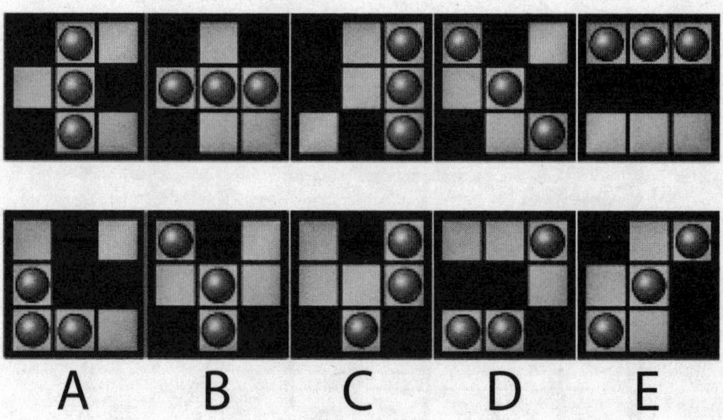

ANSWER:

Puzzle 8.18	**Difficulty rating: 3**

MAZE

Discover the logic behind the placement of the circles within the maze and choose the best location for the last circle.

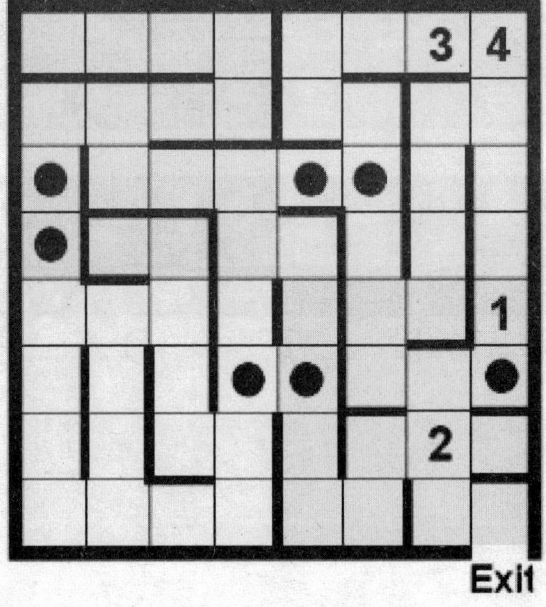

ANSWER:

Puzzle 8.19	**Difficulty rating: 4**

BALANCING ACT

Shown below is the aerial view of a see-saw perfectly balanced by weights on both sides.

What weight must be placed at the position indicated, to balance the following see-saw?

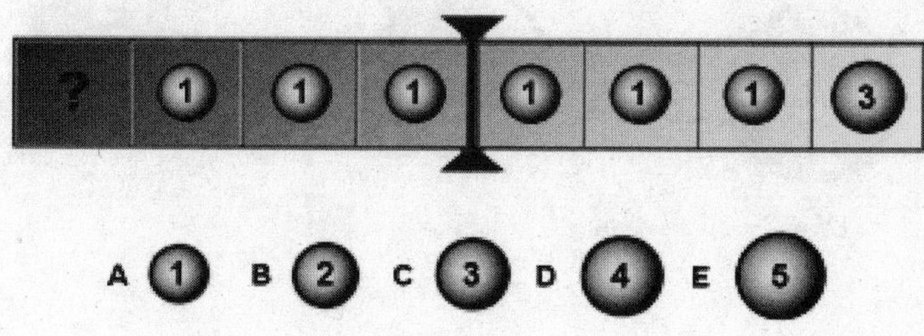

ANSWER:

Puzzle 8.20	**Difficulty rating: 2**

TURNING WHEELS

Shown below is a system of wheels connected by belts. The circumference of the outer rim of each wheel is exactly twice that of the inner rim. If wheel A turns at 100 revolutions per minute, how fast will wheel E turn?

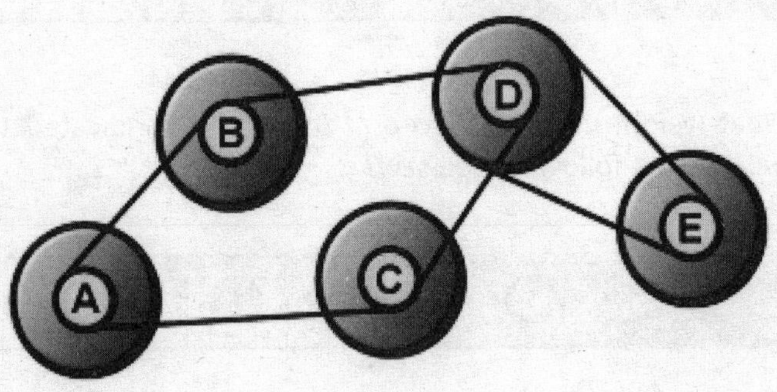

ANSWER:

Puzzle 8.21	**Difficulty rating: 3**

WORD EXTENSION

What word can be added to each of these to create three new words?

HOLE TROT HOUND

ANSWER:

Puzzle 8.22	**Difficulty rating: 2**

ACADEMIC CHOICE

HARVARD is to MASSACHUSETTS as PRINCETON is to:

A. Rhode Island
B. Delaware
C. New York
D. New Jersey
E. California

ANSWER:

Puzzle 8.23	**Difficulty rating: 2**

WORD SCRAMBLE

There are seven scrambled letters below that can be formed into four English words. You must use all the letters in the word, and they can only be used once. Can you find all four?

I A P S R D E

ANSWER:

Puzzle 8.24	**Difficulty rating: 3**

WORD ADDITION

What word inserted in the blank space will create two new words? Find at least one word for each set of words. *Example: QUICK sand PAPER*

POP _____ PIPE

KETTLE _____ STICK

ANSWER:

Puzzle 8.25	**Difficulty rating: 2**

PYRAMIDS AND SPHERES

Complete the sequence.

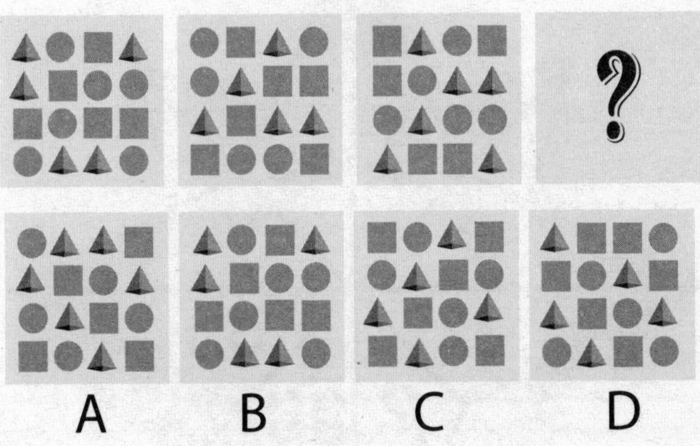

ANSWER:

Puzzle 8.26	**Difficulty rating: 5**

MISSING SEGMENT

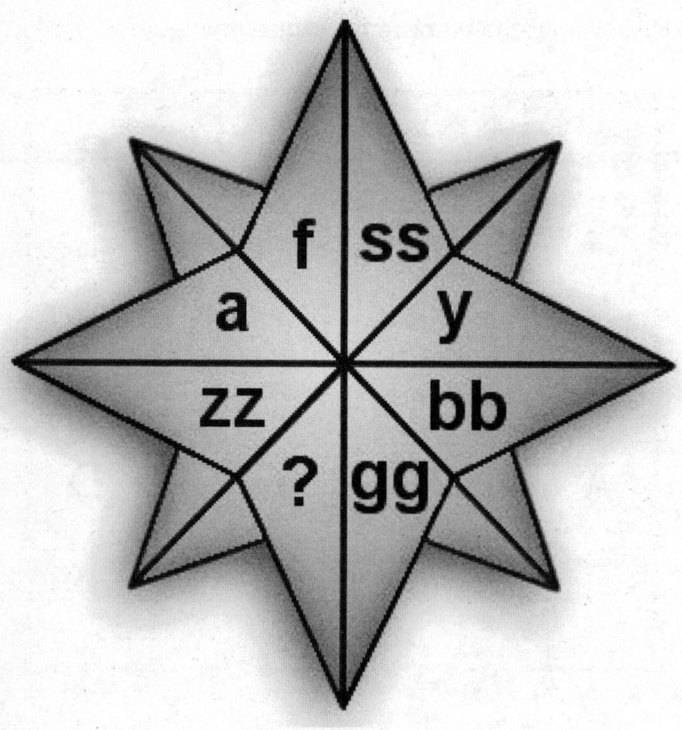

ANSWER:

Puzzle 8.27	Difficulty rating: 4

FIVE INTO EIGHT

Which item is the best continuation of the sequence?

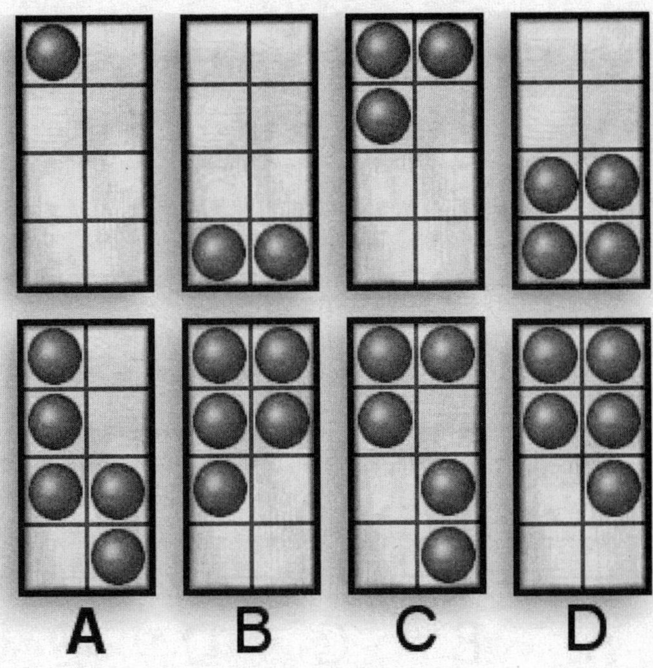

ANSWER:

Puzzle 8.28	**Difficulty rating: 4**

ANALOGY PUZZLE

Determine the item that best completes the analogy.

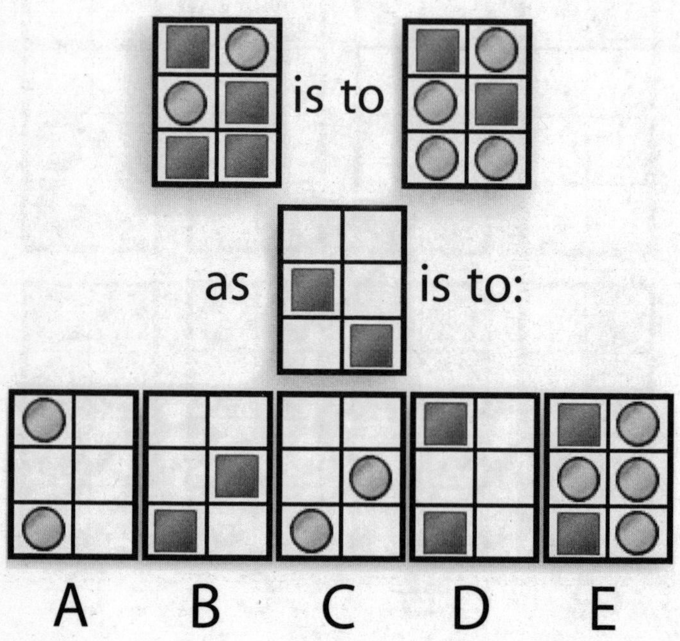

ANSWER:

Puzzle 8.29	**Difficulty rating: 4**

ARABESQUE

Determine the missing square.

A B C D E

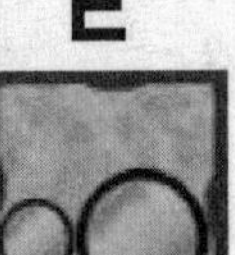

ANSWER:

Puzzle 8.30	**Difficulty rating: 4**

TRELLIS PATTERN

Determine the system used to generate numbers in the grid below, and find the missing value.

ANSWER:

Puzzle 8.31	Difficulty rating: 3

WHEELS WITHIN WHEELS

Determine the system used to generate numbers in the diagram below, and find the missing value.

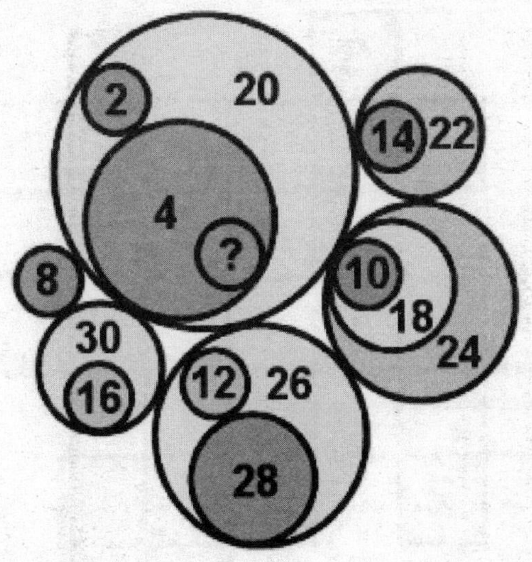

ANSWER:

Puzzle 8.32	**Difficulty rating: 5**

HIDDEN VALUES

Determine the system used to generate numbers in the grid below, and find the missing value.

ANSWER:

Puzzle 8.33	**Difficulty rating: 3**

STARBURST

Determine the relationship between the central star and the outer circles, and find the missing value.

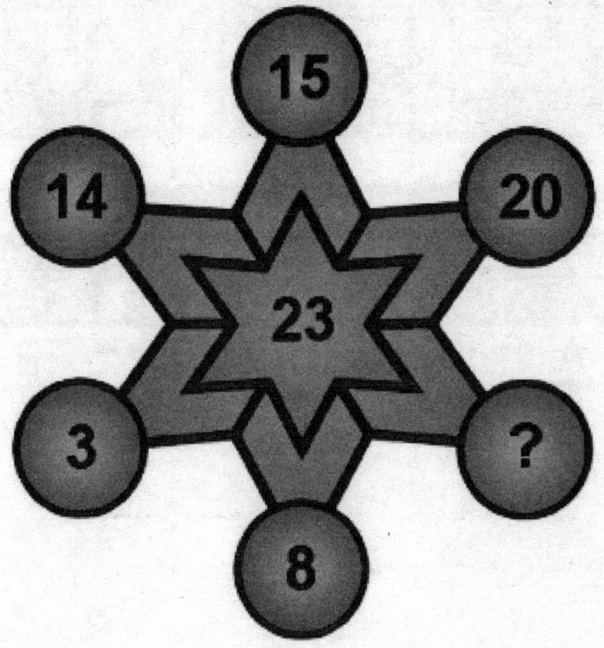

ANSWER:

Puzzle 8.34	**Difficulty rating: 3**

ODD ONE IN

Which item is most like the first five?

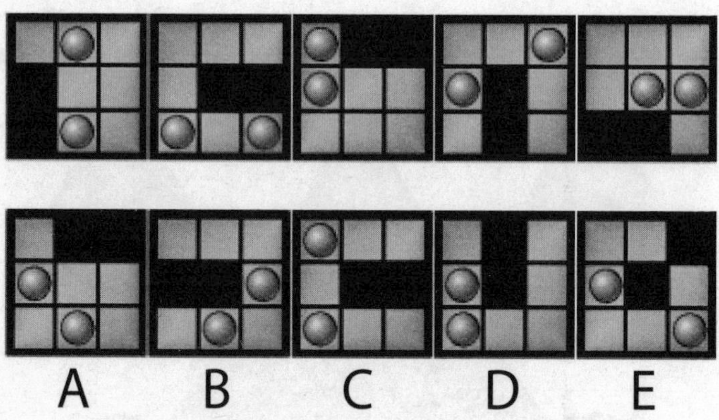

ANSWER:

Puzzle 8.35	**Difficulty rating: 3**

MAZE

Discover the logic behind the placement of the circles within the maze and choose the best location for the last circle.

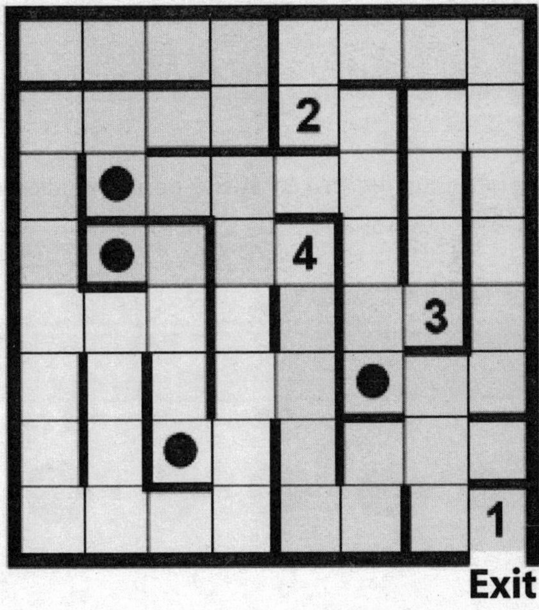

ANSWER:

Puzzle 8.36	**Difficulty rating: 4**

BALANCING ACT

Shown below is the aerial view of a see-saw perfectly balanced by weights on both sides.

What weight must be placed at the position indicated, to balance the following see-saw?

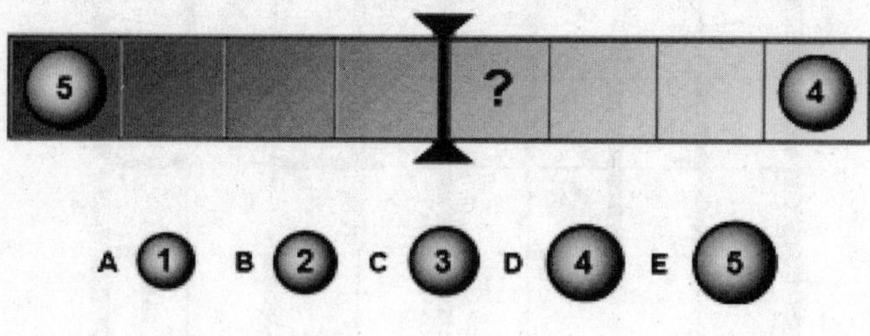

ANSWER:

Puzzle 8.37	**Difficulty rating: 2**

TURNING WHEELS

Shown below is a system of wheels connected by belts. The circumference of the outer rim of each wheel is exactly twice that of the inner rim. If wheel A turns at 100 revolutions per minute, how fast will wheel E turn?

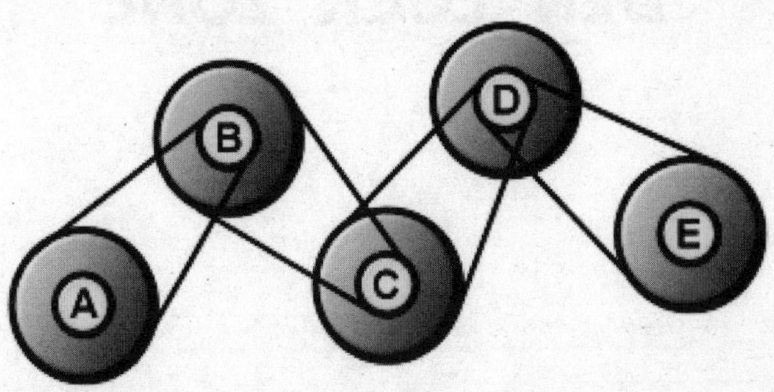

ANSWER:

Puzzle 8.38	**Difficulty rating: 3**

WORD EXTENSION

What word can be added to each of these to create three new words?

DEN LOCK ZONE

ANSWER:

Puzzle 8.39	Difficulty rating: 2

THREE SISTERS

Three sisters shared twenty-four lollipops, each getting a number equal to her age three years before. The youngest one proposed a swap.

> I will keep only half the lollipops I got, and divide the rest between you two equally. But then the middle sister, keeping half her accumulated lollipops, must divide the rest equally between the oldest sister and me, and then the oldest sister must do the same.

They agreed. The result was that each had eight lollipops. How old were the sisters?

ANSWER:

Puzzle 8.40	**Difficulty rating: 4**

CHAPTER 8 ANSWERS

8.1. 5
8.2. D
8.3. 4
8.4. B
8.5. 100 revolutions per minute.
8.6. FORE
8.7. Present, Repents, Serpent
8.8. Horse (race) car
Lamp (post) man
8.9. A
8.10. 4H
8.11. D
8.12. B
8.13. E
8.14. 6
8.15. 4
8.16. 3
8.17. 5
8.18. E
8.19. 1
8.20. C
8.21. 200 revolutions per minute.
8.22. FOX
8.23. D
8.24. Aspired, Praised, Despair, Diapers
8.25. Pop (corn) pipe
Kettle (drum) stick
8.26. B
8.27. r
8.28. B
8.29. C
8.30. A
8.31. 6
8.32. 6
8.33. 1
8.34. 9
8.35. D
8.36. 2
8.37. D
8.38. 400 revolutions per minute.
8.39. WAR
8.40. The youngest sister is 7, the middle sister is 10, and the oldest is 16.

DIFFICULTY RATING: 118

WORD ADDITION

What word inserted in the blank space will create two new words? Find at least one word for each set of words. *Example: QUICK sand PAPER*

PAPER ____ PACK

LIFE ____ LINE

ANSWER:

Puzzle 9.1	**Difficulty rating: 2**

BUBBLE TROUBLE

Complete the sequence.

ANSWER:

Puzzle 9.2	**Difficulty rating: 2**

ONE INTO EIGHT

Which item is the best continuation of the sequence?

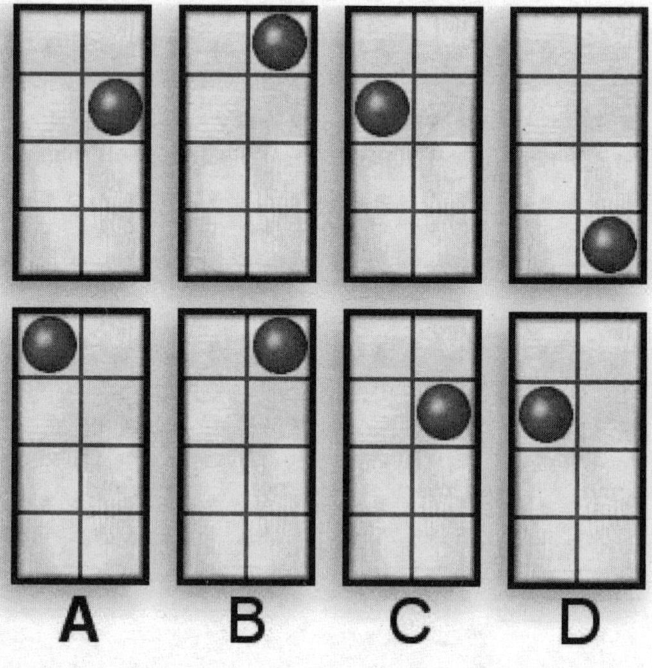

ANSWER:

Puzzle 9.3	**Difficulty rating: 2**

ANALOGY PUZZLE

Determine the item that best completes the analogy.

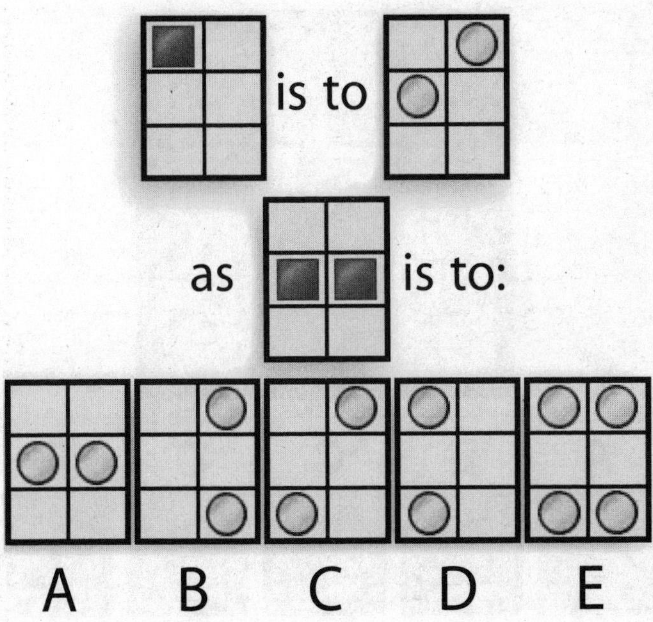

ANSWER:

Puzzle 9.4	Difficulty rating: 3

ARABESQUE

Determine the missing square.

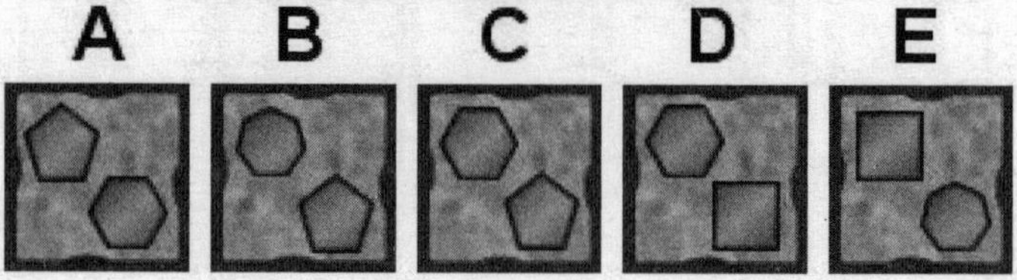

A B C D E

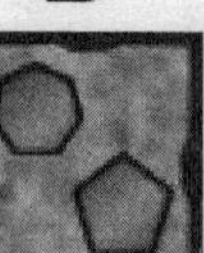

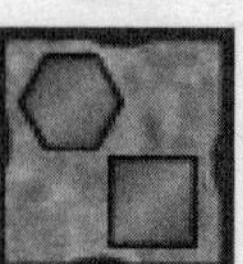
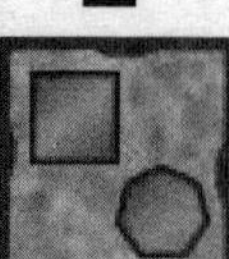

ANSWER:

Puzzle 9.5	**Difficulty rating: 4**

TRELLIS PATTERN

Determine the system used to generate numbers in the grid below, and find the missing number.

ANSWER:

Puzzle 9.6	**Difficulty rating: 3**

WHEELS WITHIN WHEELS

Determine the system used to generate numbers in the diagram below, and find the missing value.

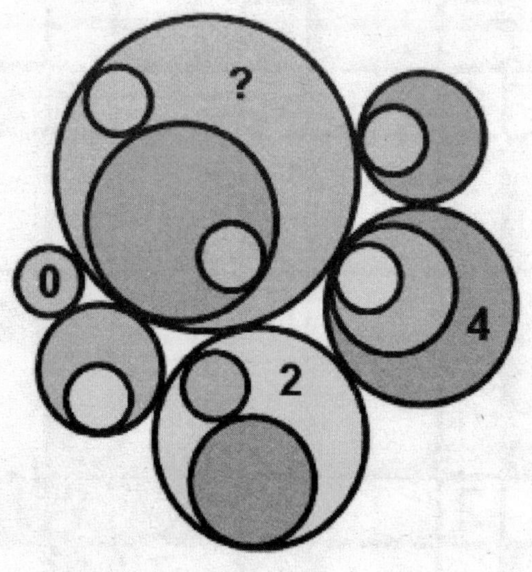

ANSWER:

Puzzle 9.7	Difficulty rating: 4

HIDDEN VALUES

Determine the system used to generate numbers in the grid below, and find the missing value.

ANSWER:

Puzzle 9.8	**Difficulty rating: 3**

STARBURST

Determine the relationship between the central star and the outer circles, and find the missing value.

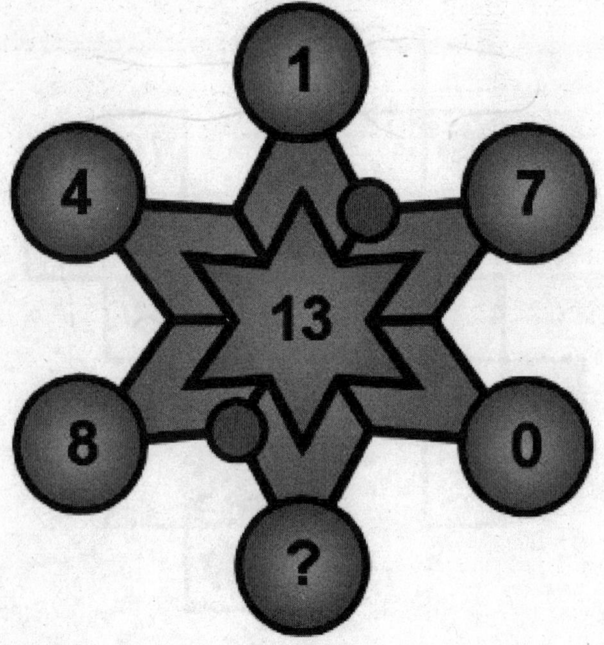

ANSWER:

Puzzle 9.9	Difficulty rating: 3

ODD ONE IN

Which square is most like the first five?

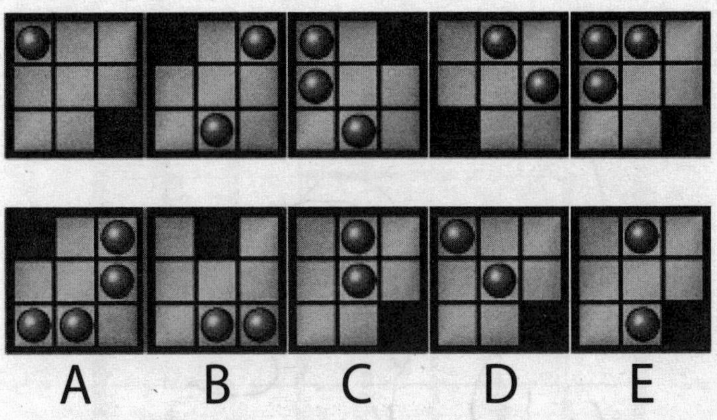

ANSWER:

Puzzle 9.10	**Difficulty rating: 3**

MAZE

Discover the logic behind the placement of the circles within the maze and choose the best location for the last circle.

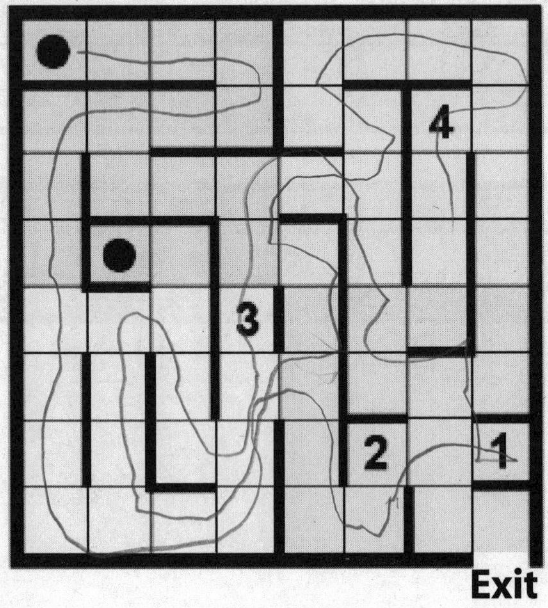

ANSWER:

Puzzle 9.11	**Difficulty rating: 4**

BALANCING ACT

Shown below is the aerial view of a see-saw perfectly balanced by weights on both sides.

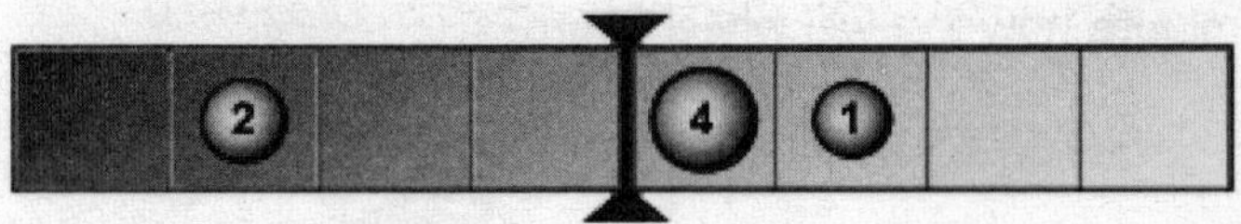

What weight must be placed at the position indicated, to balance the following see-saw?

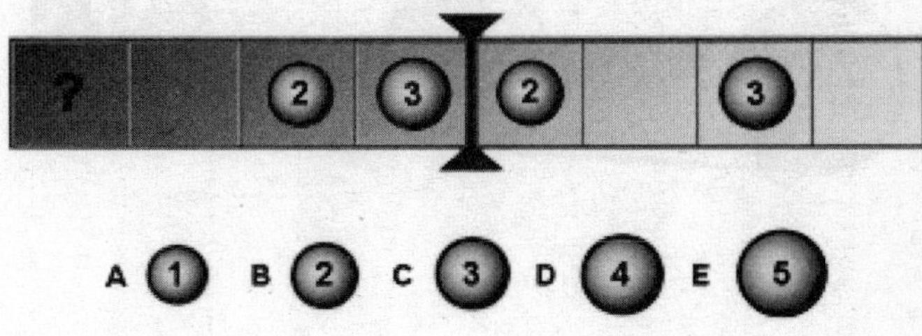

A 1 B 2 C 3 D 4 E 5

ANSWER:

Puzzle 9.12	**Difficulty rating: 2**

TURNING WHEELS

Shown below is a system of wheels connected by belts. The circumference of the outer rim of each wheel is exactly twice that of the inner rim. If wheel A turns at 100 revolutions per minute, how fast will wheel E turn?

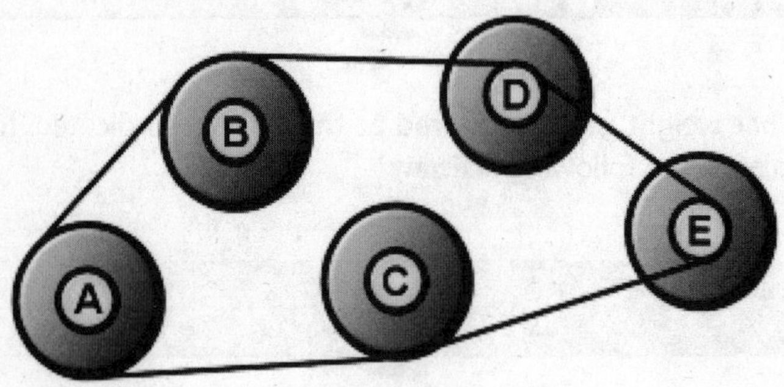

ANSWER:

Puzzle 9.13	**Difficulty rating: 3**

WORD EXTENSION

What word can be added to each of these to create three new words?

BACK TIME WAY

ANSWER:

Puzzle 9.14	**Difficulty rating: 2**

THREE SOLDIERS

Three soldiers were patrolling the jungle. Two of them, while crossing a river, got their cartridge cases wet. The three soldiers divided what good cartridges remained, equally. After each had fired four shots, the total cartridges remaining were equal to the number each had after the division. How many cartridges were divided?

ANSWER:

Puzzle 9.15	Difficulty rating: 4

WORD ADDITION

What word inserted in the blank space will create two new words? Find at least one word for each set of words. *Example: QUICK* *sand* *PAPER*

MOON _____ HOUSE

KNOCK _____ SIDE

ANSWER:

Puzzle 9.16	**Difficulty rating: 2**

HIDE AND SEEK

Complete the sequence.

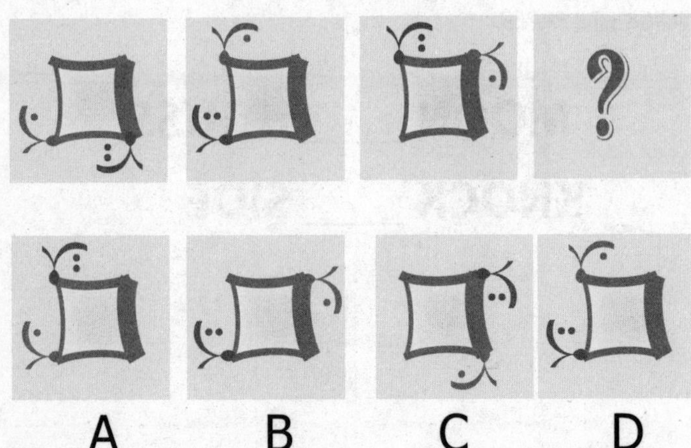

ANSWER:

Puzzle 9.17	**Difficulty rating: 1**

ANALOGY PUZZLE

Determine the item that best completes the analogy.

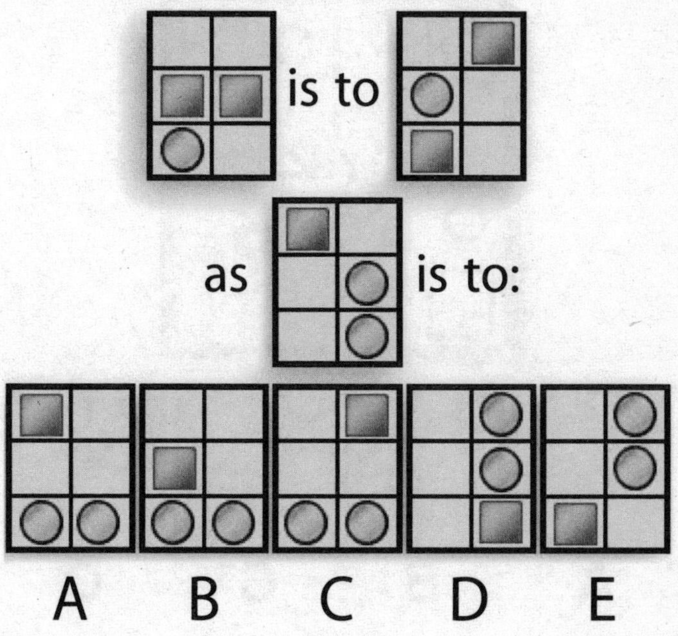

ANSWER:

Puzzle 9.18	**Difficulty rating: 3**

FINAL QUARTER

Determine the missing item.

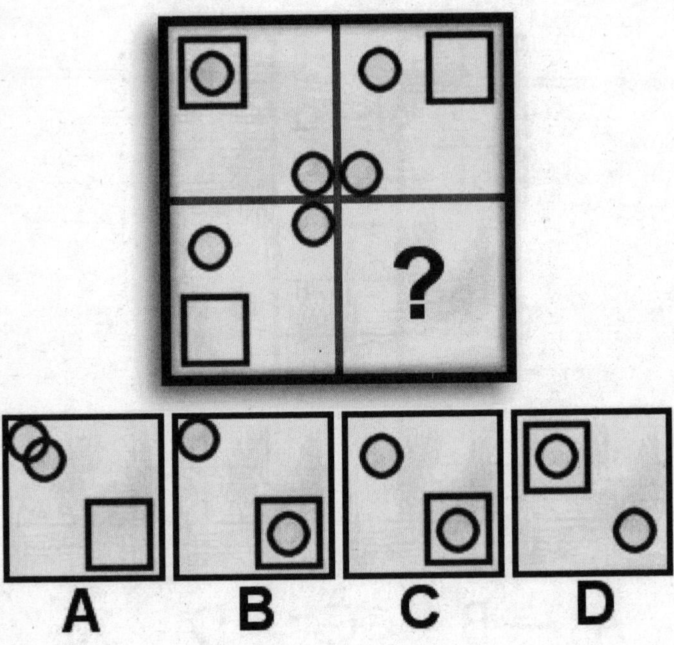

ANSWER:

Puzzle 9.19	Difficulty rating: 3

TRELLIS PATTERN

Determine the system used to generate numbers in the grid below, and find the missing value.

ANSWER:

Puzzle 9.20	**Difficulty rating: 3**

WHEELS WITHIN WHEELS

Determine the system used to generate numbers in the diagram below, and find the missing value.

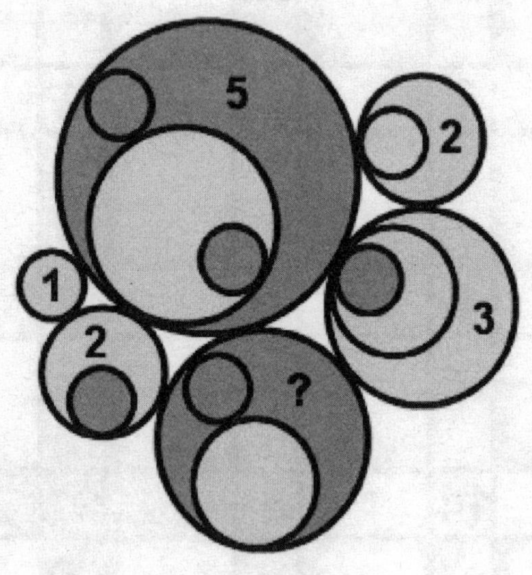

ANSWER:

Puzzle 9.21	Difficulty rating: 4

STARBURST

Determine the relationship between the central star and the outer circles, and find the missing value.

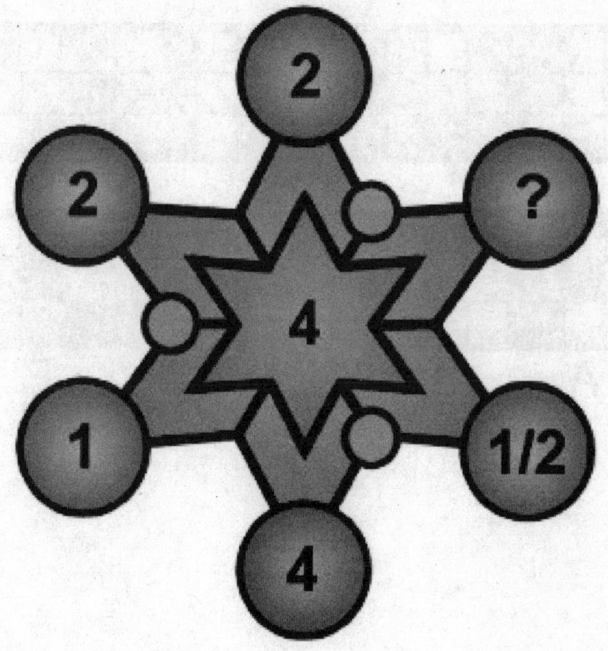

ANSWER:

Puzzle 9.22	Difficulty rating: 3

ODD ONE IN

Which square is most like the first five?

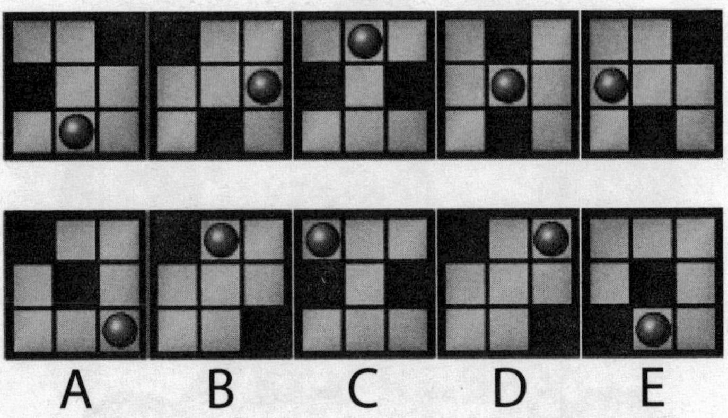

ANSWER:

Puzzle 9.23	**Difficulty rating: 4**

MAZE

Discover the logic behind the placement of the circles within the maze and choose the best location for the last circle.

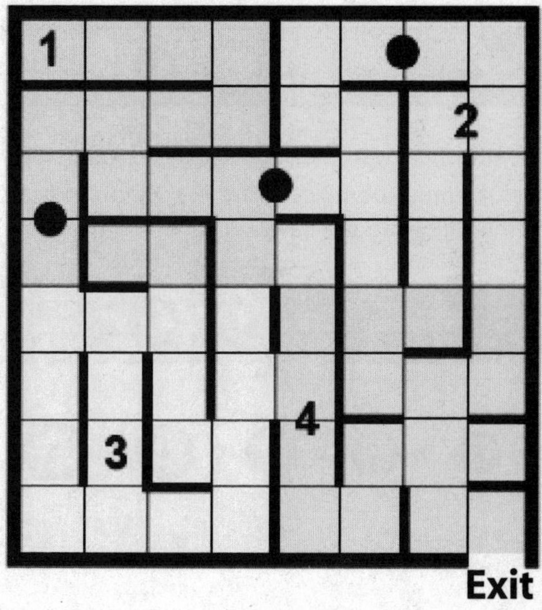

ANSWER:

Puzzle 9.24	**Difficulty rating: 4**

BALANCING ACT

Shown below is the aerial view of a see-saw perfectly balanced by weights on both sides.

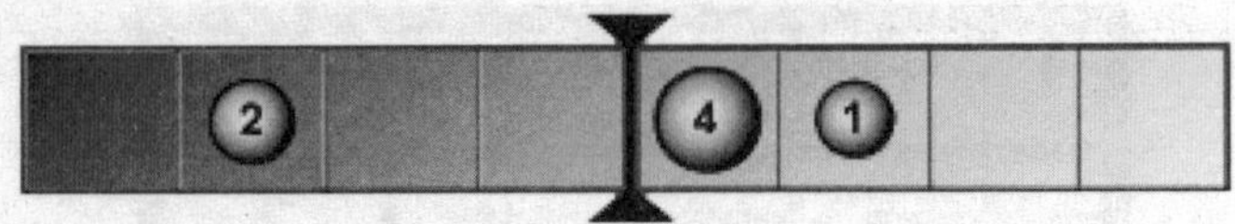

What weight must be placed at the position indicated, to balance the following see-saw?

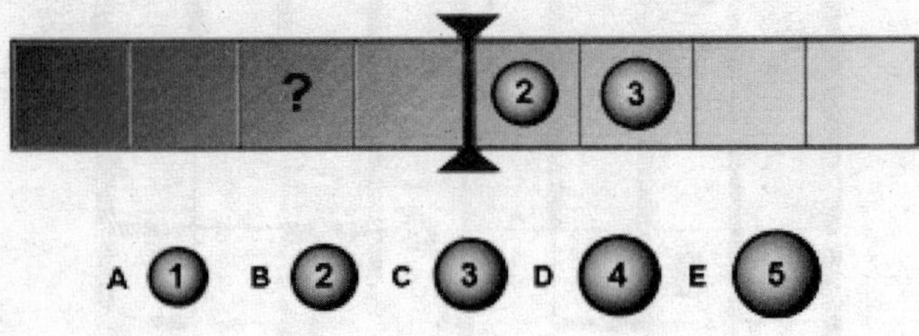

ANSWER:

Puzzle 9.25	Difficulty rating: 2

TURNING WHEELS

Shown below is a system of wheels connected by belts. The circumference of the outer rim of each wheel is exactly twice that of the inner rim. If wheel A turns at 100 revolutions per minute, how fast will wheel E turn?

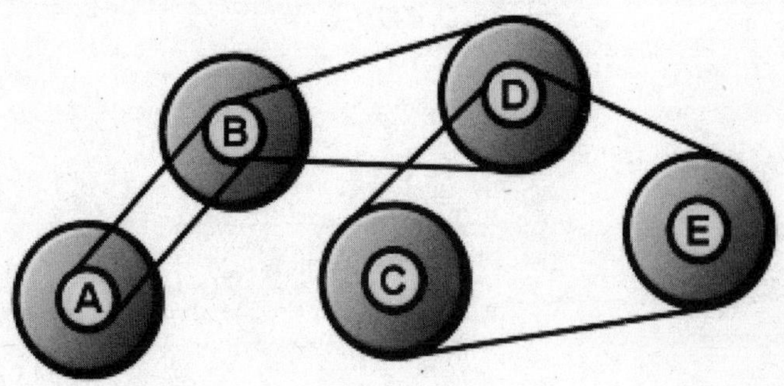

ANSWER:

Puzzle 9.26	Difficulty rating: 3

WHAT IF . . .

If cat is 3-1-20, dog is:

A. 4–15–7
B. 3–16–8
C. 4–16–7
D. 4–20–6

ANSWER:

Puzzle 9.27	**Difficulty rating: 2**

TWO OARSMEN

Scott rows on a river x miles with the current, and x miles against the current. Paul rows 2x miles on a lake where there is no current. Does Scott take more time than Paul, or less? The length of their stroke is the same.

ANSWER:

Puzzle 9.28	**Difficulty rating: 4**

WORD ADDITION

What word inserted in the blank space will create two new words? Find at least one word for each set of words. *Example: QUICK sand PAPER*

SUN ____ OUT

UNDER ____ WATER

ANSWER:

Puzzle 9.29	**Difficulty rating: 2**

ANALOGY PUZZLE

Determine the item that best completes the analogy.

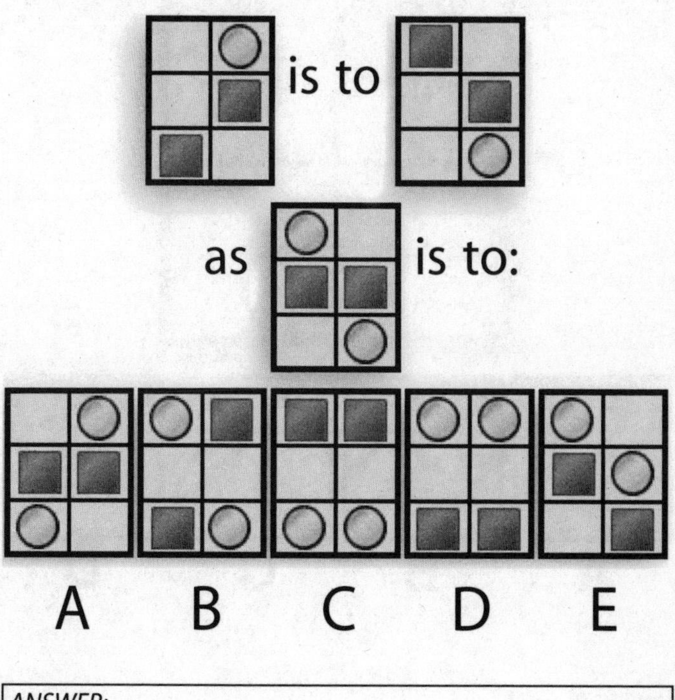

ANSWER:

Puzzle 9.30	**Difficulty rating: 4**

FINAL QUARTER

Determine the missing square.

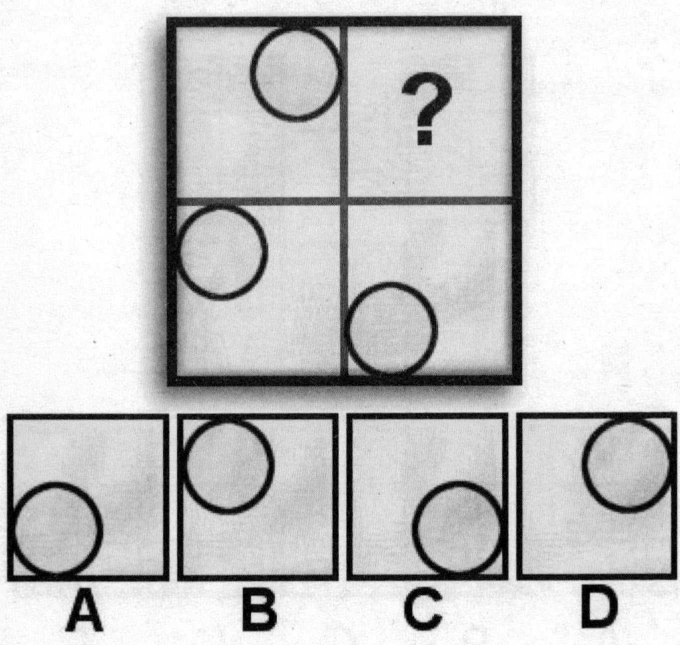

ANSWER:

Puzzle 9.31	**Difficulty rating: 2**

TRELLIS PATTERN

Determine the system used to generate numbers in the grid below, and find the missing value.

ANSWER:

Puzzle 9.32	**Difficulty rating: 3**

WHEELS WITHIN WHEELS

Determine the system used to generate numbers in the diagram below, and find the missing value.

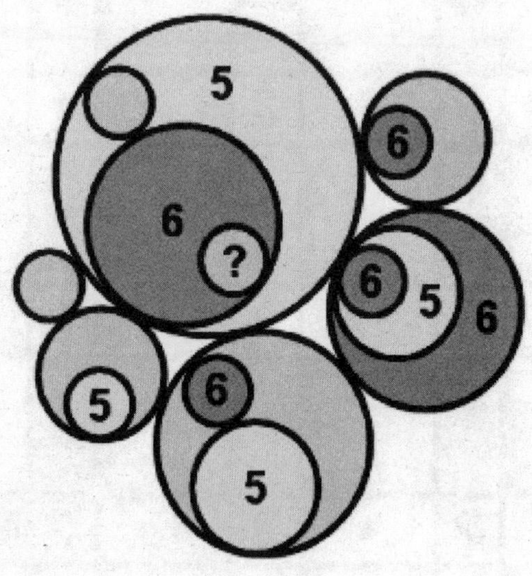

ANSWER:

Puzzle 9.33	**Difficulty rating: 4**

STARBURST

Determine the relationship between the central star and the outer circles, and find the missing value.

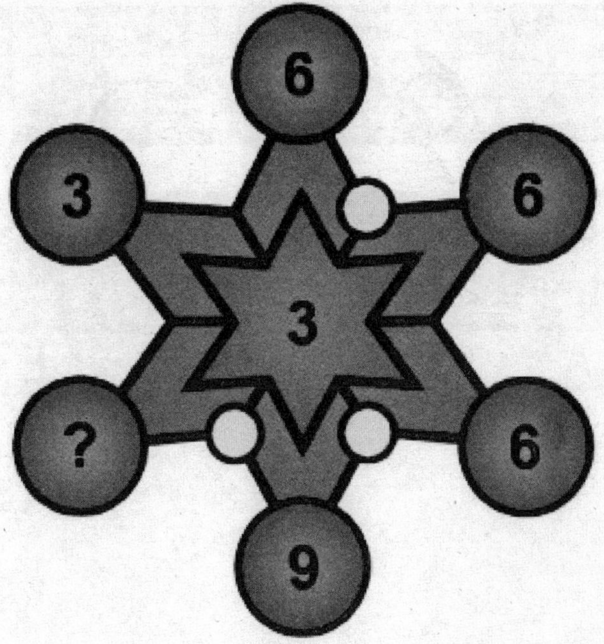

ANSWER:

Puzzle 9.34	Difficulty rating: 3

ODD ONE IN

Which square is most like the first five?

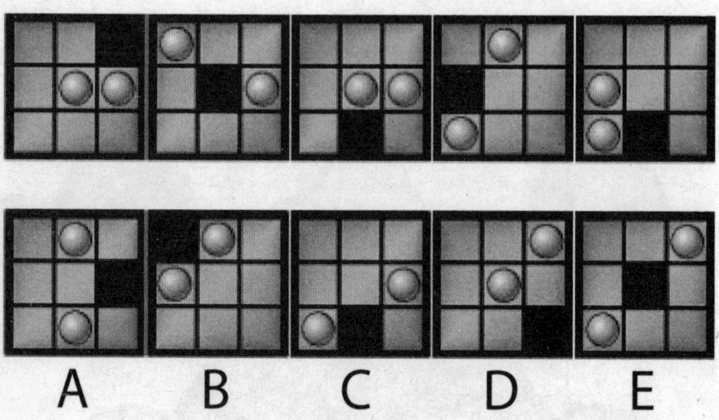

ANSWER:

Puzzle 9.35	Difficulty rating: 4

MAZE

Discover the logic behind the placement of the circles within the maze and choose the best location for the last circle.

ANSWER:

Puzzle 9.36	Difficulty rating: 3

BALANCING ACT

Shown below is the aerial view of a see-saw perfectly balanced by weights on both sides.

What weight must be placed at the position indicated, to balance the following see-saw?

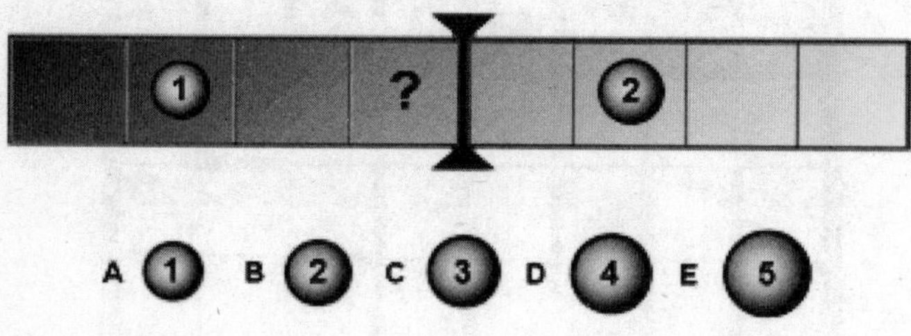

ANSWER:

Puzzle 9.37	**Difficulty rating: 2**

TURNING WHEELS

Shown below is a system of wheels connected by belts. The circumference of the outer rim of each wheel is exactly twice that of the inner rim. If wheel A turns at 100 revolutions per minute, how fast will wheel E turn?

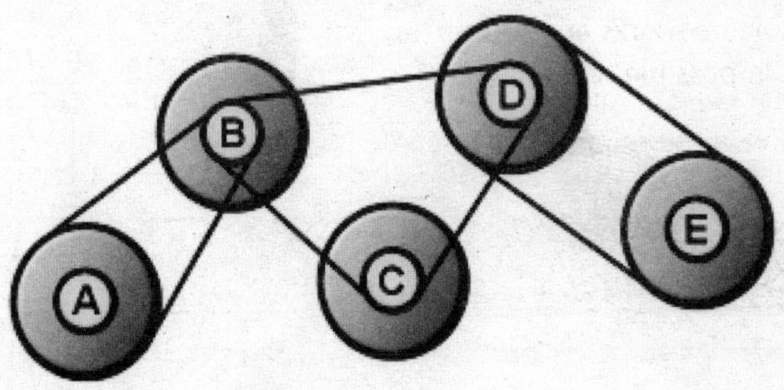

ANSWER:

Puzzle 9.38	**Difficulty rating: 3**

WHAT IF . . .

If all morks are porks and no porks are dorks, which of the following is true?

A. No Morks are dorks
B. All morks are dorks
C. Some morks are dorks
D. Impossible to tell

ANSWER:

Puzzle 9.39	**Difficulty rating: 2**

SHIPS PASSING IN THE NIGHT

Two ships leave the dock simultaneously. Ship A heads downstream and ship B heads upstream, both with the same motive force. As they leave, a life buoy falls off ship A and floats downstream. An hour later both ships are ordered to reverse course. Will the crew of ship A be able to pick up the buoy before the ships meet?

ANSWER:

Puzzle 9.40	**Difficulty rating: 4**

CHAPTER 9 ANSWERS

9.1. Paper (back) pack
Life (time) line
9.2. B
9.3. A
9.4. E
9.5. C
9.6. 1
9.7. 5
9.8. 6
9.9. 6
9.10. A
9.11. 1
9.12. A
9.13. 200 revolutions per minute.
9.14. HALF
9.15. 18
9.16. Moon (light) house
Knock (out) side
9.17. C
9.18. A
9.19. A
9.20. 4
9.21. 4
9.22. 8
9.23. B
9.24. 4
9.25. D
9.26. 25 revolutions per minute.
9.27. A
9.28. Scott takes more time than Paul does.
9.29. Sun (burn) out
Under ground (water)
9.30. A
9.31. C
9.32. 2
9.33. 4
9.34. 6
9.35. C
9.36. 2
9.37. A
9.38. 200 revolutions per minute.
9.39. A
9.40. The two ships reach the buoy simultaneously.

DIFFICULTY RATING: 126

WORD ADDITION

What word inserted in the blank space will create two new words? Find at least one word for each set of words. *Example: QUICK sand PAPER*

UP _____ HAND

TOUCH _____ PLAY

ANSWER:

Puzzle 10.1	**Difficulty rating: 2**

AUTHOR POOL

MULCIBER is to MILTON as GLUMDALCLITCH is to:

A. Swift
B. Heller
C. Dickens
D. Melville
E. Hardy

ANSWER:

Puzzle 10.2	**Difficulty rating: 4**

PRESSURE POINTS

Complete the sequence.

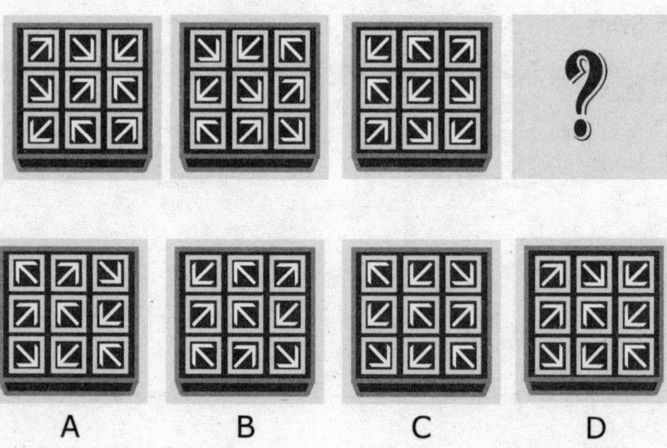

ANSWER:

Puzzle 10.3	Difficulty rating: 3

ANALOGY PUZZLE

Determine the item that best completes the analogy.

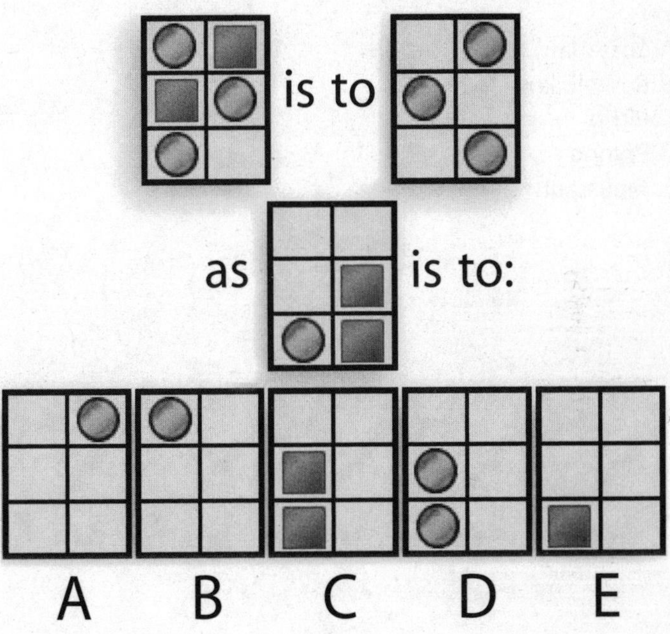

ANSWER:

Puzzle 10.4	Difficulty rating: 3

FOOT FAULT

BLOODY SOCK is to ___ as FESTERING ANKLE SORE is to WINSTON SMITH.

A. Yossarian
B. Raskolnikov
C. Pirrip
D. Prynne
E. Meussault

ANSWER:

Puzzle 10.5	**Difficulty rating: 4**

FINAL QUARTER

Determine the missing square.

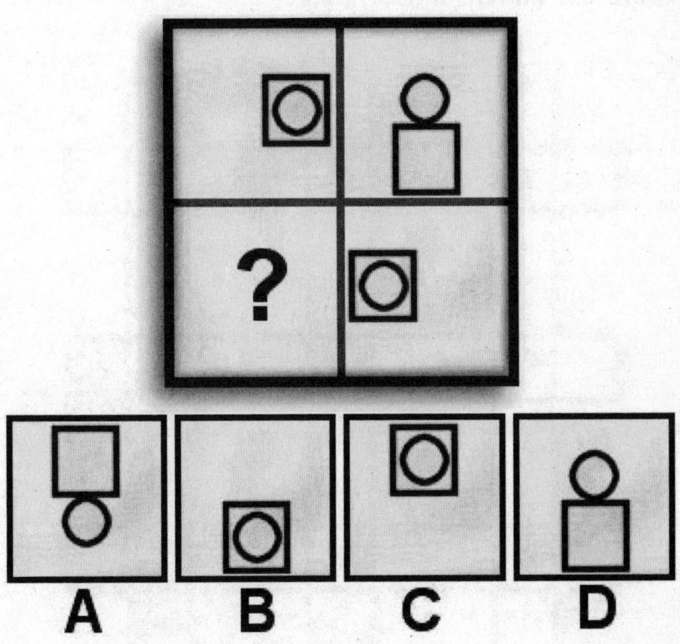

ANSWER:

Puzzle 10.6	**Difficulty rating: 3**

TRELLIS PATTERN

Determine the system used to generate numbers in the grid below, and find the missing value.

ANSWER:

Puzzle 10.7	**Difficulty rating: 3**

VERBAL ANALOGY

A TOYOTA is to A WAR AT TARAWA as ___ is to REIGN AT TANGIER.

A. Chariot
B. Jeep
C. Kayak
D. Kiribati
E. Gilbert Islands

ANSWER:

Puzzle 10.8	**Difficulty rating: 4**

WHEELS WITHIN WHEELS

Determine the system used to generate numbers in the diagram below, and find the missing value.

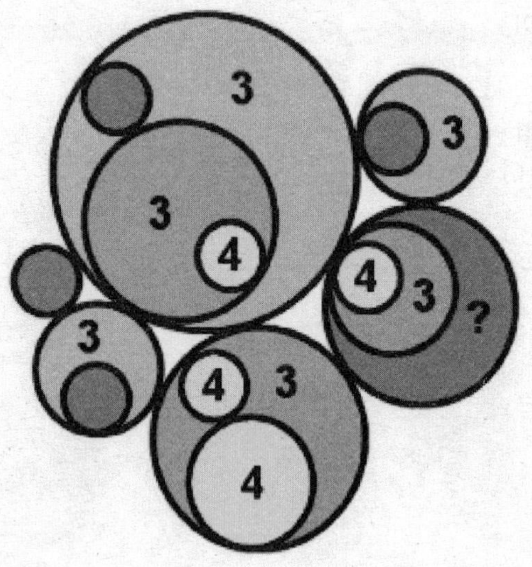

ANSWER:

Puzzle 10.9	**Difficulty rating: 4**

STARBURST

Determine the relationship between the central star and the outer circles, and find the missing value.

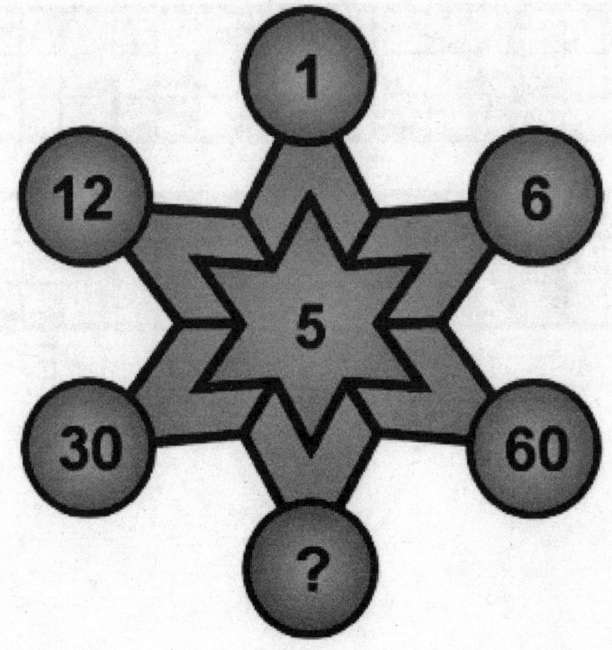

ANSWER:

Puzzle 10.10	Difficulty rating: 3

ODD ONE IN

Which square is most like the first five?

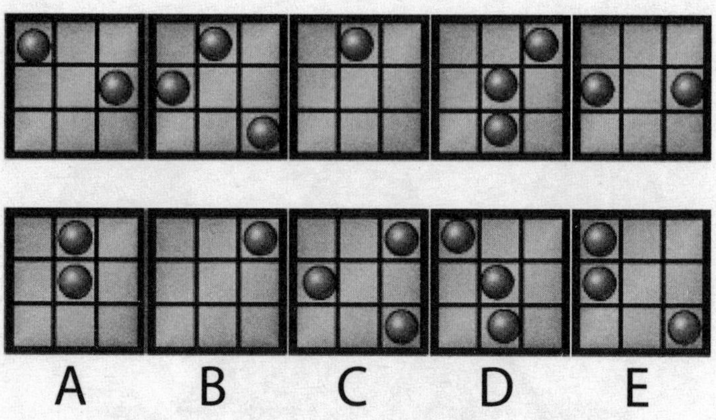

ANSWER:

Puzzle 10.11	**Difficulty rating: 3**

ROCK POOL

KIMBERLITE is to DIAMOND as ___ is to TITANIUM

A. Hematite
B. Chalcopyrite
C. Magnetite
D. Ilmenite
E. Chromite

ANSWER:

Puzzle 10.12	**Difficulty rating: 4**

MAZE

Discover the logic behind the placement of the circles within the maze and choose the best location for the last circle.

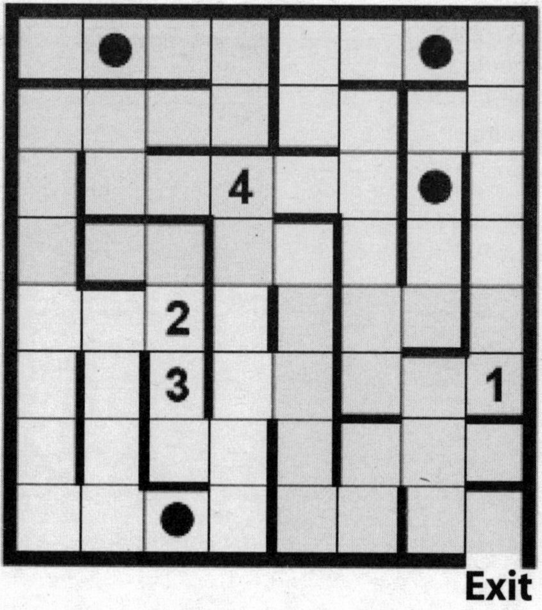

ANSWER:

Puzzle 10.13	Difficulty rating: 3

BALANCING ACT

Shown below is the aerial view of a see-saw perfectly balanced by weights on both sides.

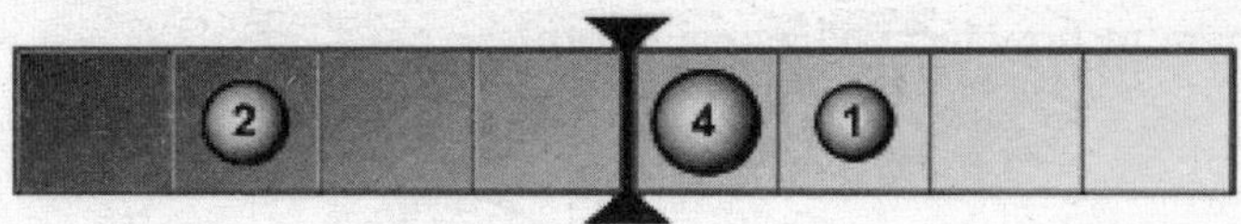

What weight must be placed at the position indicated, to balance the following see-saw?

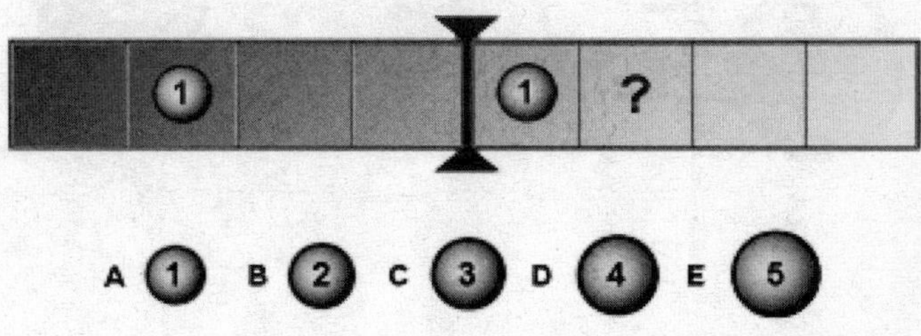

ANSWER:

Puzzle 10.14	Difficulty rating: 2

TURNING WHEELS

Shown below is a system of wheels connected by belts. The circumference of the outer rim of each wheel is exactly twice that of the inner rim. If wheel A turns at 100 revolutions per minute, how fast will wheel E turn?

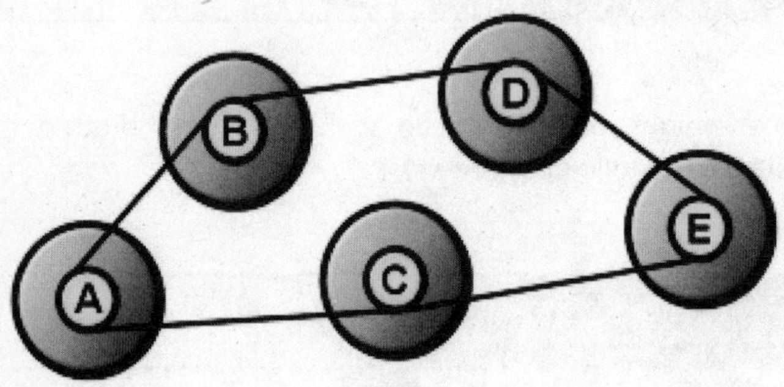

ANSWER:

Puzzle 10.15	Difficulty rating: 3

WHAT IF . . .

If no looms are pegs but some gogs are looms this means:

A. Some gogs aren't pegs
B. All gogs are looms
C. Most gogs are pegs
D. No gogs are pegs

ANSWER:

Puzzle 10.16	**Difficulty rating: 2**

CHOOSE A LEADER

CHARLEMAGNE is to PIPPIN THE SHORT as OTTO THE GREAT is to:

A. Ivan the Terrible
B. Bismarck
C. Richard the Fearless
D. Suleiman the Magnificent
E. Henry the Fowler

ANSWER:

Puzzle 10.17	**Difficulty rating: 4**

ROUND THE BEND

Complete the sequence.

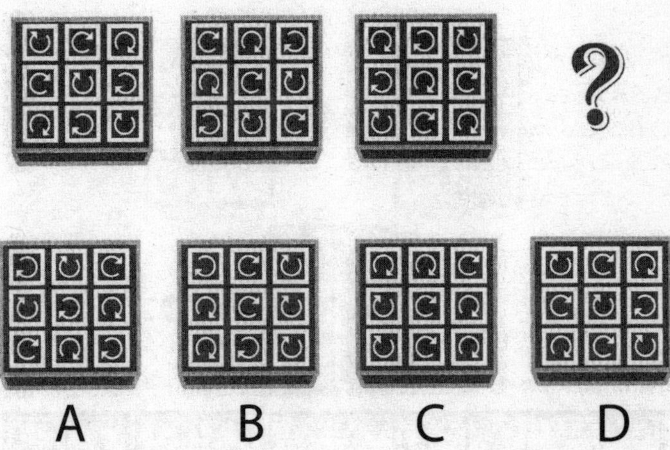

ANSWER:

Puzzle 10.18	**Difficulty rating: 3**

ANALOGY PUZZLE

Determine the item that best completes the analogy.

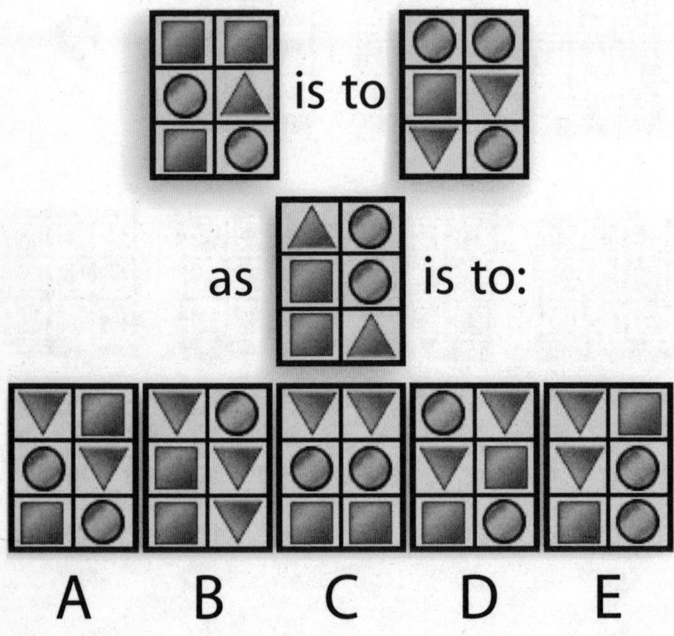

ANSWER:

Puzzle 10.19	Difficulty rating: 3

VOLCANIC ACTIVITY

KRAKATOA is to INDONESIA as VESUVIUS is to:

A. Italy
B. Pompeii
C. Etna
D. Sicily
E. Martinique

ANSWER:

Puzzle 10.20	**Difficulty rating: 3**

FINAL QUARTER

Determine the missing square.

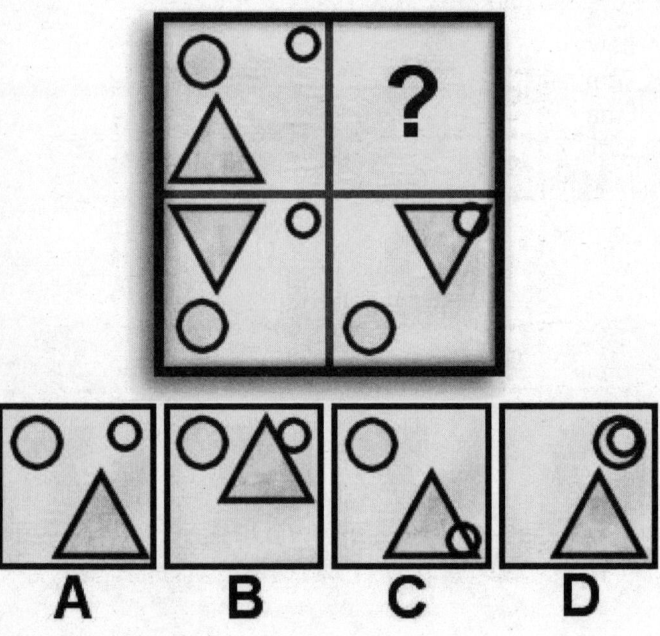

ANSWER:

Puzzle 10.21	Difficulty rating: 3

TRELLIS PATTERN

Determine the system used to generate numbers in the grid below, and find the missing value.

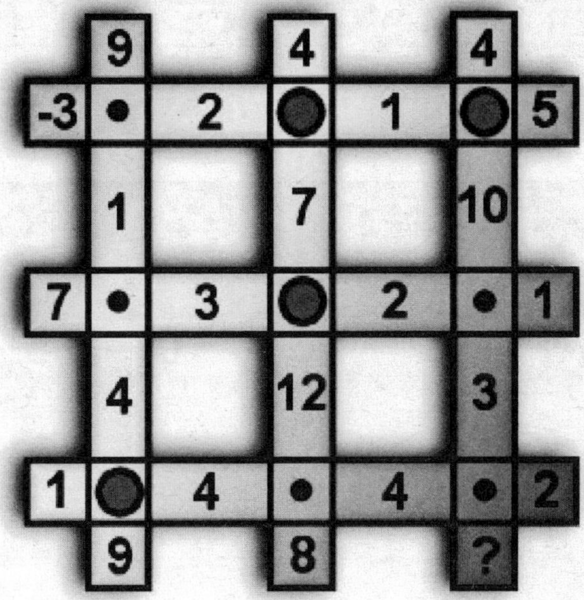

ANSWER:

Puzzle 10.22	**Difficulty rating: 4**

ODD ONE IN

Which square is most like the first five?

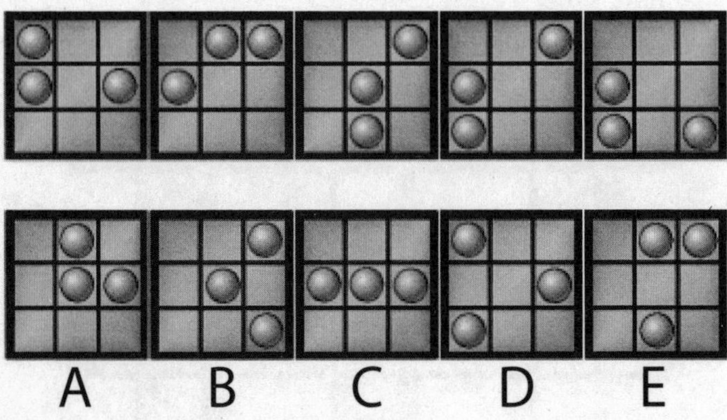

ANSWER:

Puzzle 10.23	Difficulty rating: 3

DOCTOR'S DILEMMA

STAPES is to COCHLEA as CEREBELLUM is to:

A. Brain
B. Thalamus
C. Epiglottis
D. Ear
E. Bone

ANSWER:

Puzzle 10.24	**Difficulty rating: 4**

MAZE

Discover the logic behind the placement of the circles within the maze and choose the best location for the last circle.

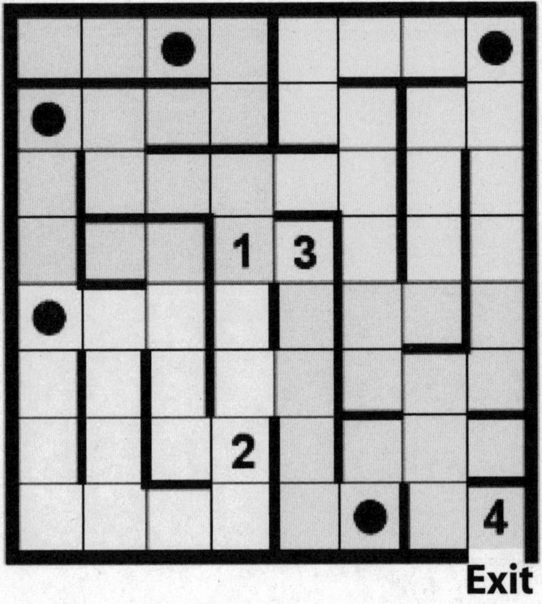

ANSWER:

Puzzle 10.25	Difficulty rating: 3

CHOCOLATE BALLS

Complete the sequence.

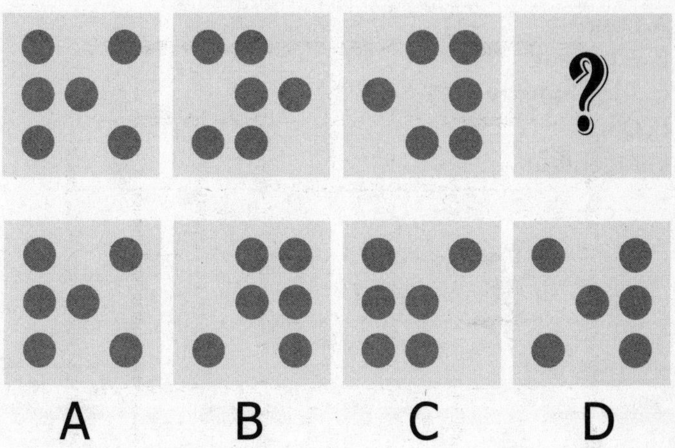

ANSWER:

Puzzle 10.26	**Difficulty rating: 3**

ALL ABOUT ANGLES

SINE is to ___, as MANTISSA is to LOGARITHM

A. Cosine
B. Exponent
C. Trigonometry
D. Obtuse
E. Algorithm

ANSWER:

Puzzle 10.27	**Difficulty rating: 4**

WHAT'S NEXT?

Complete the sequence.

6, 14, 30, 62, ?

ANSWER:

Puzzle 10.28	Difficulty rating: 3

WORD ADDITION

What word inserted in the blank space will create two new words? Find at least one word for each set of words. *Example: QUICK sand PAPER*

VINE ____ STICK

WAIST ____ AGE

ANSWER:

Puzzle 10.29	**Difficulty rating: 2**

TWO-WAY TRAFFIC

Complete the sequence.

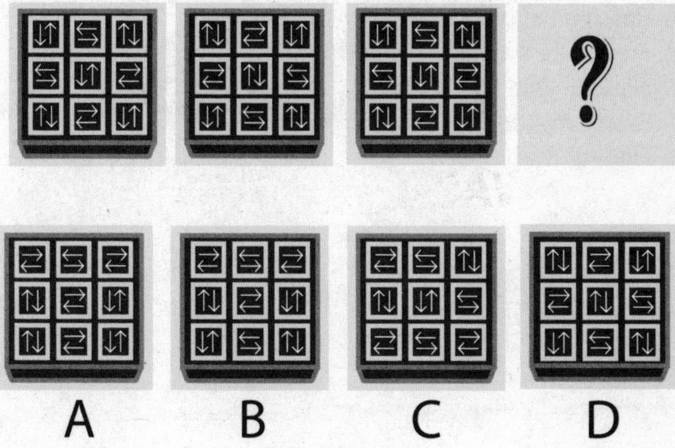

ANSWER:

Puzzle 10.30	Difficulty rating: 4

FROM PRUSSIA WITH LOVE

BORGLUM is to FOUNDING FATHERS as ROEBLING is to:

A. Russian Revolution
B. French Resistance
C. US Civil War
D. Brooklyn Bridge
E. Hoover Dam

ANSWER:

Puzzle 10.31	Difficulty rating: 4

ANALOGY PUZZLE

Determine the item that best completes the analogy.

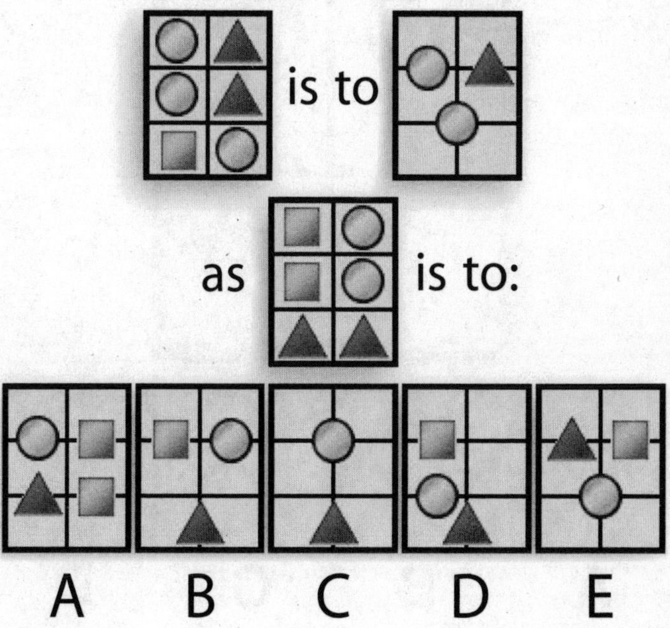

ANSWER:

Puzzle 10.32	Difficulty rating: 3

FINAL QUARTER

Determine the missing square.

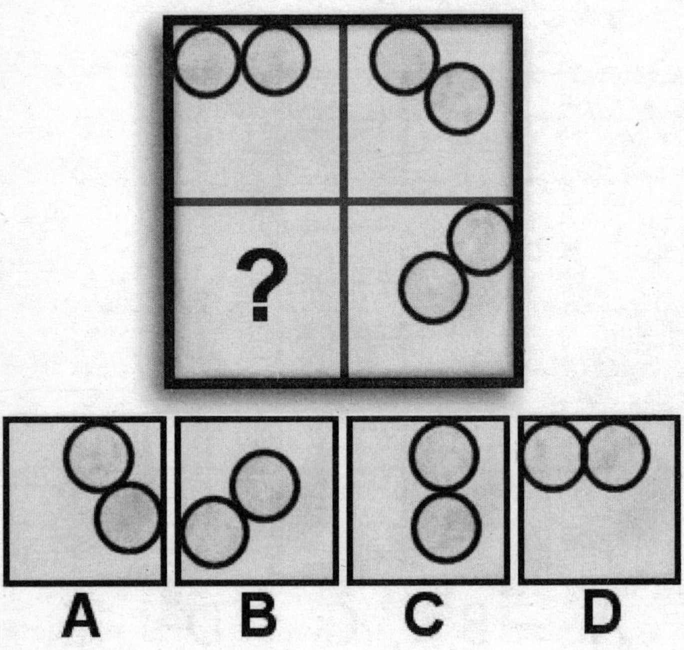

ANSWER:

Puzzle 10.33	**Difficulty rating: 3**

TRELLIS PATTERN

Determine the system used to generate numbers in the grid below, and find the missing value.

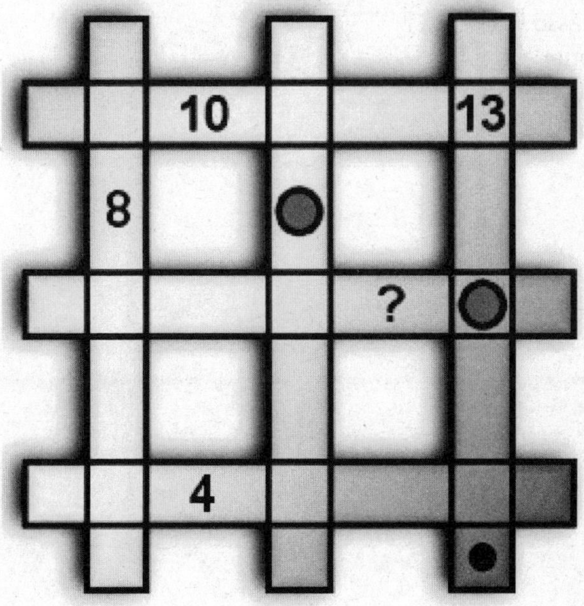

ANSWER:

Puzzle 10.34	**Difficulty rating: 3**

MASTERS' PALETTE

POLLOCK is to WARHOL as REMBRANDT is to:

A. Dali
B. Picasso
C. Manet
D. Michelangelo
E. Van Gogh

ANSWER:

Puzzle 10.35	Difficulty rating: 3

ODD ONE IN

Which square is most like the first five?

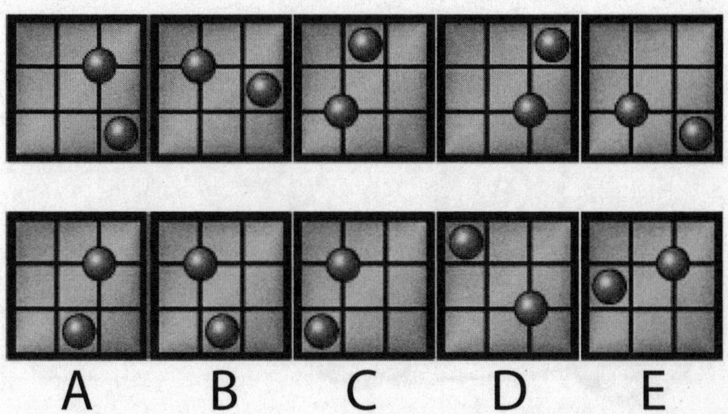

ANSWER:

Puzzle 10.36	Difficulty rating: 3

TURNING WHEELS

Shown below is a system of wheels connected by belts. The circumference of the outer rim of each wheel is exactly twice that of the inner rim. If wheel A turns at 100 revolutions per minute, how fast will wheel E turn?

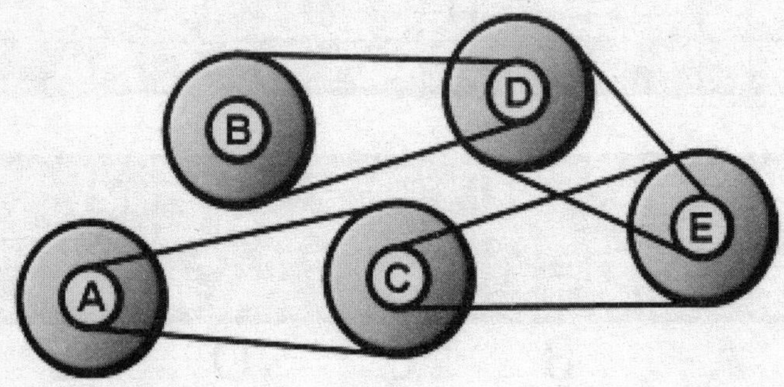

ANSWER:

Puzzle 10.37	**Difficulty rating: 3**

WORD CONNECTION

Come up with the connecting word.

EAR_____ROLL

ANSWER:

Puzzle 10.38	**Difficulty rating: 2**

SNUG FIT

Complete the sequence.

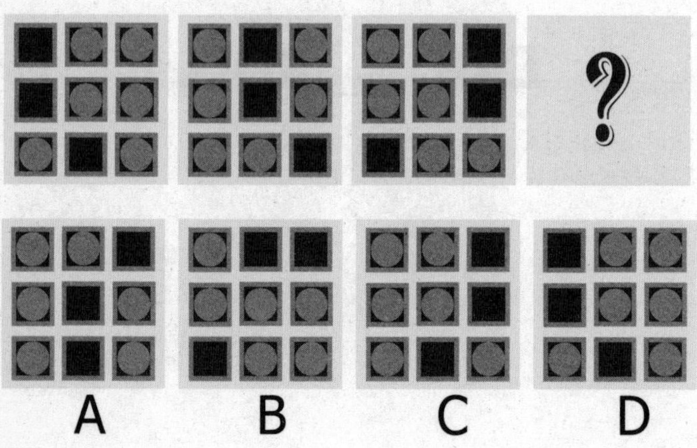

ANSWER:

Puzzle 10.39	**Difficulty rating: 3**

WORD POOL

TRIREME is to JUNK as ZIGGURAT is to:

A. Campanile
B. Viking
C. Schooner
D. Hammurabi
E. Babylon

ANSWER:

Puzzle 10.40	**Difficulty rating: 3**

CHAPTER 10 ANSWERS

10.1. Up (stage) hand
Touch (down) play
10.2. A
10.3. A
10.4. C
10.5. B
10.6. A
10.7. 4
10.8. C
10.9. 5
10.10. 5
10.11. D
10.12. D
10.13. 3
10.14. A
10.15. 100 revolutions per minute.
10.16. A
10.17. E
10.18. A
10.19. E
10.20. A
10.21. A
10.22. 5
10.23. E
10.24. B
10.25. 4
10.26. A
10.27. C
10.28. 126
10.29. Vine (yard) stick
Waist (band) age
10.30. D
10.31. D
10.32. B
10.33. C
10.34. 6
10.35. E
10.36. B
10.37. 25 revolutions per minute.
10.38. DRUM
10.39. D
10.40. A

DIFFICULTY RATING: 133

WORD ADDITION

What word inserted in the blank space will create two new words? Find at least one word for each set of words. *Example: QUICK sand PAPER*

WASTE ____ CASE

WEEK ____ GAME

ANSWER:

Puzzle 11.1	**Difficulty rating: 2**

CHOCOLATE BALLS

Complete the sequence.

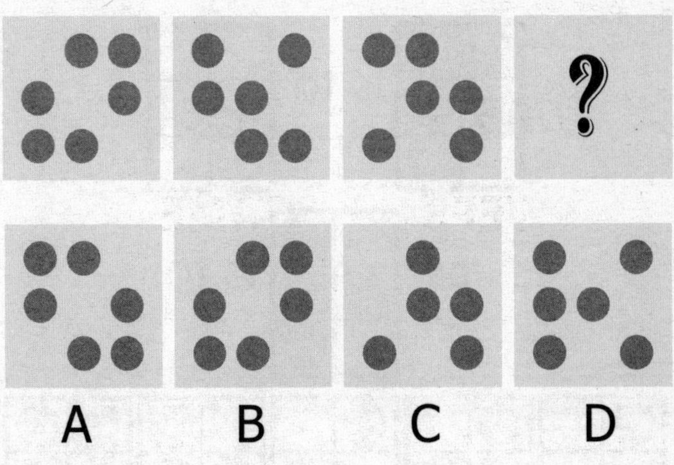

ANSWER:

Puzzle 11.2	**Difficulty rating: 3**

ANALOGY PUZZLE

Determine the item that best completes the analogy.

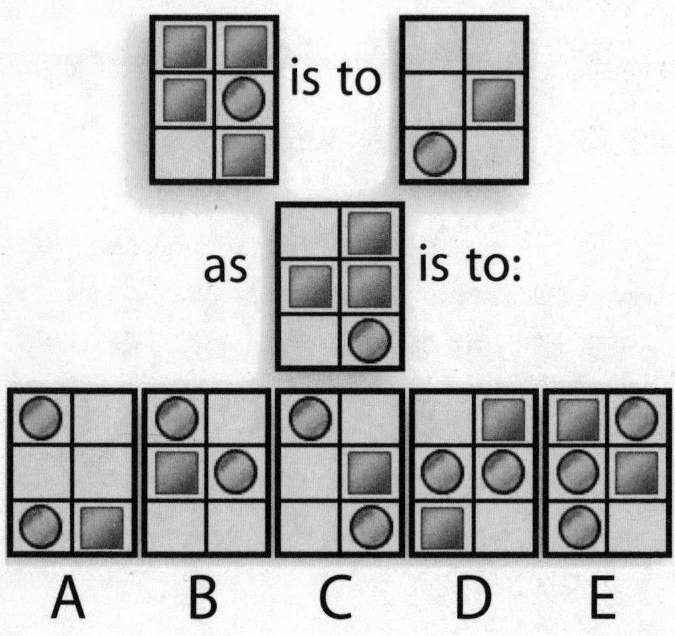

ANSWER:

Puzzle 11.3	Difficulty rating: 3

WHICH COUNTRY?

GANDHI is to HO CHI MINH as GREAT BRITAIN is to:

A. Indochina
B. France
C. Vietnam
D. India
E. Korea

ANSWER:

Puzzle 11.4	**Difficulty rating: 4**

WORD CONNECTION

Come up with the connecting word.

EYE______BEAT

ANSWER:

Puzzle 11.5	**Difficulty rating: 2**

FINAL QUARTER

Determine the missing square.

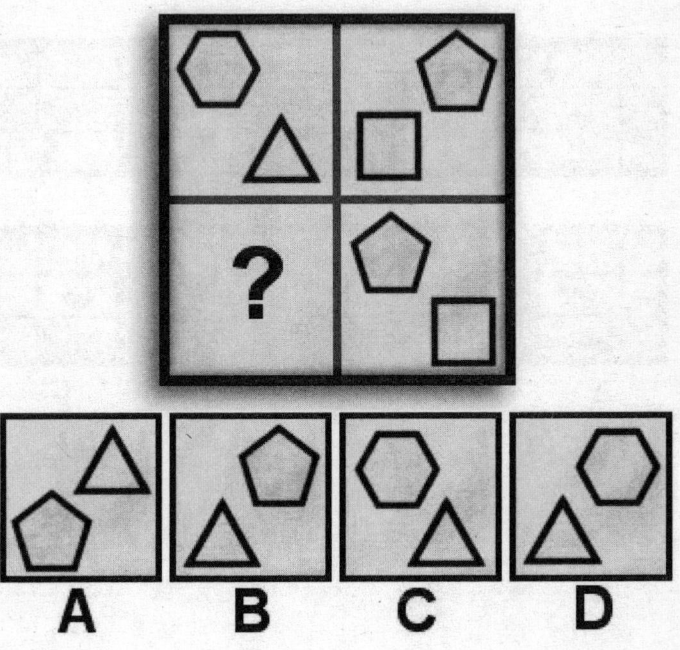

ANSWER:

Puzzle 11.6	Difficulty rating: 3

ODD ONE IN

Which square is most like the first five?

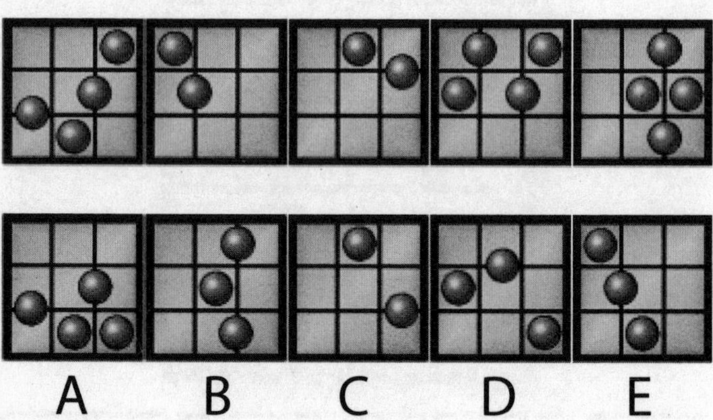

ANSWER:

Puzzle 11.7	**Difficulty rating: 3**

POGS, FROGS AND NOGS

If 50% of pogs are frogs and 25% of frogs are nogs, what per cent of pogs are nogs?

ANSWER:

Puzzle 11.8	**Difficulty rating: 3**

COMEDY OR TRAGEDY?

HAMLET is to MACBETH as MERCHANT OF VENICE is to:

A. Othello
B. Romeo and Juliet
C. Taming of the Shrew
D. Julius Caesar
E. King Lear

ANSWER:

Puzzle 11.9 | **Difficulty rating: 4**

TURNING WHEELS

Shown below is a system of wheels connected by belts. The circumference of the outer rim of each wheel is exactly twice that of the inner rim. If wheel A turns at 100 revolutions per minute, how fast will wheel E turn?

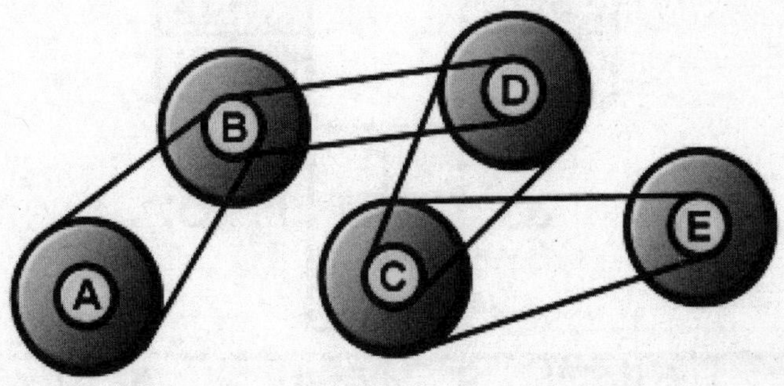

ANSWER:

Puzzle 11.10	Difficulty rating: 3

ANALOGY PUZZLE

Determine the item that best completes the analogy.

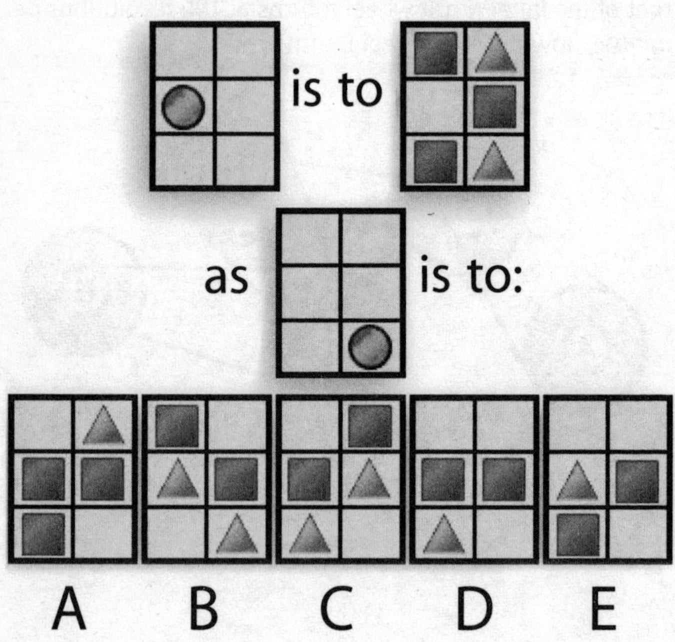

ANSWER:

Puzzle 11.11	**Difficulty rating: 3**

SPELLING BY NUMBERS

123 is to ABC as 629 is to:

A. FBI
B. FAC
C. EBK
D. FBK

ANSWER:

Puzzle 11.12	Difficulty rating: 3

FINAL QUARTER

Determine the missing square.

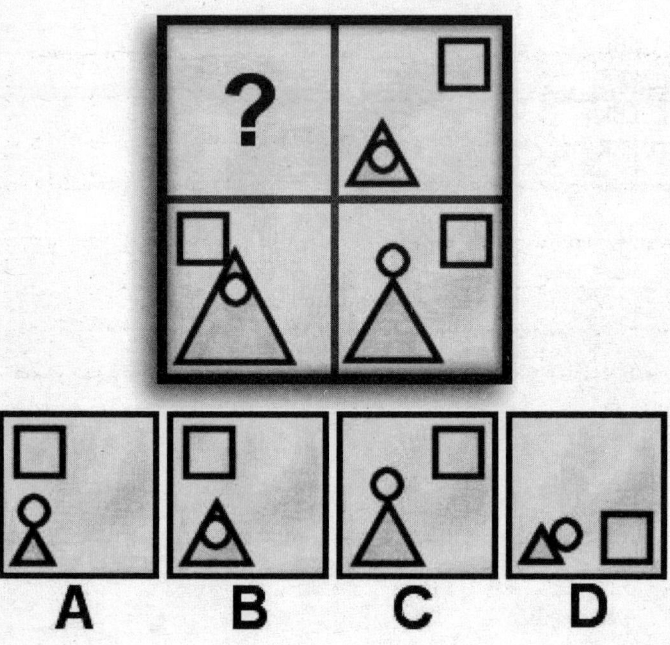

ANSWER:

Puzzle 11.13	Difficulty rating: 3

ODD ONE IN

Which square is most like the first five?

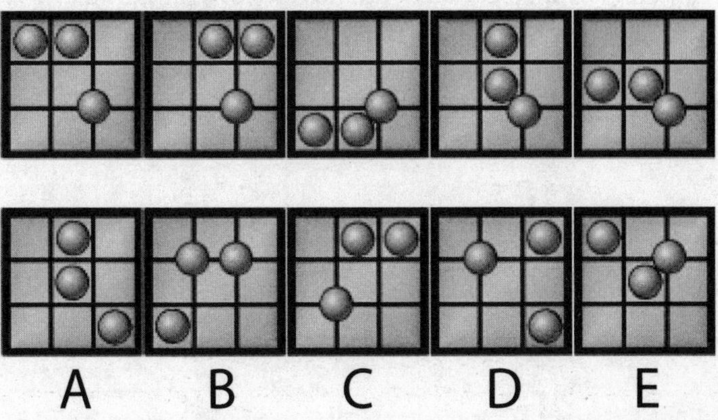

ANSWER:

Puzzle 11.14	Difficulty rating: 3

WINTER TIME

Winter is approaching at a small town in Siberia. As the soil will soon freeze, they need to dig enough graves in the town cemetery in anticipation of the number of deaths. The town's population is 1,000 and it is assumed that each person has a one per cent chance of dying during winter. What is the least number of graves they should dig so that the probability of having enough is at least ninety per cent?

ANSWER:

Puzzle 11.15	**Difficulty rating: 5**

LEAGUE OF NATIONS

SEATO is to MANILA as LEAGUE OF NATIONS is to:

A. New York
B. Precursor
C. Treaty
D. Versailles
E. NATO

ANSWER:

Puzzle 11.16	**Difficulty rating: 4**

BLACK AND WHITE

Complete the sequence.

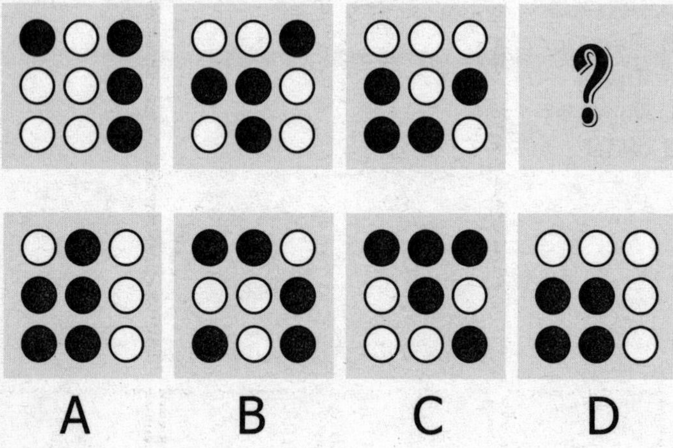

ANSWER:

Puzzle 11.17	**Difficulty rating: 3**

Determine the missing square.

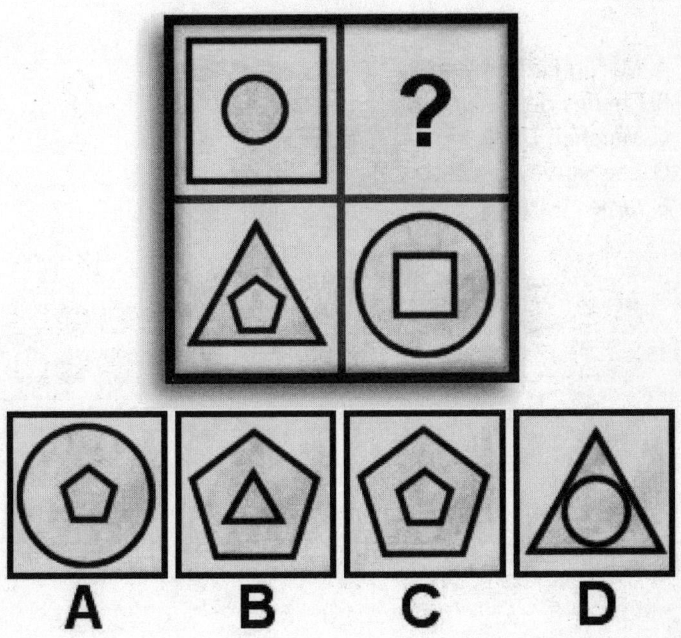

ANSWER:

Puzzle 11.18	Difficulty rating: 3

BASS GUITEAU

GAVRILO PRINCIP is to ARCHDUKE FERDINAND as GUITEAU is to:

A. Martin Luther King
B. Charles de Gaulle
C. Marshall Tito
D. Lee Harvey Oswald
E. James Garfield

ANSWER:

Puzzle 11.19	**Difficulty rating: 4**

ODD ONE IN

Which square is most like the first five?

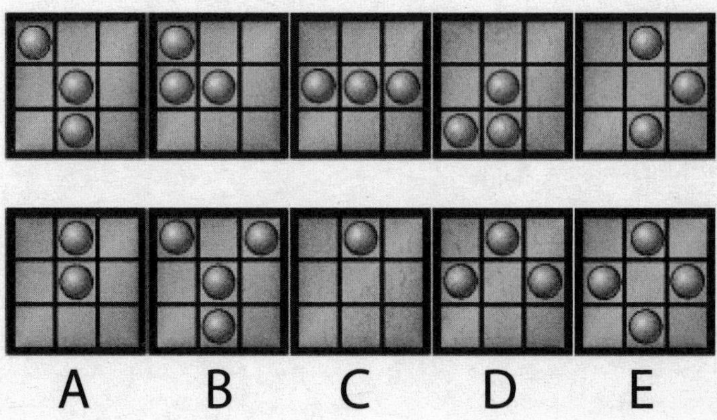

ANSWER:

Puzzle 11.20	**Difficulty rating: 3**

SPECIES POOL

ABALONE is to MOLLUSCA as EARTHWORM is to:

A. Platyhelminthes
B. Annelida
C. Porifera
D. Arthropoda
E. Cnidaria

ANSWER:

Puzzle 11.21	**Difficulty rating: 3**

SCIENCE OF PEARLS

Complete the sequence.

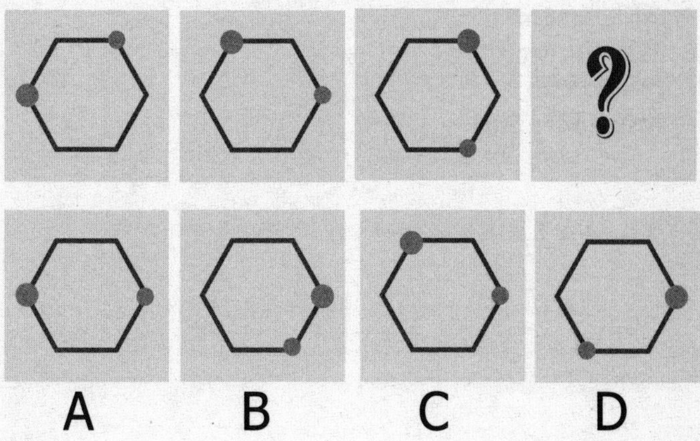

ANSWER:

Puzzle 11.22	**Difficulty rating: 1**

SCHOOLS OF THOUGHT

HOBBES is to ENLIGHTENMENT as KIERKEGAARD is to:

A. Reformation
B. Existentialism
C. Romanticism
D. Creationism
E. Post Modernism

ANSWER:

Puzzle 11.23	**Difficulty rating: 4**

FINAL QUARTER

Determine the missing square.

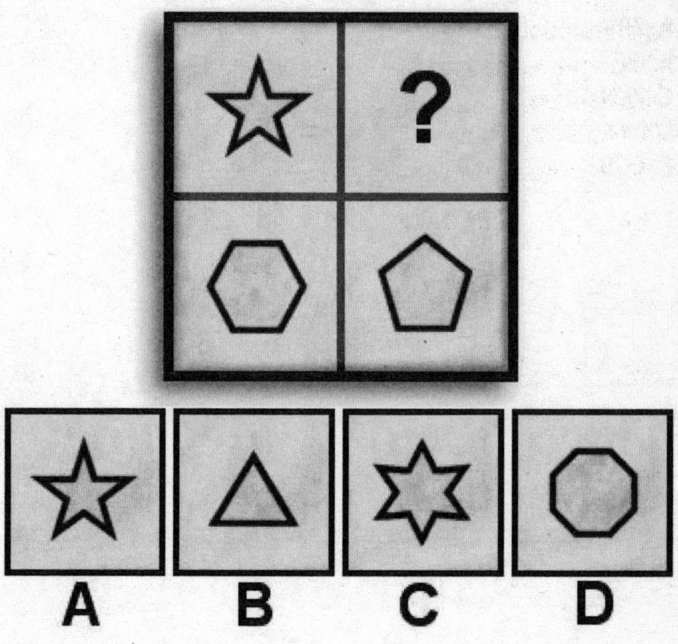

ANSWER:

Puzzle 11.24	**Difficulty rating: 1**

INITIAL THOUGHTS

IEU is to QMP as FNJ is to:

A. ZRV
B. IBF
C. PKN
D. PXT
E. CGB

ANSWER:

Puzzle 11.25	Difficulty rating: 3

IDENTICAL BOXES

Imagine two identical boxes. One is filled with twenty-seven steel balls and the other one is filled with sixty-four smaller-sized steel balls. If all the balls are made of the same material, both boxes are filled exactly to the top, and both boxes are the same size, which box would weigh more?

ANSWER:

Puzzle 11.26	**Difficulty rating: 5**

SNUG FIT

Complete the sequence.

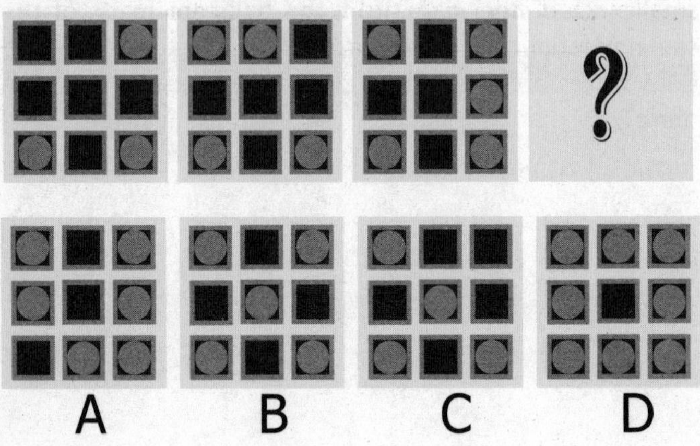

ANSWER:

Puzzle 11.27	**Difficulty rating: 3**

SLEEPY PASSENGER

Alex fell asleep on a plane halfway to his destination. He slept till he had half as far to go as he went while he slept. How much of the whole trip was Alex sleeping?

ANSWER:

Puzzle 11.28	**Difficulty rating: 4**

BORDERLINE CASE

SAN MARINO is to ITALY as ___ is to SOUTH AFRICA

A. Eritrea
B. Great Britain
C. Pretoria
D. Lesotho
E. Cape Town

ANSWER:

Puzzle 11.29	**Difficulty rating: 4**

ALL FENCED IN

Complete the sequence.

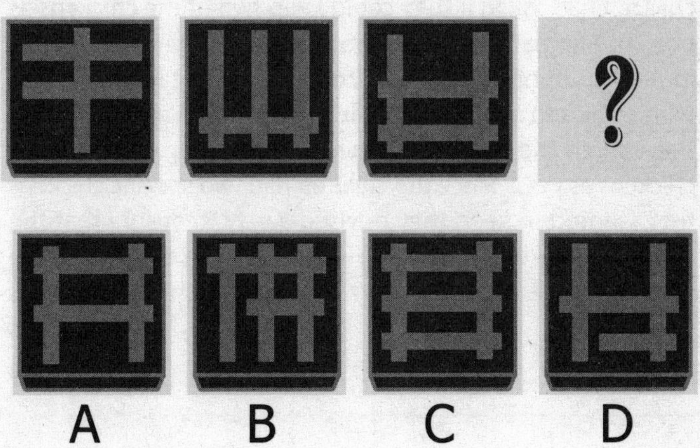

ANSWER:

Puzzle 11.30	**Difficulty rating: 3**

CHICKENS

A farmer had twenty chickens in individual cages that he was planning on selling at the market in the morning. His two children had asked if they could keep two of the chickens as pets. The farmer said, "Tomorrow morning line up the cages in a row. Counting from left to right, open each fifth cage with a chicken in it and place it in the truck. When you reach the end of the row, start over. You can keep the last two chickens as pets." Since the children had two specific chickens they wanted to keep they devised a way to ensure that the last two chickens remaining would be the two that they wanted. Which cages did they put the two chickens in?

ANSWER:

Puzzle 11.31	**Difficulty rating: 5**

A QUESTION OF ECONOMICS

GINI COEFFICIENT is to INCOME INEQUALITY as HERFINDAHL INDEX is to:

A. Opportunity cost
B. Industry concentration
C. Economy of scale
D. Supply and demand curve
E. General equilibrium

ANSWER:

Puzzle 11.32	**Difficulty rating: 5**

SET SQUARES

Complete the sequence.

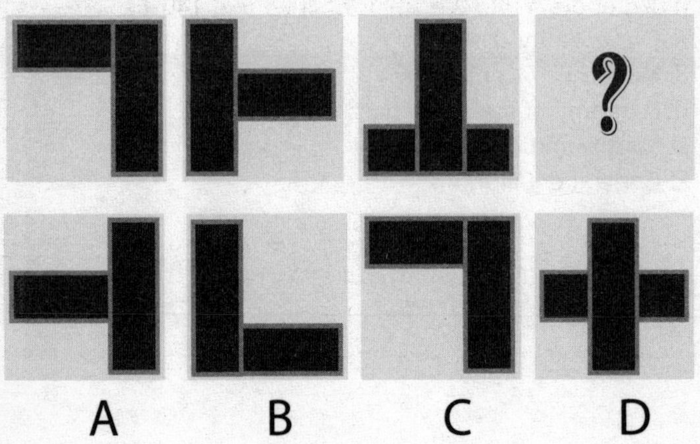

ANSWER:

Puzzle 11.33	**Difficulty rating: 2**

BUSHELS OF GRAIN

A scale has only two weights that can be used for weighings – a 1kg weight and a 4kg weight. In only 3 weighings, divide 180kg of grain into 2 bushels of 40kg and 140 kg.

ANSWER:

Puzzle 11.34	**Difficulty rating: 4**

HOROLOGY ANALOGY

METEOROLOGY is to WEATHER as HOROLOGY is to:

A. Horoscopes
B. Food
C. Religion
D. Shape of the skull
E. Time

ANSWER:

Puzzle 11.35	**Difficulty rating: 3**

DOT GAIN

Complete the sequence.

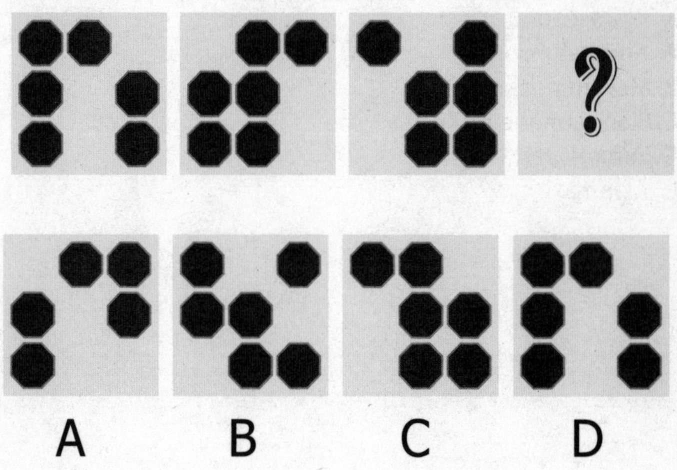

ANSWER:

Puzzle 11.36 | **Difficulty rating: 4**

OCCUPATIONAL HAZARD

DECOMPRESSION SICKNESS is to THE BENDS as PNEUMOCONIOSIS is to:

A. Athlete's Foot
B. Morning sickness
C. Black Lung
D. Lung Water
E. Asthma

ANSWER:

Puzzle 11.37	**Difficulty rating: 4**

ODD ONE IN

Which square is most like the first five?

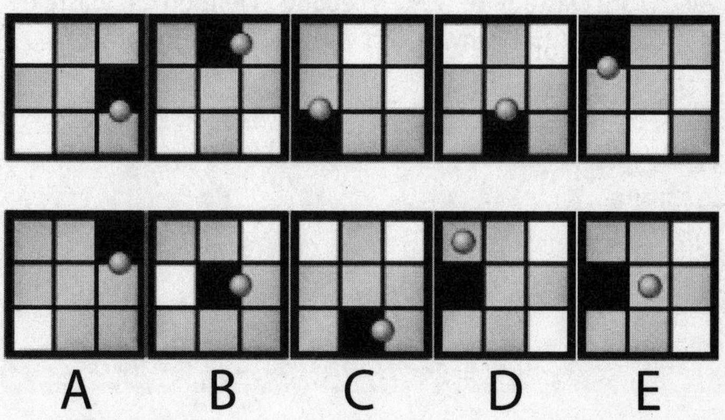

ANSWER:

Puzzle 11.38	**Difficulty rating: 3**

HOOVER DAM

Several years after the generators were installed in the Hoover Dam, someone invented a new generator that cut electricity wastage by 30%. A second invention cut waste by 45%; a third, 25%. How much waste was cut in total?

ANSWER:

Puzzle 11.39	**Difficulty rating: 4**

SOLDIER'S MARCH

A one-mile-long column of soldiers are marching back to the base at a constant rate. The soldier at the front of the column has to deliver a message to the soldier at the rear. He breaks rank and begins marching toward the rear at a constant rate while the column continues forward. The soldier reaches the rear, delivers the message and immediately turns to march forward at a constant rate. When he reaches the front of the column and drops back in rank, the column has moved one mile. How far did the soldier delivering the message march?

ANSWER:

Puzzle 11.40	**Difficulty rating: 4**

CHAPTER 11 ANSWERS

11.1 Waste (basket) case
Week (end) game
11.2. B
11.3. A
11.4. B
11.5. BROW
11.6. D
11.7. A
11.8. 12.5%
11.9. C
11.10. 200 revolutions per minute.
11.11. E
11.12. A
11.13. A
11.14. C
11.15. 14
11.16. D
11.17. D
11.18. B
11.19. E
11.20. D
11.21. B
11.22. D
11.23. B
11.24. C
11.25. D
11.26. The two boxes weigh the same.
11.27. A
11.28. Two-thirds of one-half of the whole trip, or one-third.
11.29. D
11.30. B
11.31. From left to right, the seventh and fourteenth cages.
11.32. B
11.33. C
11.34. Divide the 180kg between the 2 pans of the scale. Then remove the grain from one pan and divide the other pan's 90kg of grain between the 2 pans. You now have 45kg on each pan. Then remove 5kg from one of the pans by using both the weights on the other side. You now have 40kg left.
11.35. E
11.36. D
11.37. C
11.38. C
11.39. 71.125%
11.40. 2.4142 miles